Kenneth P. Kirkwood (1899-1968), Canadian Ambassador
photograph 1941, copyright Karsh of Ottawa

THE DIPLOMAT AT TABLE

*A Social and Anecdotal History
Through the Looking-Glass*

by
KENNETH P. KIRKWOOD

The Scarecrow Press, Inc.
Metuchen, N. J.   1974

other books by the author:

HISTORY:
Turkey (Modern World Series)
In collaboration with Arnold
J. Toynbee
Preface to Cairo: A Survey
of pre-Cairo in History
and Legend.
Renaissance in Japan: A
Cultural Survey of the
Seventeenth Century.

TRAVEL:
Under Argentine Skies

BIOGRAPHY:
A Garden in Poland (Notes on
Chopin)
The Immortal Memory (of
Robert Burns)
Unfamiliar Lafcadio Hearn

ESSAYS AND CRITICISM:
Abstractions (thoughts and
comments)
Did Shakespeare Visit Den-
mark?
Excursions Among Books
Maud: An Essay on Tenny-
son's Poem.
Ophelia of Elsinore

POETRY:
In Gardens of Proserpine
Lyrics and Sonnets
Song in My Heart
Time's Tavern
Travel Dust

ACKNOWLEDGEMENT

I wish to acknowledge the contribution of my friends,
Irena Rowinski and A. Brian Buchanan, who proofread the
text and prepared the index. I am indebted to them and
here express my gratitude for their valuable work.

--Christine Kirkwood

Library of Congress Cataloging in Publication Data

Kirkwood, Kenneth Porter, 1899-1968.
The diplomat at table.

1. Kirkwood, Kenneth Porter, 1899-1968. 2. Dinners
and dining. 3. Diplomatic etiquette. I. Title.
D413.K57A3 1974   395'.3   74-2416
ISBN 0-8108-0714-9

TABLE OF CONTENTS

BIOGRAPHICAL NOTE
by Christine Kirkwood

How many of us bring to this world dreams and ideals which so often, unfulfilled, vanish with time.

My husband achieved more than the realization of a dream--he managed to touch the stars as a poet. Arnold J. Toynbee wrote in his foreword to my husband's Renaissance in Japan, "Kenneth Kirkwood was an admirable diplomatist because he was a scholar and an author as well."

During his thirty-one years of diplomatic service he reached the summit. However, this was not an easy or spectacular career, for he disliked politics and kept away from them. His achievements were based on merit; his greatness was in modesty. He never worked for his personal glory, for he always considered himself "an obedient servant of Government and Country," which he served with zeal and devotion. He belonged to that calibre of diplomat who seems to be vanishing nowadays under political and economic tensions, both domestic and international.

Born in Brampton, Ontario, in 1899, he was educated in England and in Canada. His father, John C. Kirkwood, descendant of Scottish immigrants, editor and journalist, was known as an advertising and marketing authority. His mother, Lottie V. Porter of Nova Scotia, daughter of a Baptist minister, was a teacher at Moulton College in Toronto.

Taken to England by his family at the age of six, Kenneth P. Kirkwood attended various private and county schools in and around London till the age of eleven. At the age of nine he won the British National Essay Prize and later two of his stories were printed in the school magazine. On his return to Canada he studied at the Harbord Street Collegiate Institute, Toronto, and graduated with honors. He then immediately enlisted in the University of Toronto Canadian Officers Training Corps (C. O. T. C.) in April of

v

1917 and completed training as a lieutenant of infantry. Transferred to the R. N. A. S. as a probationary flying officer, he took training in England and in France. With boyish enthusiasm he had written the following lines:

> February 19, 1916. A thrill of patriotism floods through me sometimes. Oh that I might do my share in my country's cause, to fight in the cause of right and justice!   How I long to have my name connected with the greatest war on this planet! But I am chained, I am not yet of military age.... December 8, 1916: How one's heart beats and chafes to be in the active service of the Empire! How tiresome it is to stick here at school, doing practically nothing, when our friends are doing heroic deeds on the field of battle in the greatest war in history

But then the dream materialized. He wrote in Vendôme, France, on April 2, 1918:

> A wonderful day to-day, when one seems absolutely in love with life and the beauty of earth. Oh glorious life--this free wholesome outdoor life in the sunny warm heart of France! Oh glorious sport--flying through these azure depths on man-made wings almost as good as nature's birds! ... Once again under the magic spell of this glorious weather, I am in tune with life and the world, and am happy, happy! And yet, or because of this feeling, I am content to perform any duty that may be put upon me, heedless of death and fate. Not often have I felt so happily resigned to anything that may come. I have had, and have, cherished dreams of a golden future of my life. I have felt a strong desire, a passion, for a safe exit from this war, that I may realize my vision and grow to the power of my dreams. But to-day, with the spring warmth and air in my blood, I am ready to take anything Fate may have in store for me. My ambitions for the future cannot be better than a glorious death in the sunshine of beautiful France, a death gained in glorious conflict with invading hordes. Can anything excel an aerial battle in a golden light of an afternoon sun? Or can any death be greater than that received in a grapple with a messenger of Satan? [From Toronto to Taranto--Memories of an Aviator (unpublished manuscript)].

Commissioned as a flight sub-lieutenant (pilot) to the Royal Air Service early in 1918, my husband served in anti-submarine coastal patrol in England; and then in the Mediterranean (H. M. S. Riviera)--Malta, Sicily and Italy--until the Armistice. He took a bomber training course in England (R. A. F.); returned to Canada in 1919 as pilot officer, R. A. F. , and joined the new R. C. A. F. Seconded as senior subaltern, Queen's Own Rifles (Militia) in Toronto, he then became military instructor for the C. O. T. C. of the University of Toronto. After his First World War Service, he entered University College (studying chemistry and later political science) and graduated in 1922 (with a B. A.). He spent the academic year 1922-23 reading Near-Eastern history at London School of Economics; also, as a roving student, he attended lectures at Oxford, Cambridge, Edinburgh, Aberdeen and Glasgow.

In 1923-25 my husband taught English, history, economics and literature at the International College, Smyrna, Turkey (operated under the American Board of Foreign Missions). There he met Dr. Arnold J. Toynbee who was visiting Smyrna and who made him the flattering offer of collaboration on his projected book on Turkey (published in 1926 by Ernest Benn in London, and by Scribners in New York in 1927). In 1925-26 my husband taught history at Appleby College, Oakville, Ontario. The book with Toynbee resulted in an invitation from Columbia University, where my husband spent two years (1926-28) as an instructor in American and European history, also lecturing at Brooklyn Law School and Long Island Medical School. Later he became substitute lecturer in Near-Eastern history at Columbia University Graduate School (1927). At the same time he was continuing postgraduate studies in public law and obtained his M. A. in 1927.

Awarded a Columbia University Fellowship in Public Law (1927-28), he completed the requirements for Ph. D. , but before completing his thesis he joined the Canadian Diplomatic Service. He gained this appointment by ranking among the four highest candidates out of sixty who wrote the first civil service examinations ever held in Canada for diplomats.

As a diplomat, he helped to open, or opened, eleven Canadian diplomatic missions. He served as second secretary in Washington, D. C. (1928-29), and when he took his first post in this original Canadian mission, his chief, the

Honorable Vincent Massey, warned him: "Let me tell you that in the diplomatic career you are on duty 24 hours a day; there is no interlude when you can forget your role, rank and representational character, and become a private individual." After one year in Washington, he was transferred to Tokyo (1929-39). This long sojourn in a remote area cut him off automatically from influential and personal contacts at home, but it did have a strong impact on his artistic nature. He developed a deep admiration for Japanese art and the charming countryside and traditions of old Japan. After a number of years there, he assumed that the Government would keep him at this distant post forever and he began to learn Japanese, but as soon as he had become more or less fluent, his superiors suddenly transferred him to Holland! This was but a short posting from 1939 to 1940, when he was caught by the German invasion and evacuated by British destroyer to London in 1940, along with the Netherlands Court and Government. From there he was immediately assigned (June 1940 to July 1941) as Canadian Consul to Greenland to help protect that Danish colony from the German menace. In his notes on Greenland, called "Arctic Intermezzo," my husband wrote:

> Off the beaten paths of the world of mankind is the Arctic on the periphery of the habitable world, the ultimate fringe of civilization. It is the remnant of another age, the vestige of the Glacial Epoch, the unchanged region primeval and primordial, of a prehistoric, geological era. The origin of Man, the creation of the human race, brought a new and revolutionary condition into God's Earth; but in the Arctic that epochal event has hardly made an impression. The Arctic is a world, not of Man, scarcely of beast, but of physical and geological and meteorological attributes only; it belongs to the universe of first creation, but not to the universe of last creation; of the First and Second Days, not of the Sixth Day.

> From the civilized world of men and machines, of science and art and culture, I was suddenly transposed. From the languid ease, the orchidaceous luxury of the sub-tropics--steaming summers of Japan, the swimming, malarial heat of midsummer in South China, Canton, Hong Kong, the paradisial clemency of Hawaii, the soft allurements of the Mediterranean islands and littoral, that I have known--I was transplanted; from the metropolitan world of

symphony concerts and operas, cathedrals and temples,
beautiful women in evening gowns and rare perfume,
the halls of gaiety and bright lights and dancing and
champagne, the roar of traffic and the hum of machinery, the shriek of speeding trains and the drone of
gleaming aeroplanes--I was translated from the civilized world to which I had been born, in which I was
experienced--I was ejected suddenly into this barren,
virgin, uncorrupted, unsophisticated world of the
Glacial Age. For fourteen months I have dwelt in
the silent zone on the perimeter of the habitable
earth. For a large period of that time I lived in a
long wintry black-out, when even the interminable
landscape of snow was sombre and dark instead of
light and white; I lived within the fortress of ice or
Arctic Sea; I lived amongst a handful of other white
folks and a cluster of semi-natives in an isolated
realm; I was in exile beyond my own civilized world
of gregarious society and multitudinous friends....
I may never experience these moods again. They are
unique in my life and sui generis; the moods and impressions engendered by a vacuum-like realm; the
thin and attenuated music of an Arctic Intermezzo.

From 1941 to 1946 my husband was assigned to
Brazil, and Chile, and to Argentina, where he was first
secretary, counsellor and chargé d'affaires in Buenos Aires,
and co-operated in Allied wartime intelligence work in these
countries. Buenos Aires was like another Paris during the
Second World War, a center of musicians and other artists
from all over the world. Life was full of cultural activities
and involvements which he had always particularly enjoyed.
After returning from South America and a short (as usual)
stay in Ottawa, in the Consular Division of the Department of
External Affairs, he was named Canadian Delegate to the
United Nations Passport and Visa Conference in Geneva in
1947, and then spent three and a half years behind the Iron
Curtain--in Poland, as the first Canadian chargé d'affaires
with the rank of minister (1947-50). This was, of course,
a hardship post and rather difficult, not only from the political point of view, but also physically and emotionally.
There were shortages of food and of everyday needs and
accommodation, and it was depressing to live in Warsaw at
that time; the city had been 75 per cent destroyed as a result of the war and the 1944 uprising. It was like a tragic
cemetery, with hundreds of people buried in the ruins and
the survivors rising like phoenixes from ashes. Their brave

spirit and determination were admired by foreign missions'
representatives but the general atmosphere was underlined
with sadness.   My husband's sensitive mind could hardly
bear this situation and surroundings.   In addition to this,
his own life was uncomfortable, for both the Canadian Legation and his personal lodging were situated in a half-destroyed
hotel, with no cooking facilities and little privacy.   This had
a temporary effect upon his health.

        At the end of 1950 he returned to Canada and was for
a few months Acting Head of the Consular Division and
temporary Head of Commonwealth Division at the Department
of External Affairs in Ottawa.   But he was soon appointed
High Commissioner for Canada to Pakistan in 1951-54 (and
also delegate to the Colombo Plan Conference in Karachi).
The climate was unhealthy, but he enjoyed the friendly attitude of the government and people toward Canada, and the
typically Oriental hospitality and atmosphere.   On his way
back to Ottawa, he toured the Arab Middle East, Egypt,
North Africa, Gibraltar and Spain, with short visits to Paris
and London.   In 1954 he spent some time as Canadian delegate to the U. N. General Assembly in New York before
leaving for his new post as first Canadian Ambassador to
Egypt and Minister to Lebanon (1954-56).   The Cairo post
was a rather hot one politically, but also very interesting
and--from the personal point of view--fascinating to my husband who was an expert in Middle Eastern affairs and pas-
sionately interested in archaeology.   He left Egypt on July
26, 1956 (an historic date) for his new post as High Commissioner for Canada to New Zealand (1956-57).   This was
a post of leisure, with beautiful scenery and a mild,
pleasant climate, full of cultural activities, as the High
Commissioner was expected to deliver university and other
addresses and take part in the openings of agricultural and
various other expositions.   In 1957-59 he was on assign-
ment in Ottawa, writing the early history of the Department
of External Affairs.

        This brief personal summary shows my husband's
busy life and his many and varied experiences.   He also
experienced at first hand the following historical events:
war conditions in France in 1918 and the bombardment of
Paris by "Big Bertha" and Gotha and Zeppelin raids over
London.   He saw part of Mussolini's "March on Rome" in
Milan in 1922; the Turkish nationalist Revolution under
Mustapha Kemal Ataturk; the Greco-Turkish exchange of
populations in 1922 and 1923; Civil War in China (1933)--

he travelled to Hankow under danger; Japanese-Chinese War in Manchuria--he travelled through the war-zone at some peril. He witnessed political rebellions, uprisings and assassinations in Japan in 1929-39; the fall of Bruening in Germany, preceding Hitler's seizure of power; the German blitz and invasion of Holland (he spent four days under German occupation before escaping); the 1941 Peron coup d'état in Argentina; the Communist takeover in Poland; Ismailia (Suez Canal) fighting--while passing through the Canal on January 1, 1952; several riots in Karachi (1952-54); the rise of Nasserism in Egypt (1954-1956) and the expropriation of the Suez Canal on July 26, 1956, while he was passing through it on his way to New Zealand.

His participation in cultural and social activities embraced a wide area. He was active in Sunday-school teaching in Toronto; as an undergraduate he was Canadian delegate to succeeding Student Christian-Movement Conferences in England, Holland, Switzerland, Bavaria and Hungary, and was International Relations Secretary of the British Student Christian Movement, with headquarters in London. He gave courses in English poetry at the YWCA in Tokyo; and other frequent courses and addresses in Japan, Argentina, Poland (the British Council in Warsaw), Pakistan, Egypt, New Zealand, Canada and the U.S.A. My husband contributed articles to various periodicals in Canada, England and the States. While in Turkey, he was special correspondent for the London Economist, Egyptian Gazette and Manchester Guardian Commercial Supplement. While in New York, he reviewed books for the American Journal of Political Science and the New Republic, and contributed to other journals as well.

Seventeen books and several pamphlets were published during my husband's teaching and diplomatic service and his wanderings around the world, and many unpublished manuscripts and mimeographed works have been left among his papers for the Public Archives of Canada. Each period and country contributed to his literary inspiration and scholarly endeavors and achievements.

First among the published books was Turkey (Modern World Series), written in collaboration with Arnold J. Toynbee; then the following works were published in Japan: Abstractions (book of thoughts and comments), Meiji Press, Tokyo 1937; In Gardens of Proserpine (poems), 1930; Lyrics and Sonnets, Tokyo 1934; Renaissance in Japan--A Cultural

Survey of the Seventeenth Century, Meiji Press, Tokyo 1938,
and Charles E. Tuttle, Tokyo 1970 (this second edition was
included in the American Reference Books Annual for 1971).
Also: Song in My Heart (poems), Tokyo 1932; Time's
Tavern (poems), Meiji Press, Tokyo 1935; Travel Dust
(poems), Tokyo 1932; and Unfamiliar Lafcadio Hearn (bio-
graphical notes), Hokuseido Press, Tokyo 1936.   Among
the pamphlets are: Discoverers of the Japanese Alps; Harunobu
and Hogarth; Mountaineering in Japan; Mountains and Mountaineering in Yezo, Japan; Lafcadio Hearn's Ancestry.

     Did Shakespeare Visit Denmark? was written in Hol-
land and published later--in 1953 in Karachi; so was Maud--
an essay on Tennyson's poem--conceived in Holland; it was
published in 1951 in Ottawa.   Some of the poems created in
Japan, Greenland and Argentina were mimeographed in
Buenos Aires in the years 1941-43; these include: "Arctic
Intermezzo, " "Harp of Aeolus, " "On An Oriental Screen, "
"Pacific Tapestry, " "Until in God's Good Time, " and "Wind
Vane and Hour Glass. "

     Argentina is said to have a good atmosphere for
artists and their creative moods.   During his five years
there, my husband wrote and published Excursions Among
Books, Mitchell, Buenos Aires 1945; and Under Argentine
Skies, Artes Graficas, Buenos Aires 1945.   Poland inspired
notes on Chopin: A Garden in Poland, published a few years
later, in Karachi in 1953; and various notes (unpublished)
on Polish theatre and music, Polish personalities, Tatra
Mountains, and his diaries and impressions: Warsaw in
Ruins--A Point in History, and others.   Preface to Cairo--
A Survey of Pre-Cairo in History and Legend was written
in Cairo and published later in Ottawa in 1958.   The Immortal Memory (of Robert Burns) was published in Ottawa
in 1958, and so was Ophelia of Elsinore, a product of many
years of my husband's meditations and research.   He was
fascinated by the genius of Shakespeare and knew Hamlet by
heart.

     Among the early notes and unpublished journals are
the following typed or mimeographed copies: From Toronto
to Taranto--War Memories of an Aviator (1916-1918);
Turkish Journal--Smyrna Blue (Turkish travels and impressions: 1922-25); Foot Loose--Essays on Travel (Tokyo,
1931); Fair House--A Bachelor's Musings (Tokyo 1931);
Journal of Travel Through the United States of America (February 1932); A Journal of Travel Through

Soviet Russia, Siberia and Manchuria (May 1932); Journal of the Tour Through Formosa (October 1932); Journal of a Tour of China (September 1933); Journal of a Tour of Korea (July 1935); Report of a Trip Through Yezo (Hokkaido), Japan (July 1930); Report of a Trip Through Northern Japan (Mining regions, August 1930); Report of a Trip Through Kyushu, Southern Japan (May 1931); Journals of Travels in Japan, Summer 1934; The Buddhist Pantheon in Japanese Art (August 1935); and Diplomatic Journals, Tokyo 1929-39.

Apart from literature, my husband was interested in music and theatre; he played violin in university and church orchestras; acted in amateur performances at International House in New York; and was secretary-manager of the Tokyo Amateur Dramatic Club. He developed a taste for oil painting in Japan, and continued it sporadically, especially in Argentina. Some paintings were donated to the Canadian Embassies in Tokyo and Buenos Aires. He was a connoisseur of art and a collector of Oriental prints, jade, ceramics and Persian bronzes and rugs, and gathered a personal library of 4000 books.

Later in life, after his retirement from the public service of Canada at the age of sixty, he collaborated with the Centennial International Development Programme; the Committee on Election Expenses; the Royal Commission on Bilingualism and Biculturalism; the Overseas Institute of Canada, and the United Nations Association, Ottawa Branch, among others.

He was awarded two War Medals (1914-1919); the George Jubilee Medal; the George and Elizabeth II Coronation Medals; Japanese Red Cross Order of Merit and other foreign medals. His name was nominated for inclusion in the 1970 edition of the Blue Book--Leaders of the English-Speaking World, but he passed away before publication, destroyed by cancer in September of 1968.

He was formerly a Fellow of the Royal Geographical Society, the American Geographical Society, and the Canadian Geographical Society; was formerly active with the International YMCA; co-founder of the Wilsonian Club, Columbia University; and a member of various Asian Societies, several Canadian learned societies, the National Education Committee, W. F. U. N. A. Committee (Canadian delegate to Geneva Conference in 1961).

My husband was a bachelor until the age of sixty. All his books were written at night (between 11 p. m. and 5 a. m. !) and during the weekends, with the exception of The Diplomat at Table which is one part of a very long unfinished manuscript, "Diplomat Through The Looking Glass-- A Social and Anecdotal History of the Side Lines of Diplomacy, " written after his retirement from the diplomatic service.   His preface to that manuscript reveals his intent in writing it.   He said in part:

> History is normally the account of great affairs of state; and most diplomats' memoirs and reminiscences deal in part with historical episodes and affairs of state in which they had some small and passing role.   But, in the way of life there are also the sidelines of diplomatic life, the trivial and the comic, the incidentals and diversions--though each may have some unapparent significance.   Dining is important in diplomacy; and even wining; and cocktails have taken the place of the important coffee shops.

In his Excursions Among Books my husband revealed some of his philosophy and his passion for books:

> The true world, of course, is life; but when Life becomes too real, and too earnest, we turn to the mirror of Life, either in dreams or in books.

He wrote mostly for his own diversion and amusement.   "One may have dreams; and one may have books; they are each a world behind a world. "

Once in a nostalgic mood he expressed his thoughts in a poem he called "Philosophy":

> You wonder what I think, in this my life,
> Of hermitage, of bachelor solitude;
> What love imagined, with what dreams endued,
> What Beauty visioned, and, in inner strife,
> What firm philosophy brings seeming truce
> To ill-adjusted senses, blood and brain,
> And weaves, not warps, the tension and the strain
> Of human nature to a concord use.
>
> You wonder what I think.   I'll not explain
> My inward discords and my harmonies;
> For all I know is living dutiful

To daily tasks, not asking what the gain,
Knowing that life is not a course of ease,
But knowing, too, its heart is Beautiful.

(from Time's Tavern)

Christine Kirkwood

Ottawa, May 1973

PREFACE

"Diplomat Through the Looking Glass"

My diplomatic career commenced in 1928. After passing--side by side with my old friend Lester B. (Mike) Pearson--the qualifying examinations for External Affairs, I was tipped off that I would shortly receive a telegram instructing me to report on September 1st to our new Washington Legation, then about six months old, headed by the Hon. Vincent Massey. I never received the telegram, but in anticipation I proceeded to Washington, and on that date presented myself. The minister was away, First Secretary Hume H. Wrong was absent, and the other first secretary, Laurent Beaudry received me with some obvious perplexity. He had never heard of me, and had received no instructions or notification from Ottawa. He asked me to wait over the Labor Day week-end, while he telegraphed for information. The following Tuesday he telephoned inviting me to call around. I did so. This time his welcome was much more cordial. He told me he had received a reply from Ottawa, confirming my appointment. I expected, as a new recruit, to be made third secretary; but he surprised me by telling me that I had been appointed as second secretary. After a little friendly chat, he looked at his watch, found it was just past noon and therefore outside office hours, and surreptitiously invited me to join him in a glass of sherry (extracted from the medicine cabinet in his office washroom) and then invited me to lunch with him.

When we returned to the chancery--situated, along with the Massey children's nursery, on the fourth floor of the legation and minister's residence at 1746 Massachusetts Avenue--I was assigned to a large vacant room, barely furnished, which evidently had recently been used as a bedroom. There was a large fireplace, a desk and a chair and a carpet. My host suggested that, until some files could be extracted from the file-room for me to study for some initiating background, I might make myself as comfortable as possible and read anything that I could find at hand. After

1

a brief search around the room, I found it completely devoid of any reading matter except one book.   It lay casually
on the mantelpiece over the unlighted fireplace.   It was
evidently displaced from the nursery at the other end of the
hall, where young Hart and Lionel Massey romped with their
sometimes vocative dog.

It was entitled Alice in Wonderland and Through the
Looking Glass.   Faute de mieux, I sat down and read it
from cover to cover.

It was my first day's occupation.   It was my initiation into a long diplomatic career.   In some respects, it
was symbolic, and perhaps even premonitory.

As I perused this little book of fairy-tale and parable,
I felt that like Alice I too was about to enter a Wonderland
and explore a strange world like her Looking-Glass House.
I felt akin to her when she talked to her Kitty and said
"I'll tell you all my ideas about Looking-Glass House.   First,
there's a room you can see through the glass--that's just the
same as our drawing-room, only the things go to the other
way, I can see all of it when I get upon a chair--all but the
bit just behind the fireplace.   Oh! I do so wish I could see
that bit! ... Well, then, the books are something like our
books, only the words go the wrong way: I know that, because I've held up one of our books to the glass....   Now
we come to the passage.   You can just see a little peep of
the passage in Looking-Glass House, if you leave the door of
our drawing-room wide open; and it's very like our passage
as far as you can see, only you know it may be quite different on beyond.   Oh, Kitty, how nice it would be if we
could only get through into Looking-Glass House!   I'm sure
it's got, oh! such beautiful things in it!"

Having commenced my diplomatic career with the
perusal of Alice, I have now reached the period when I can
regard that story again.   Before, I saw through the Glass
darkly; now I can see myself and my career, face to face.
And the Looking-Glass has many queer facets, such as those
which puzzled Alice.   She had her encounters with Kings and
Queens and Duchesses; she learned to play croquet, chess
and cards; she attended tea-parties and dinners, sometimes
with wine at the table; she travelled on railway trains.   She
met the Hatter, with his oversize topper; she met the Footman Frog, dressed in bright yellow with enormous boots on.
She observed the birds in the garden, and learned about fish.

So, too, the retired diplomat remembers the queer things out of his experience; royalties, princes and potentates he has met, the card-playing, the dinners and receptions and cocktail parties, the oddities of official dress; and many other strange aspects that give the profession of diplomacy a fairy-tale-like quality, like that droll quaint world of Looking-Glass House through which Alice wandered and adventured.

Through 31 years of a varied diplomatic life, I have had my adventures; and the whole span has been one great adventure. The time now has come to make a few notes upon it. Like Alice, I might say: "When I used to read fairy tales, I fancied that kind of thing never happened, and now here I am in the middle of one! There ought to be a book written about me, that there ought! And when I grow up, I'll write one--but I'm grown up now--at least there's no room to grow up any more." But then she had some doubts. The Gryphon said: "Come, let's hear some of your adventures." "I could tell you my adventures, beginning from this morning; but it's no use going back to yesterday, because I was a different person then."

"Explain all that," said the Mock Turtle.

"No, no! The adventures first," said the Gryphon in an impatient tone: "explanations take such a dreadful time."

History is normally the account of great affairs of state; and most diplomats' memoirs and reminiscences deal in part with historical episodes and affairs of state in which they had some small and passing role. But, in the way of life, there are also the sidelines of diplomatic life, the trivial and the comic, the incidentals and diversions-- though each may have some unapparent significance. Dining is of importance in diplomacy, and wining; and cocktails have taken the place of the important old coffee shops. Costume has been symbolic of changes of social philosophy and the effects of democracy, égalité and republicanism. Means of communication have changed and speeded up and with them has come usurpation by the press correspondent of the ambassador's place. Personal adventures are no longer so much in safaries, tiger-shooting, elephant-hunting, and similar past diversions of the diplomat; but are found in other hobbies and pursuits. These are the "incidentals" of diplomacy; the backstage "properties and lights"

that function in the great dramas of history that the world
watches.   As any actor knows, the backstage is as fascinating and curious as the stage itself; there is importance
among the properties and curtain ropes and switchboards;
there is laughter in the dressing room; there is stimulation
in the Green Room or actors' lounge.

Danièle Varé, the former Italian Minister to China
and other countries, noted in his diary: "Had an audience
with the King [of Italy]. . . . He asked me what I had been
writing lately, and when I answered 'A Comedy for Marionettes,' he smiled and shook his head, as if to imply that I
had been wasting my time (which was doubtedly true)"
[Laughing Diplomat, p. 294].   That would have made a good
title for this book--"A Comedy for Marionettes"; but I do
not wish to steal it from its respected author.   Indeed, having ventured to recall my first initiation into my profession,
determined to entitle my manuscript and memories "Diplomat Through the Looking Glass." But in some cases, re-
versing the Gryphon's choice, I have placed the explanations
before the adventures; and in so doing, I find that I have
ventured into the great wide field of the social historian.

I have made Alice's adventures the little silver thread
on which to string my comments and recollections, because
even this long after its publication in 1865 and 1871, it is
still a timely parable.   As a Canadian reviewer observes:
"Could not the White Rabbit, watch in hand, muttering over
his lateness ('Oh, my ears and whiskers, how late it's getting!') be any Member of Parliament dashing from committee meeting to Commons session?   Could not the Mad Hatter's tea party be duplicated in the chit-chat and nonsense
of a cocktail party where 'all things beginning with M--
mouse-traps, moon, memory, muchness, much of a muchness' are discussed interminably?   The mock trial of the
Knight for stealing the tarts might have its counterpoint in
many a modern court case.   'If there's no meaning in it,
that saves a world of trouble, as we didn't try to find any'
says the King of Hearts blithely.   And hasn't the oft-repeat-
ed cry of 'off with his (her) head' a familiar ring?   The
Dodo's 'I move that the meeting adjourn for the immediate
consideration of more important remedies' will surely ring
a bell for any parliamentarian, and the Eaglet's crisp response 'Speak English' brings an echo" [Ruth Campbell,
Ottawa Journal, August 27, 1960].

And so, in the pages of this part of my notes, The

<u>Diplomat at Table</u>, I shall wander through the dinner tables and cocktail parties of Wonderland, often finding Alice there, and often giving the explanations before the adventures. Retrospect is quite as amusing and interesting as prospect, when one has passed middle-age, and anecdotage is the accompaniment or forerunner of dotage. The telescope is for the lookers-to-the-future, and for those who search the prospect; the looking-glass is that which produces reflections, and, sometimes, the opportunity to "see ourselves as others see us." As Shelley said, "we look before, and after." This book is the scene seen "after," through more eyes than mine own. To recall the familiar lines of <u>Ulysses</u>:

> Much have I seen and known;--cities of men
> And manners, climates, councils, governments,
> Myself not least, but honor'd of them all, ...

But in this experience, I have been only "a part of all that I have met"; and others besides myself have found in the sidelines of the diplomatic career the strange discoveries and experiences that ten-year-old Alice encountered in her Odyssey.

Kenneth P. Kirkwood
Ottawa, the 1960s

DIET IN HISTORY

Politics, diplomacy and gastronomy go together. History most often deals with the prosaic narratives of politics and statecraft, diplomatic negotiations and treaty-making. The gastronomic interpretation of history has never been fully written, even by those who interpret history in terms of economic determinism, dialectic materialism, or "social" rather than political science. There is also to be found "dietetic materialism." The pages that follow are a random effort to bring into the historical picture of politics and diplomacy some aspect of this other side, the social and gastronomic side, as it may be found in social annals, as well as in personal experience. A lifelong diplomat knows only too well that man's gustatory tastes and habits and uses underlie much of the business of history. The great chef Brillat-Savarin said, "The destiny of nations depends on the manner in which they are fed."

So basically influenced are we by this matter of food and drink [wrote Lin Yutang] that revolutions, peace, war, patriotism, international understanding, our daily life and the whole fabric of human social life are profoundly influenced by it. What was the cause of the French Revolution? Rousseau and Voltaire and Diderot? No, just food. What is the cause of the Russian Revolution and the Soviet experiment? Just food again. As for war, Napoleon showed the essential depth of his wisdom by saying that 'an army marches on its stomach.' And what is the use of saying 'Peace, Peace,' when there is no peace below the diaphragm? This applies to nations as well as to individuals. Empires have collapsed and the most powerful regimes and reigns of terror have broken down when the people were hungry. Men refuse to work, soldiers refuse to fight, prima donnas refuse to sing, senators refuse to rule the country when they are hungry [The Importance of Living, Chapters iii, iv].

Professor James I. Shotwell, writing on "History" in the Encyclopaedia Britannica [11th ed.], said: "The definition of history as 'past politics' is miserably inadequate. Political events are mere externals. History enters into every phase of activity, and the economic forces which urge society along are as much its subject as the political result. " Included in these economic forces is this one which is generally neglected by historians. It is the influence of diet and taste on world development and civilization. The tastebuds in the palates of men have, like the proverbial horseshoe nail, affected kingdoms and changed the shape of empires. Many a war has been fought over some economic or political casus belli; but occasionally war has also been fought over what Professor Durant has called a "casus belly. " This interesting and neglected thesis could be expanded at length; but here are given only a few suggestive illustrations.

Let us admit that mankind is, generally speaking, both carnivorous and herbivorous; that is to say, throughout history, man has been a meat and fish eater; and at the same time, or afterwards, an eater of cereals and vegetables. His tastes along these lines have influenced his social development and progress. The story of civilization involves the various stages from nomadic hunting and herding, to settlement animal husbandry and agriculture and community living; and by projection of his food demands, to maritime trade and commerce, involving navigation and exploration and colonization and empire. From being a homeless nomad, man became a settled social animal; tribes, and then nations, arose and expanded by conquest into empires. One of the driving impulses was food.

The earliest men were wandering hunters, seeking their food with slingshot, bow and arrow, and spear. They can still be found among the bushmen of Australia, Africa, Borneo and such places. The vanishing gauchos of the Argentine pampas still hunt down animals with bolos, and the vanishing western Red Indians were masters at capturing fleet game with lassos.

At a later stage, while still nomadic, men collected and bred herds and flocks of animals for meat and milk. They had no fixed base, but drove their animals from place to place to find seasonal pasturage. The herdsmen and shepherds lived in temporary tents, made of the skins of their animals. I have seen the desert Bedouins existing thus; and in the Khyber Pass the Pathan-Afghan shepherds move their flocks hither and thither across the political frontier as seasonal pasturage shifts. These nomadic herdsmen represent a primitive and early stage of civilization, but one which still endures in various parts of the world. Their mobility and migrations are based mainly on food requirements.

The word nomad, "wanderer," is particularly used of tribes who shift continually from place to place in search of pasture (Greek: νέμειν). The νομάδες of ancient Greek writers meant particularly the pastoral tribes of North Africa, hence the Latin name of the Numidians.

Many nomadic migrations and invasions and conquests are known in history. It is probable that the whole aboriginal population of America evolved from migrating Mongol peoples moving across the Bering Straits in search of "new pastures" more promising than Siberia and Mongolia. Of such nomadic tribes was the powerful one composed of the race of Huns, emerging into recorded history in the 4th century. The Huns, a nomadic people of the steppes north of the Caspian, migrated according to grazing facilities for their horses and cattle; their wanderings took them down into Persia, and westward toward what is now Europe. Thus, led by such men as Attila, they moved beyond the Urals and the Straits into Europe and almost destroyed the incipient civilization of the West. They pushed into the Danube basin, into what is now Bulgaria; into Greece, and westward as far as the Rhone, and there came into conflict with the Burgundians. Attila might have become the successor of the God-Caesars, after he had brought Constantinople under Theodosius II to tribute, sacked most of the towns of France as far as Orleans, and in spite of his resounding defeat at Troyes (A.D. 451) overrun North Italy, burning Aquileia and Padua and looting Milan. But Attila died in 453, and the Hunnish Empire disappeared out of history. It may not be an exaggeration to say that the original urge that impelled Attila toward Europe was the search for new pasturage for his enormous entourage of tribesmen with their steeds, and their herds; ultimately he was infected with the urge for political conquest in the manner of Alexander the Great.

MEAT

Whether among the nomadic herdsmen, or among the more settled peoples who domesticated their animals and

went in for animal husbandry, it is historically evident that
meat was a principal diet of Homo carnivora. Among the
foods usually claimed to be desirable in ancient times was
flesh.   Even the gods were supposed to love the smell of
fried or roasted meat, ever since Prometheus had brought
the gift of fire to mankind.   A meat diet was necessary especially for those engaged in physical activity, such as warriors, laborers, slaves and athletes.   The cattle-driving
gauchos of the Argentina pampas, ever in the saddle, were
such meat eaters, and their cattle so numerous, that when
hungry or camping, they thought nothing of killing a steer,
cutting off the portions they desired, roasting them in an
asado, and abandoning the rest of the unstripped carcasses
to the stars.   The killing of big game and domesticated animals for food permeates human history.

I myself was once leading a party of Turkish students
in a mountain expedition in Asia Minor when we lost our
way, and, being short of food, had recourse to killing a goat,
amateurishly cooking the carcass over a bonfire, and staving
off hunger until we refound a civilized community.   Almost
every adventurer, traveller in the wilds, or isolated hunter,
has met with the same necessity.

The late Dr. T. R. Glover, a professor of Latin at
Queen's University at Kingston Ontario, once contributed a
learned yet interesting article on the relation of diet and
history ["Diet in History," Queens Quarterly winter 1951,
p. 25-50].   He showed how the ancient Greeks, who had
been meat eaters, found their resources retreating, and
therefore struck out into colonial expansion.   Athenaeus,
about A.D. 200, in his book Gastronomers, referred to the
meat-eating predilection in the days of Homer.   He noted
that the meal was always a roast, generally beef, though
possibly also pig.   Many as are the meals Agamemnon gave
to his chieftains, whatever the occasion, the roast meat was
one big dish--no entrees served on fig leaves, no rare tid-
bit, or milk-cakes, or honey-cakes does Homer serve as
choice dainties for his kings, but only viands by which body
and soul might enjoy strength.   Even the suitors, insolent
though they were and recklessly given over to pleasure, were
not represented as eating fish or birds or honey-cakes.
Priam rebuked his sons for taking the lambs and kids for
their countrymen.   Even though Homer described the Helles-
pont as teeming with fish, the Phaeocians as devoted to the
sea, Ithaca as rich in creeks and islands full of fish and
wild fowl, he apparently never had those things on the table.

Meat was the customary dish and contributed to the after-
dinner athletics, the discus and the spear. Penelope kept
geese--obviously to be eaten; on Circe's island Odysseus
killed a stag for his men.

    Men, comments Dr. Glover, can kill off wild animals
more quickly than these can reproduce themselves, as is
seen in the diminishing game in Europe, North America and
Africa, and when men have destroyed the obvious supply that
nature gave, they have to search elsewhere. As human
population spreads, the wildlife recedes, and a land once
abundant may become one of scarcity or even starvation.
Athens became an urban center, without common demesnes
or common fields for domesticated animals, and with no wildlife. Through its seaport Piraeus, it resorted to seaborne
supplies and then took to fish eating. Much of the fish was
dried fish imported from the Black Sea. This dependency
on overseas sources, as a result of the Greek populations
outgrowing the home food supplies, and of the deforestation
by charcoal burners and goats led not only to overseas mer-
cantilism but to migration and colonization. Solon tried to
substitute for inefficient agriculture and husbandry a system
of manufacturing and commerce; his conviction was that
Athens need not raise her own food if she could hold the
sea. Colonization relieved the pressure at home, it offered
food and dwellings for the overflow and further growth of
population and its needs, which in its turn meant increase
of activity and production, and expansion of commerce.
Colonization extended the Greek world and helped to create
the Hellenic Age, with its resplendent movements in art and
philosophy. "We need not regret too much the meager table
of the Greek," drily remarks Dr. Glover. For it led to
commerce and colonization, and ultimately to Hellenic civilization.

    If the Greeks built up their Hellenic Empire by coloni-
zation, followed by the Romans, the British also--sea-locked
and insufficiently productive enough at home to nourish their
rapidly expanding population, went into the business of navigation, overseas trade, and colonization, and came to depend
on foreign imports and thus a control of the mercantile seas.
They turned to manufacture at home, largely for export and
trade, and relied on overseas sources, both in their own
colonies and in foreign countries, for their food sustenance.
As Rudyard Kipling expressed it ["Big Steamers"]:

'Oh, where are you going to, all you Big Steamers,
    With England's own coal, up and down the salt seas?'
'We are going to fetch you your bread and your butter,
    Your beef, pork and mutton, eggs, apples and cheese. '

'And where will you fetch it from, all you Big Steamers,
    And where shall I write you when you are away?'
'We fetch it from Melbourne, Quebec and Vancouver,
    Address us at Hobart, Hong-Kong, and Bombay. '

'For the bread that you eat and the biscuits you nibble,
    The sweets that you suck and the joints that you carve,
They are brought to you daily by all us Big Steamers,
    And if anyone hinders our coming, you'll starve. '

Beef has always been a favorite item of meat diet in
England, supplemented by mutton.   England, and particularly Wales, was a sheep-raising country, and developed its
famous woolen industry, with English or Welsh mutton or
lamb as a culinary by-product.   But beef came first, often
eaten with Yorkshire pudding in later times.   Henry VIII
dubbed his juicy joint Sir Loin of Beef; the Yeomen of the
Guard, used especially as Wardens of the Tower, are still
nicknamed "Beefeaters. "   When enclosures, the reduction of
pasturage, and industrialization reduced cattle-raising and
husbandry below the consumption level, and as a result of
expanding population, importation of beef from abroad became
essential to English life.   From Australia, New Zealand and
Canada went the cattle ships; for before days of refrigeration, cattle were shipped on the hoof to England.   Even in
my younger days, many a student or poor traveller worked
his passage to the British Isles and Europe by employment
on those wretched, noisy, smelly ships.   Then, to meat-
hungry Europe, the cattle of Argentina were as enviable as
gold was to the Spanish conquistadors or spices to the East
India Company.   On those vast pampas, there have been cattle for hundreds of years.   Along the railway tracks one
sees the white dry skeletons that mark the generations of
cattle indiscreet enough to challenge the intrusion of trains
into their domain; in places even the fences are built up of
skulls, bleached and ghostlike.   In fact cattle bones might
form a characteristic mark of the Argentine landscape, a
symbolic signature of the major product of the country.
Have we not W. H. Hudson's vignette of this in the outskirts
of Buenos Aires during his boyhood?

One extraordinary feature of the private quintas or

orchards and plantation in the vicinity of the Saladero
was the walls or hedges. These were built entirely
of cow's skulls, seven, eight or nine deep, placed
evenly like stones, the horns projecting. Hundreds
of thousands of skulls had been thus used, and some
of the old, very long walls, crowned with green
grass and with creepers and wild flowers growing
from cavities in the bones, had a strangely picturesque but somewhat uncanny appearance. As a rule
there were old Lombardy poplars behind these strange
walls or fences. In those days bones were not uti-
lized; they were thrown away, and those who wanted
walls in a stoneless land, where bricks and wood for
palings were dear to buy, found in the skulls a useful substitute.

Surely this glimpse is enough to impress one with the vast
number and cheaply discarded remains of the country's cattle. The fences were made to constrain the cattle, until
the cattle made the fences. If Alexander's bones might stop
the bung-hole of a barrel, or imperial Caesar's might stop
a hole to keep the wind away, as Hamlet ruminated, what
can be said of these infinite skulls and skeletons used in
place of bricks and stones? The tens of thousands of skeletons so used, and the millions of carcasses that have rotted
and fertilized the Argentine plains, are mere symbols of
those inexhaustible herds that have populated the pampas
through the centuries. During the gran seca, or great
drought, of 1827-30, Darwin tells us, countless thousand
herds of cattle rushed into the Parana and being exhausted
by hunger were unable to crawl up the muddy banks and thus
were drowned; their carcasses, several hundred thousand,
filled the river and were deposited in the estuary of La
Plata. The lowest estimate of the loss of cattle in the
province of Buenos Aires alone at that time was taken as a
million head. Darwin then adds: "I noticed that the smaller
streams in the Pampas were paved with a breccia of bones,
but this probably is the effect of gradual increase, rather
than of the destruction at any one period." After the gran
seca, great rains and floods helped to bury the carcasses
and skeletons. Truly the measure of the cattle of olden
days is the relict of their bones. Argentina is the cattle
country par excellence.

In desperate need of more beef, the British discovered these resources of Argentina and conquered the country. They built up a near monopoly. They built railways

to bring the cattle to the coast; they supported the railways with shipments of English coal.   They built, on the coast, huge packing houses, or frigorificos, where the meat, when not shipped on the hoof, was chilled for easier shipment to England.   Vast, enormously rich estancias prospered, largely owned by English cattle-barons.   This monopolistic control over the most important aspect of Argentina economy gave the land a nickname of "England's Sixth Dominion," although since 1830 Argentina was politically an independent Republic.

But the interruption of maritime traffic during the years of the two World Wars broke some of this reciprocal trade relationship; the ogre of nationalism rose in Argentina, and expropriation began.   British investment, once the stimulant to Argentine progress, declined through lack of the great cattle-producing estancieros.   The lack of supplies of English coal to operate the railways left the Argentinians to depend on their own inefficient cornhusks for fuel.   The urgent British need for beef led the Argentine nationalists to demand extortionate prices and conditions.

During World War II, when the European markets for Argentine beef were partially closed, an effort was made to find a market in the U.S.A.   Ray Joseph recorded in the 1940's, "Plans are under way here and in Washington to open the hitherto tightly closed United States market to lower priced Argentine beef.   The proposals are being developed for two basic reasons.   The first is economic: the present critical, war-borne United States meat shortage and Argentina's vast, practically untapped supply of what she claims is the world's best meat.   The second is political-- the fact that if Uncle Sam opens the door to Argentine beef, a door long barred on the grounds that the pampa cattle are carriers of hoof-and-mouth disease, Argentina may, in return, drop her old belief that it is still possible to do business with Hitler, and sever the last vital swastika link to this hemisphere.   Mixing meat with the gravy of diplomacy and handing out one-way tickets to the Berlin, Rome and Tokyo diplomats in return for a hefty beef contract may seem far fetched to some norteamericanos.   But to those who know Argentina's meat complex, who know that meat is the No. 1 industry, the No. 1 export item and top wealth producer, is not at all strange.   Meat is a king here" [Argentine Diary].

The British taste for beef indeed led to diplomacy:

while I was in Argentina, several high-level British commercial missions came to Buenos Aires and the British Ambassador was mainly concerned with negotiations over beef shipments to England.   There was also much diplomatic discussion between Argentina and the United States government, as
mentioned above.

Argentina is generally regarded as the principal Latin American cattle country.   Nevertheless Richard Condon
has recently reminded us that Mexico has a similar reputation.   "Mexico is such a meat-and-salsa picante (hot sauce)
country that its cattle industry virtually invented the United
States cowboy, his equipment, methods, and much of his
speech, thus sustaining the North American television industry through some twelve years of programming.   Fifty years
before the Pilgrim invasion of New England in 1620, the
cattle business was flourishing in northern Mexico" ["An
Old and Exotic Cuisine," Holiday, Oct. 1963, p. 104].

We may mention the effects of a certain tuber in
English husbandry.   Dr. Glover draws a far-stretched link
between the real foundation of the work of Reynolds and
Romney and Gainsborough and the other great painters of
their day, with turnips!   In brief his line of argument is
the following: cattle, used for food, were, because of shortage of pasture land and fodder, poor beasts, ill-bred and
ill-fed.   There was not enough meadow land to raise the
hay needed to keep them alive through the winter, and they
had to be slaughtered in November.   The introduction of
Swedish turnips provided winter fodder.   The commons were
enclosed experimentally with clover and turnips, and today's
English hedgerows are monuments of a victory for scientific agriculture and husbandry.   The gain was fresh meat
all winter and an obvious gain in national health.   "The improvements [said Dr. Glover] enabled England to meet the
strains of the Napoleonic wars, to bear the burdens of additional taxation, and to feed the vast centres of commercial
industry, which sprang up as if by magic, at a time when
food supplies could not have been provided from another
country."   And so, thanks to the introduction of the lowly
turnip, the great prosperous landlords and farmers had
their wives and daughters painted by the great portraitists,
and England was richer forever, even if the originals sometimes cross the ocean.

FISH

From early times Europeans had generally been eaters of fish, a relatively cheap food. Northern Europe had its fisheries; England, an overpopulated island had a strong fisheries industry. Indeed, economic interpreters of history suggest that while the Church, on religious grounds favored one meatless day a week as a sort of fast and a fish-eating day as a sort of ritualistic observance, the political authorities in London encouraged the eating of fish on Fridays as a means of using up the stocks of perishable fish in the dockside fish markets before a non-commercial Sabbath should allow the stocks, lacking cold storage, to decay.

The Catholic religion and the High Church set aside certain days of the week of fasting, on which days fish might be eaten in place of meat. Friday in particular was a fish day. But the strict observance of this practice by all good followers of the Church was also associated, in mediaeval times, with more mundane economic considerations. Thomas Cogan, in his Haven of Health (1596), wrote:

> Now concerning fish, which is no small part of our sustenance in the realme of England. And that flesh might be more plentifull and better cheape, two daies in the week, that is Friday and Saturday, are especially appointed to fish, and now of late yeares by the providence of our prudent Queen Elizabeth, the Wednesday is also in a manner restrained to the same order, not for any religion or holiness supposed to be in the eating of fish rather than flesh, but only for the civill policie as I have said....

This "civill policie" would seem to have been an effort to encourage and support the fisheries industry of England, and also to protect the fish-dealers from losing their perishable stock in their sheds and shops through decay if unsold, since there was no cold storage, or other preservation. Moreover, as fish was cheaper than meat, the poorer classes, rather than be impoverished by high expenditure on meat and game, or be left hungry, were recommended to make fish their diet. Fish was also a popular article of diet in southern France, in Portugal and Spain; and the fishing boats and fishermen were kept busy around the coasts and further abroad.

Adventurous sailors got across the Atlantic as far as

the Newfoundland banks, where they discovered a plentitude of codfish; and soon each season, fleets of European fishing boats were at work.   To a continent which never had quite enough to eat, a new source of food supply was literally more valuable than gold.   Consequently, after John Cabot's return to Bristol, others flocked out for the fishing, and the harbor of St. John's, Newfoundland, has never been empty of ships.   Settlement in Newfoundland, based on codfish, came in time, but it was a long time.   Meanwhile French and English merchants from west country parts, like St. Malo and Bristol, brought some cargoes of the new food, or better still sent them down to Spain and Italy, where they sold them for Spanish gold.   There developed two types of fishery: the green fishery of cod caught off-shore, split and salted and thence carried to Europe, and the dry fishery, of cod mainly caught inshore, cleaned, salted and dried in the sun on the "flakes" still to be seen in any Atlantic coast village, and shipped to whatever market seemed to offer best.   Later on, after West Indian industry had become well organized and the slave population there had grown considerably, dried codfish from the north proved to be a cheap and economical food, so that another branch was added to this first northern staple trade.   It was naturally the dry, or inshore, fishery that gave rise to settlement.   Local settlement gave rise to exploration of the rivers, like the St. Lawrence, and inland penetration; and thus the beginnings of the exploration and conquest of the New World by Europeans were initiated. Again, we may trace this historic outcome backwards to its source, the taste of Europeans for codfish as a nutritious and inexpensive diet.

SPICES

From meat and fish, there was the world-history influencing development of the spice trade.   For those European peoples who ate meat, in the late Middle Ages, there was the problem of preservation.   Normally meat was seasonal.   Wild animals bred in certain seasons, or migrated: hunting was limited to season.   Unless meat could be preserved out of season, eaters of it went short or starving; or there was famine, leading to depleted health, or to political agitation.   Throughout the Middle Ages in Europe, the supreme necessity of the prevailing meat diet, if it were to be palatable, was spice--not only in England (as the common name Spicer reminds us), but in Germany and France as well.   Pepper, ginger--anything to get the stuff down; and certain spices to preserve some flavor in decaying meat.

The Venetians and the Genoese were the great middlemen who supplied the North with spices from the Orient. But in the 15th century Constantinople fell to the Turks, who won a new hold on the Mediterranean and the overland caravan spice routes. Meanwhile the West was beginning to think of sea routes in place of the closed land routes to the lands of spice in the Orient. Under the stimulus of Henry the Navigator, the Portuguese Vasco da Gama opened the long way to Calicut, in 1498. Admiral Ballard says that a supreme step in history had been taken, and ever since those seas have been more and more dominated by Western merchantmen protected by Western navies. This maritime spice trade flourished until Portugal and her dominions fell under the Spanish rule, which was more interested in gold than in spice. Then in religious zeal Philip II forbade Lisbon to sell pepper and spices to heretics. The Dutch thereupon established their own trade and set up outposts throughout the Orient. When they put up the price of pepper and spice, London resented it, and formed its own East India Company, which led, under Clive and Warren Hastings, to the British Indian Empire, surrendered only in 1947. "If ever diet affected history, it was surely when bad English meat and high Dutch prices drove Englishmen to fetch their own pepper; leading to the search for a short route to the spice-lands of the Orient, either across the isthmus of Suez and through the Red Sea, or around the Cape, or across the isthmus of Panama, or in search of a passage to China through the rivers or Arctic seas of North America" [W. R. Young, Life Nov. 23, 1962, p. 113]. Thus the need for spices among the countries with a meat diet changed the map of the Earth.

It is said that the wealth and power of King Solomon, of the Princes of Arabia and of the merchants of Venice all rested upon the spice-trade. "In search of the fabled but mystery-cloaked Spice Islands from which oriental traders said they obtained the coveted supplies of cloves and cinnamon, pepper and nutmeg, Marco Polo toured the East, Columbus discovered America and Magellan launched his circumnavigation of the globe. And when Europeans finally located the pepper vines on the Malabar coast of India, the cinnamon tree on Ceylon, and the clove and nutmeg groves on the Moluccan Isles, savage competition and ruthless battles were set off among the Portuguese, Dutch and English" [W. R. Young, Life].

SUGAR

Another example is that of sugar, which in many forms, including rum, is an important article of diet and confectionery. Indian sugar was known to the Hellenic world, but only used as medicine; the Crusaders esteemed it especially for chest troubles. Throughout the ancient world honey was the popular sweetener of food; the bee was honored and worshipped, as in the fourth Georgic. Sugar cane was early introduced from India to Persia, and thence the plant was carried by the Arabs to Egypt, North Africa, and then to Spain. The Portuguese took it to Madeira, the Spaniards to the Canary Islands; and thence the cane was transplanted to the West Indian islands, which came to dominate the market. Under the Spaniards, native labor was wanting on the plantations, and negroes were imported. Sugar was not the sole cause of West Indian negro slavery, but it was among the initial causes. From there slavery spread to the mainland of America, where sugar growing was supplemented by tobacco and rice cultivation and ultimately cotton. "Not all the consequences of African bondage must be put down to sugar, but on sugar the whole struggle for emancipation centered in the days of Clarkson and Wilberforce, and indirectly from sugar, came the American Civil War, and the hideous troubles involved in the presence of the African in North and South America. ... Diet, it will be allowed, can have amazing consequences in history," remarks Dr. Glover.

This same conclusion is given by Professor A. R. M. Lower of United College, Winnipeg.

Europe hungered for good things. One of the best was sugar. Men everywhere have sweet tooths but before sugar became available, few there were who could satisfy their tastes. It was no accident that it was the Queen who sat in the parlor eating bread and honey; ordinary people had to get along as best they could with beer and fat meat. Once sugar appeared it added greatly to the joy of living and to the profit of the country which controlled the delectable lands from which the new supplies came, the West Indies or 'sugar islands.' With sugar, an agricultural product, came the need for labor. Lordly Spaniards did not go to the colonies to toil, so that it became necessary to find others to work for them. The native Indian seemed the natural solution, but he proved

too proud or too tender and as an alternative to
slavery, died.   A satisfactory substitute was eventually found in the African Negro.   On gold, sugar and
slaves the Spanish and Portuguese colonies grew up.
They were founded from Europe and they existed for
Europe" [From Colony to Nation, p. 4].

Thus, to the European taste for cane sugar, mainly
from the West Indies, can be attributed the slavery controversy, the American Civil War, Abraham Lincoln's fame
and General Grant's tomb on Riverside Drive.   The taste
for this American sweetener brought its sour and sorry aftermath.

But, says Dr. Glover, we are not quite done with
sugar.   Pitt captured the Caribbean sugar-islands, and cut
France off from her supplies of what had become in two or
three centuries absolutely necessary to life.   Napoleon, to
meet the emergency, mobilized French botanists, horticul-
turalists and chemists, to make France independent of the
Indies and sugar cane, by giving her a new type of sugar
and a new industry, whose staple was the beet.   A bounty
was given for the manufacture of beet sugar, which then became so cheap that it found an increasing market in England.   But then an English government, anxious to help its
dependencies, discriminated against the bounty-fed or subsi-
dized French beet sugar, failing to realize, at least initial-
ly, how large a part in national life was held by cheap sug-
ar--on the table, indeed, but far more in sweets, choco-
lates (which became almost a monopoly of Quaker manufac-
turers like the Rowntrees, Cadburys and Frys), other confectionery, and jams.   The struggle between beet sugar and
cane sugar continued.   Hawaii changed its complexion by the
introduction of sugar cane, which brought it into the orbit of
the United States; and the Cuban sugar trade with America
has lately suffered such blows in our own day that Russian
influence and Communism crept into the Caribbean.

"A lot of politics, industry, human life, and human
suffering, war and peace and prosperity--all affected by a
single article of diet which was quite unknown to the ancients.   On such trifles turn the fate of nations--if they are
trifles. ...   That there is a field for historical study in the
common dishes and tastes of the people, in their necessi-
ties, we may agree--if it was ever really disputable"
[Glover, "Diet in History," op. cit.].

SALT

Having mentioned spices and sugar, we may make
passing reference to the universal condiment salt, which also has its political implications.   Early in the agricultural
societies evolving from nomadic ones, salt became a necessity; often, many societies, or nations, had to import salt
from abroad.   Local sources were considered gifts from the
gods, and wars were fought for salt springs.   The Germans
believed that an area with salt in the earth was particularly
sanctified--a place where prayers were most readily heard.
The customary use of salt is directly linked to the changes
from nomadic to agricultural life; and it was precisely this
advancement that most informed the religious life of almost
all ancient nations.   The gods were worshipped as providers
--especially of the cereals--and in many languages throughout the world, the words (and concepts) "bread and salt" commonly go together.   Salt, then, has come to be widely associated with ceremonial or spiritual offerings.   Some of the
oldest trade routes were probably those for commerce in
salt.   Along with incense, a religious necessity of the ancient world, salt plays a great part in what we know of ancient highways.   One of the oldest roads in Italy is the
Via Salaria, by which salt from Ostia was brought up into
the Sabine country.   Herodotus's account [iv, 181 ...] of
the caravan routes among the salt oases of the Libyan desert indicates clearly that the route existed mainly for the
trade in salt.

"In like manner the ancient trade between the Aegean
and the coasts of southern Russia was largely dependent on
the salt pans at the mouth of the Dnieper and on the salt
fish brought from this district.   In Phoenician commerce
salt and salt-fish--the latter a valued delicacy in the ancient
world--always formed an important item.   The vast salt-
mines of northern India were worked before the time of Alexander, and must have been the center of a widespread
trade" [Britannica (11th ed.), "Salt"].

The "salt of the earth" has two forms.   In many
coastal countries, the brine of the sea is dried in huge salt
pans or evaporation beds; I have seen them in India, at
Aden, and in Japan, and elsewhere.   The desiccating sun
does the work; and the product is vast quantities of bleached
salt.   In many other countries there are large rock salt de-
posits, which are quarried or mined by hand.   The "salt-
mines" of Russia and Siberia are notorious for the utiliza-

tion of slave and (political) prisoner labor. Rock salt, which
is easily destroyed if exposed to erosive and corrosive elements, is, if protected underground, an easily-worked crys-
talline salt. In one famous salt mine at Wieliczka, near
Cracow, which I visited in Poland, the excavation of sub-
terranean salt has gone on from ancient times; and by now
has, in one sector, left a vast cave that has been modelled
as a cathedral or large chapel, complete with an altar, effi-
gies carved in the side niches, and illumination by indirect
electric lighting. There may be other such constructions in
the salt mines of Europe. In 1963 it was reported that a
new salt mine in Louisiana contains enough salt to supply
the world's needs for centuries. Canada ranks about eighth
among world salt producers; and Ontario accounts for almost
90 per cent of the nation's production. The first Canadian
production of salt for commercial purposes was in Manitoba
in 1820. Settlers found a salty spring, boiled the water in
iron pans over wood fires and recovered the salt. Rock
salt, which is coarser than brine salt, is largely used to
melt ice, but salt is also an important raw material source
for the chemical industry. Rock salt accounts for about 40
per cent of Canada's total production. At the great Ojibway
mine, near Windsor, big rubber-tired diesels wheel 15-ton
loads through spotless, well-lighted underground chambers,
20 feet high in some places.

Another illustration of the political importance of salt
has recently come [via Ottawa Journal, January 5, 1963] from
Vietnam. In one of the anti-Communist villages inhabited by
Montagnards, the enemy of the tribesmen is as much the
disease, goiter, as it is Communist guerrillas. The Montagnards have built a village, created an economy, set up a
miniature hospital, started a school. But nothing is more
basic to their health and life than salt, which is hard to come
by. Generation after generation of Montagnards have suffered from goiter and sickness has impaired their hunting
prowess. Regulations govern how much salt they may take
out for fear it will end up in Communist hands. The Americans have been the main source of salt sent to this village.

But apart from other commercial uses, salt resem-
bled spices, inasmuch as it helped to preserve meat and fish
from decay. The trade in salted meat and fish was an essential part of maritime commerce, aimed ultimately at en-
abling half-starving countries to have an additional source of
food and general sustenance. Before the modern era of refrigeration, most overseas supplies of meat and fish to Eu-

rope were in the form of dried and salted cargoes.

GRAIN

The role of meat and fish in history has led us to spices, and thence to cane sugar and beet sugar. We may therefore, by this transition, consider other aspects of the vegetarian tastes of man. From time immemorial, since mankind became agricultural, primitive religion has been based on a consideration of crops and fertility. Ceres was a principal goddess in the Roman pantheon, but she had her counterparts in every primitive society, as Sir James Frazer has shown in The Golden Bough. Long-established fertility rites of primitive peoples have been transmuted into religious holidays of, for example, Christian and Jewish significance.

Animal husbandry had in some parts shifted to agriculture; and man became as much an herbivorous animal as carnivorous. Out of these vegetarian tastes came more examples of change in the development and political history of the world. The nomadic aspects of early mankind gave place to agriculture, more stable settlement, community living, and social life. If we assume that the cultivation of cereals signalized the first stages of "civilization," we may note that it was somewhere in Egypt or Mesopotamia that its cultivation began, and spread over the entire eastern hemisphere. The growing of wheat had spread in neolithic times from the Atlantic to the Pacific coast, even before the beginnings of civilization. Civilization is something more than the occasional seasonal growing of wheat. It is the settlement of men upon an area continuously cultivated and possessed, with a common rule and a common community city or citadel. Along with these was required a permanent supply of water and fodder for the animals. In Mesopotamia and Egypt such conditions originally existed. Here was a constant water supply with enduring sunlight, trustworthy harvests year by year; in Mesopotamia wheat yielded, says Herodotus, two-hundredfold to the sower; Pliny says that it was cut twice and afterwards yielded good fodder for sheep; there were abundant palms and many sorts of fruits. Men took root; population increased rapidly; and civilization commenced, because of the security of food supply. (See H.G. Wells, Outline of History, p. 132.)

The era of the ploughshare and iron was the era of this second stage of civilization. Man was no longer generally a savage, a cunning hunter or a nomadic herder. He

became a settled agriculturalist who domesticated his livestock for food and service and who tilled his soil to raise
food crops and feed his cattle.   He became partly vegetarian.   As civilization progressed, so also widened the circle
of supply upon which indeed much of civilization depends.

When Rome came into ascendancy, its Roman population required more food than southern Italy could produce.
Expansion of empire was not only an economic necessity,
but a political one; the people often suffered hunger, even
famine; this led to discontent and agitation.   To keep the
population quiet, the emperors offered them panem et cir-
censes ("bread and amusements").   But grain was scarce
in Italy and overseas sources had to be sought.   Among
these was Egypt, which had grown cereals from the most
ancient times.   This was one explanation why the Roman
conquest of Ptolemaic Egypt made it its 'Eastern Province."
Egypt became and long continued to be the granary of the
Roman empire, and twenty million bushels of corn was the
life-sustaining tribute that she annually poured into the
storehouses of Imperial Rome.   Neither Romans nor Gauls
were, until a late period, acquainted with the method of
making fermented bread.   The hand mill was one of the
trophies which the Roman eagles bore back with them from
Asia.   Mola, the goddess charged therewith, looked to the
well-meaning of mills (moulins), millers and bread.   The
Roman conquest of Egypt was mixed up with complicated
dynastic intrigues between Julius Caesar and Pompey; Caesar and the Ptolemies and Cleopatra; Caesar and Antony;
Antony and Cleopatra; Octavia and Antony; and Octavia
and Cleopatra.   It was also characterized by great battles,
especially the decisive naval battle of Actium.   But, behind
all this political manoeuvring for power and imperial alliance or conquest on behalf of Imperial Rome, was the need
of Egypt as a granary for the cereal-poor Romans.   (What
a falling off was there!   Today [1963], half the wheat consumed in Egypt comes from the fertile American plains.)

There has been a decline in the ancient civilizations
of the Middle East, largely because the disappearance of
their forested areas suspended natural soil moisture and ir-
rigation except along the rivers; agriculture and livestock
raising became ever more difficult as the lands became
desert; and human populations diminished and deteriorated.
Where are the great civilizations of North Africa, Egypt
and Mesopotamia now; their great cities like Babylon and
Ur, their great Pharaohs and Nebuchadnezzars?   The jungle

growths have vanished; the grass for pasturage has dried up;
the wind passeth over it and it is gone.

An outstanding example of the extinction of a civilization through the drying up of grain supplies is to be found
in the Mayan civilization which flourished between the 6th
and 12th centuries A.D. in Yucatan, Honduras and Guatemala. That civilization produced magnificent edifices, pyramids, temples, great sculptures and reliefs, and the first
and best calendrical system. But it had been unable to invent the plough. Its agricultural support of the city and
temple centers was extremely primitive. The jungle trees
and bush were cut down, allowed to dry out, then burned
shortly before the onset of the rainy season. Corn or Indian maize--the staple diet--was planted by the use of pointed
planting-sticks. After the fields were worn out, the farmer
moved to another clearing. Gradually the available land
supply became exhausted. The fallow period needed for a
field to become once more overgrown with trees and bushes,
after which it could be recleared by burning, steadily increased. A necessary consequence was that the Mayan
farmer had to go farther and farther into the jungle to find
suitable woodlands to clear for cultivation, and so farther
and farther away from the cities it was his duty to nourish and
which could not live without him. The great culture of the
Old Empire of the Mayas collapsed as the agricultural fun-
dament slowly proved inadequate. The lack of maize, and
pangs of hunger finally drove the Mayans to migrate, after
the cities were completely surrounded and ultimately linked
together by areas of dry, grassy steppe. Meanwhile the
jungle crept back into the forsaken temples and palaces.
Fallow wasteland again became forest, and the old abandoned cities were hidden from view for a thousand years.
Those of us who have visited Yucatan and Guatemala, and
have seen the rediscovered ruins concealed in deepest jungle,
may meditate on how the lack of grain production brought to
an end a remarkable civilization of culture and art in pre-
Columbian America.

BREAD

One of the economic causes of the French Revolution was the misery of the underfed peasantry. Tithes and
taxes and surrender of a part of their crops left them as
starving serfs; grain crop failures and natural disasters left
them hungering and famished; and the cry went up to Ver-

sailles for "Bread, bread!"* The most fatuous and inept
remark ever made was the retort by the frivolous Queen,
Marie-Antoinette, of Austrian rather than French blood:
"If they lack bread, let them eat cake." This callous attitude fired off the Revolution, lost the Bourbons their crown,
and their heads under King Guillotine. Thus the greatest
event in modern history, the French Revolution, may be
said to have been caused by the people's unfulfilled desire
for bread, the scriptural "staff of life."

It was hunger that led Jean Valjean, like so many of
his French countrymen, to steal a loaf of bread to feed his
starving sister and her family, a capital crime in 1815; and
on this incident Victor Hugo introduced and built up his magnificent epic story of Les Misérables. It was his master-
piece, written after fourteen years' labor, which appeared
simultaneously in eight capitals of the world, and brought
its author the sum of 400,000 francs. The figure of Jean
Valjean is one of the great achievements of the human imagination, and his story is a treasure of the revolutionary
movement in every modern land. It was symbolic, once
again, of bread and its consequences.

The beginnings of the Bolshevik Revolution which
overthrew the Romanov monarchy were characterized by riots breaking out in St. Petersburg, the capital. There were
several causes or pretexts for these disorders. One was a
shortage of bread, due mainly to unusually heavy snowfalls
during the first week of March 1917 which had hampered
communications and deprived many bakeries in Petersburg
of fuel. (There seems to have been no lack of flour.) Organized female textile workers marched through the streets
chanting subversive slogans like "Down with the war" and

---

*How Carlyle put it: "If we look now at Paris, one thing is too evident:
that the Bakers' shops have got their Queues, or Tails; their long strings
of purchasers, arranged in tail, so that the first come be the first served,
--were the shop once open!... In time we shall see the art, or quasi-art,
of standing in tail become one of the characteristics of the Parisian People,
distinguishing them from all other Peoples whatsoever. But consider, while
work itself is so scarce, how a man must not only realize money, but
stand waiting (if his wife is too weak to wait and struggle) for half-days in
the Tail, till he gets it changed for dear bad bread! Controversies, to the
length sometimes of blood and battery, must arise in these exasperated
Queues. Or if no controversy, then it is but one accordant Pange Lingua
of complaint against the Powers that be. France has begun her long Curriculum of Hungering ... which extends over some seven most strenuous
years. As Jean Paul says of his own life, 'To a great height shall the
business of Hungering go'" [The French Revolution, book vi, chapter iv].

"Give us Bread." Soon workers began looting the bread
shops. Thus, at its beginnings, the Russian Revolution was
a series of scattered bread riots in the capital. (See Edmond Taylor, The Fall of the Dynasties, p. 259.)

The transformation of British economic policy from
protectionism to free trade, during the ministry of Sir Robert Peel, can be traced to the famine in grain crops in
England and in the potato crop in Ireland in the years 1845-
46, leading to bread-riots and hunger-marches, death, misery, and emigration. In a period of relatively small population the wealthy landowners who comprised the aristocracy of England, and their yeomen tenantry, produced enough
grain for English consumption and even a surplus for export; they kept their privileges and profits by the high protection tariffs of the Corn Law (1815) against cheaper importations. As industrialization caused the population to increase, there was a domestic shortage of grain, especially
after crop failures in 1816-1819, and in 1845, resulting in
riots demanding imported wheat and flour. "Give us this
day our daily bread!" After bitter political struggles between the protectionists and the free traders, restrictions
of the Corn Law had to be repealed, but Sir Robert Peel's
admirable ministry suffered downfall in consequence. The
Duke of Wellington, when asked for comments, said: "Rotten potatoes have done it all; they put Peel in his damned
fright." Disraeli, visiting Paris when he heard the news
of Peel's betrayal of the protectionists and his proposal for
the abolition of the Corn Laws, reflected: "These rotten
potatoes are going to change the fate of the world."

One result was the decline of the great landed aristocracy, after imports usurped their domestic monopoly.
Another result was the development of the great grain producing countries like Canada, the United States, Australia
and Argentina, which now found markets opened in Britain.
In Canada it resulted in the development of railways, the
growth of great wheat centers like Winnipeg, and shipping
ports like Vancouver, Port Arthur, Port Churchill and
Montreal.

Grain hunger had similar effects on the economic
life of the United States. Frank Norris wrote his realistic
novel The Octopus as an epic of wheat-growing in the West
(and its bitter relationship with the railroads that carried
the wheat to ocean ports). Marine commerce in the Great
Lakes, the building of chains of locks (at Sault St. Marie

and Welland), of canals (the Erie Canal), of ports like Du-
luth, and the St. Lawrence Seaway, and more recently Port
Churchill, were largely based on the grain trade, which was
made possible by the repeal of the Corn Law in England,
caused by domestic crop failure at home and increasing population. Economic history is a long chain of connected circumstances, and of cause and effect with endless consequences. The British demand for bread, as part of its established diet, lay at the root. It affected overseas history,
and gave the impetus to the development of countries in the
New World.

Referring to the rise of wheat-connected settlements
in Canada, A. R. M. Lower wrote:

> All staples are similar in that they must be obtain-
> able in large quantities, be of fairly uniform quality
> in dependable grades and arise in response to a large
> demand. Wheat met these requirements perfectly,
> and in addition it was easily transportable because it
> was almost a liquid: it could be poured and pumped
> almost like oil. All great staples have thrown up
> high-colored exploitive societies like wildfire, and
> have rapidly subjugated all the country fit for produc-
> ing them. Wheat was to be no exception to the rule.
> It called for men and for railroads, and it soon got
> both [From Colony to Nation, p. 423].

A great dietary revolution has lately occurred in Japan and China, formerly predominantly rice-growing and rice-
eating countries. The forcible introduction, especially by
Australia, the United States and Canada, of a new taste for
bread, has changed the dietary habits and the trade patterns.
The change of dietary habits was internal as well as external. The Canadian commercial attaché in Tokyo in my time,
Mr. James P. Manion, explained it this way:

> While we have always thought of Japan as being in
> the rice area, the fact is that increasingly bread
> grains have become the staple foodstuff. There have
> been several contributing factors, the principal one
> being that up to thirty per cent of cereals had to be
> imported, and that during the post-war years rice
> cost up to two hundred dollars a ton against wheat at
> about eighty dollars. Secondly, the white-collar
> worker in the larger cities found it more convenient
> to eat bread or bring sandwiches to the office. In

addition, the government had instituted a school
lunch programme, and bread is far more easy to
handle than rice.   Finally, there is undoubtedly
among the young people a sort of emulation of the
occupation troops, all of whom must have looked like
Texans and therefore worthy of being imitated [A
Canadian Errant, p. 28].

The enormous disposable surpluses of wheat and
flour in Australia, the United States and Canada led to pressure in the search for new markets, especially in the Far
East.   When I was in Japan, the Canadian government made,
through its Minister Sir Herbert Marler, a tremendous effort to break into this potential market, but in the 1930's
it was a relative failure because of the government's inflex-
ible demand for dollar cash payment, while the countries
concerned wished long-term credit arrangements.

In the 1950's and early 1960's, however, famine and
food needs overcame the former reluctance, and payment arrangements were liberalized, so that export of wheat, both
to Japan (which reexported quantities of it to South East
Asia) and to Communist China, were dramatically increased.
Once having acquired the Westerners' taste for bread, the
Far East changed its trade-pattern, and the West discovered new outlets for its ever-increasing grain surpluses.
I remember thinking in the 1930's that the West's efforts to
change the dietary habits of those countries might be sowing
dragon's teeth and preparing a boomerang effect.   Once they
adopted wheat in place of hand-labor rice cultivation, they
might, with their cheap wages and excess manpower, begin
to cultivate their own wheat, at cheaper cost, and ultimately begin to inundate the West with their own cheaper product;
but this has not come to pass, since home consumption in
the Far East will for long exceed production and exportable
surpluses.

POTATOES

Europe quite early had supplemented its meat diet
with vegetables.   Some thought that vegetarianism was more
wholesome.   A meat diet was justified perhaps for those engaged in physical activity, for the military, the laborers
and the athletes or sportsmen.   But the notion grew up that
it was rated lower as a brain-food, and the "intellectuals"
sometimes settled for fish or vegetables.   This notion was
noted by Shakespeare: as Sir Andrew Aguecheek said in

Twelfth Night, "I am a great eater of beef, and I believe it
does harm to my wit," to which Sir Toby Belch replied "No
question!" George Bernard Shaw was among the most prominent of 20th-century wits to follow rigidly a vegetarian diet.
Besides, meat in Europe was becoming scarce and therefore
more expensive. Among the popular vegetables, besides
cabbage and Brussels sprouts, was an introduced tuber, the
potato.

The common potato was indigenous to Chile, Peru and
Mexico. It was probably brought to Spain from Quito by the
Spaniards in the early part of the 16th century. In 1598 it
arrived at Vienna, and from there spread across Europe.
One authority declares that it was not known in North America in 1586, the period at which Raleigh's colonists in Virginia are said to have sent it to England; and in England it
was not known until long after its introduction into Ireland.
Cobbett cursed the root as being the ruin of Ireland, where
it is said to have been first planted by Raleigh on his
estate at Youghal, near Cork. Its introduction into England
is described as the consequence of the wrecking of a vessel
on the coast of Lancashire, which had a quantity of this
"fruit" aboard. Meanwhile, in England the sweet potato was
the "delicate dish" at English tables, long before the introduction of the ordinary potato. It was imported in considerable quantities from Spain and the Canaries. The Irish having in the 18th century been introduced to the potato, proceeded in true Malthusian fashion to breed up to the limits
of potato subsistence. The humble vegetable gives so much
in return for so little that the population in the course of
half a century rushed from 4.5 million to over 8 million on
32,000 not too fertile square miles; at least 4 million lived
on potatoes and nothing else but potatoes. In 1845-46 the
crop failed, and Irishmen began to die like flies.

Adam Smith pointed out that, weight for weight, potatoes were more economical and more nutritious, and that
vines, fruits and tuber-vegetables were even more valuable
than the stock-in-trade of corn (i.e., wheat).

> That a vineyard, when properly planted and brought
> to perfection, was the most valuable part of the
> farm, seems to have been an undoubted maxim in the
> ancient agriculture, as it is in the modern, through
> all the wine countries.... A rice field produces a
> much greater quantity of food than the most fertile
> corn [wheat] field.... The food produced by a field

of potatoes is not inferior to that produced by a field
of rice and much superior to what is produced by a
field of wheat.   Twelve thousand weight of potatoes
from an acre of land is not a greater producer than
two thousand weight of wheat.   Allowing half the
weight of this root to go to water, a very large allowance, such an acre of potatoes will still produce
six thousand weight of solid nourishment, three times
the quantity produced by the acre of wheat [Adam
Smith, Wealth of Nations, vol. i, chap. xi].

In consequence of this fact, the potato became the major
crop in Ireland where the population was pressing on food
resources.   But when that crop failed, there was national
hunger.

In 1846 at least half the Irish peasantry would have
to be fed on corn. ("Corn" was and is the English term for
wheat, sometimes including also oats, rye and barley.) But
the English corn crop, protected by the Corn Law, was also
a failure.   In 1846 Sir Robert Peel, the British Prime Minister, wrote: "The accounts of the state of the potato crop
in Ireland are becoming alarming.   I have no confidence in
such remedies as the prohibition of exports, or the stoppage
of distilleries.   The removal of the impediments to import
is the only effectual remedy."   Amid widespread political opposition of the Protestionists in England, Peel succeeded in
passing legislation repealing the restrictive Corn Law. But
it was too late to save the starving Irish.   Between 1846
and 1851 nearly a million people died at home and a million
people left the shores of Ireland.   In the half-century between 1831 and 1881 the Irish population decreased by 32
per cent, while that of England and Wales increased by 87
per cent.   Besides, hundreds of thousands of Irishmen emi-
grated to the New World, under the most tragic hardships.
In 1847 over 17,000 Irish emigrants died of "ship fever"
alone.

The Irish exiles who reached the United States, suffered tragedies similar to those 200,000 or more that came
to the shores of the St. Lawrence, but in the end hundreds
of thousands fleeing the Emerald Isle settled in the United
States.   Most of them remained in the cities of the Atlantic
coast; New York City alone had 133,000 Irish immigrants in
1850.   The American anthropologist Carleton S. Coon remarked, "thus we can thank the Indians of southern Chile
for much of our Irish population."

Thus, as the repeal of the Corn Laws led to serious
changes in English policy and, indirectly, to the agricultural
development of North America, Australia and later Argentina, and their prosperity based on the grain trade, so the
failure of the potato culture in Ireland led to the peopling of
the United States and Canada by Irish immigrants, with their
ultimate political influences, while the depopulation of Ireland led to its permanent impoverishment. National taste,
and inadequate food-supply, affected the patterns of the
world.

TEA

The English adoption of tea as a national drink had
its vast though remote repercussions, in the Boston Tea
Party, the American Revolution and independence from British sovereignty, the creation. of the United States of America, the development of the clipper ships and maritime trade
of New England, and a host of others, some of which are
referred to in a later chapter.   On the other side, the tea-
drinking salons of England in the 19th century became centers of literature and domestic politics, which left their
permanent mark on England's cultural and political history.
The Rev. Sydney Smith (1771-1845) once exclaimed: "Thank
God for tea! What would the world be without tea? How
did it exist? I am glad that I was not born before tea."
Nor should we forget that the tea ceremony, based on the
custom of tea-drinking introduced from its native source,
China, was elaborated as a symbol of the upper class dominion in Japan in the Hideyoshi-Tokugawa era.   The elaborate tea ceremony, which is still performed as a ritual
among the conservative traditionalists, was a symbol of the
aesthetic age of 16th-century Japan.   Although under the
leadership of Hideyoshi--the greatest of Japanese warriors
who was at the same time a patron of art in the extravagant
manner--a lofty, imaginative and imposing style in art and
architecture was cultivated, there was on the other hand a
continued development of the simpler classical style.   It was
this almost spartan style, for example, that was manifested
in and influenced by the tea ceremony--then popular among
the military class.   For the dignified, restrained, and highly ritualistic ceremony, a small and simple building called
sukiya, or cha-shitsu, was developed, the architecture of
which was one of studied rusticity and simplicity.   Even the
tea utensils were of archaic simplicity, indicative of a return to almost primitive, yet chaste and graceful modera-
tion.

COFFEE

Coffee also has entered into the history as well as
diplomacy of nations as much as wines have.   Coffehouses
were the forerunners of the modern news sources.   Europe's
taste for coffee since the 17th century not only created many
social forces emanating from the widespread vogue of cof-
feehouses, but also brought economic prosperity to many
coffee producing countries, both Arabic and Latin American.
The fortunes of countries like Colombia and Brazil rose and
fell with the overseas demand and markets for coffee.   In
the mid-20th century, after oil, coffee is reported to, be the
biggest commodity in world trade.   It became of such international concern that delegates from 71 nations met in conference at the United Nations headquarters in New York in
August 1962, in what was called the biggest kaffee-klatsch
in history.   (See Time, Aug. 31, 1962, p. 51.)   Latin
Americans were angry at Common Market nations for putting high tariffs on coffee from South America yet almost
none on coffee from France's former African colonies.   Latin Americans wanted very strict quotas for export.   Afri-
cans, whose beans are used mainly for "instant" coffee and
whose trade is booming on the trend for instant, wanted
quotas that would expand or contract with world trade.   All
the forty or more coffee-producing countries wanted the
Europeans to lower their high tariffs on coffee.   An international and worldwide Coffee Council was created to stabi-
lize export quotas, control overproduction, and regularize
trade and prices.   Thus, the beverage that accompanies almost every diplomatic repast, whether café-au-lait or café-
noir or the demitasse, conceals its history of the economic
rise and fall of nations, the intergovernmental quarrels or
disputes over tariffs and taxes, the international conferences, and the commercial diplomacy that an oriental taste
carried over into Europe several centuries ago has bequeathed.

FOOD REDISTRIBUTION

Before passing on to the aspects of dining and wining,
we may also remind ourselves of the vast chasm that lies
between the underfed nations and the overfed.   For the first
time in history, we are told, the U. S. has produced a society in which less than one-tenth of the people turn out so
much food that the government's most embarrassing problem is how to dispose of 100 million tons of surplus farm
products.   Refrigeration, automated processing and packag-
ing conspire to defy the seasons.   Overproduction does not

necessarily imply underconsumption, for according to Department of Agriculture statistics the U.S. food consumption had
in 1959 averaged 1488 pounds per person, which, allowing
for the 17 million Americans that President John Kennedy
said go to bed hungry every night, means that certain glut-
tons on the upper end must somehow or other consume 8
pounds or more a day.   But still there is a production surplus.   Similarly, when I was in Argentina in the war years
1941-1946, the production of the staple food, beef, was so
far above consumption that thousands of tons were spoiled and
wasted, since overseas export markets were closed.   Yet the
other side of the medal shows food-deficiency and near-star-
vation in the more under-developed countries of Asia and Africa, which the United Nations Food and Agricultural Organization (F.A.O.) and other agencies are doing their best to
remedy, preventing or fighting famine conditions which in
Malthus's day were asserted to be one of the automatic checks
on population pressure.   Whether this huge chasm between
the undernourished peoples of the world and the overnourished
peoples is being narrowed by international action, emergency
relief, and technical food and agricultural assistance is hard
to assess.   Gains made through F.A.O. efforts are offset by
population increases gained through W.H.O. efforts of health,
hygiene and lowered mortality.   The concept of a vast international "food-bank" or reservoir has been mooted in international political and economic circles.   It would not only
provide a means of equitable distribution or sharing among
the "have" countries and the undernourished "have-not" countries, but might even reduce the impulses of hungry countries toward conquest, imperialism or colonialism, or economic dominance, which underlay past history.

At the present time, the conscience of mankind is involved in what is often called a campaign of "Freedom from
Hunger"--a means of sharing the over-producing countries'
resources and food-wealth with the poorer countries of non-
abundance and under-production.   In this respect, peaceful
cooperation may take the place of ancient food wars and revolutions, and thus contribute to a more peaceful world.   History, as we have seen, includes dietary struggles over food
supply.   Future history, under universal cooperation, as represented in the United Nations and its F.A.O., with headquarters in Rome, may diminish, under modern improvements
of communication, relief, and food exchange, the past dangers
of imperialism and colonialism and hunger.

While we have mentioned grain, flour, and bread-eating habits of the ancient and modern world, we should not forget that about half the people in the world live mostly on rice. Most of the rice-eating people are poor, and their nations, over-populated; rice, which is generally both planted and harvested by hand, is an easy and economical source of food. Rice therefore is a key to the main problem of survival in many overcrowded parts of the world. The government of India is host to a Rice Research Station, sponsored by the F. A. O. and ten other Asian countries. The adaptation of various species of rice to various climatic and topographical conditions is under serious study, in order to get the largest yields under primitive hand labor. As the new seeds are introduced, the people will see an exciting change in their own lives, when the same land and the same year's labor will bring forth twice as much to eat. For people who are almost always hungry, that will seem something to build a new world upon, without necessarily disarraying the political pattern of our globe.

Perhaps enough has been said, in these random illustrations and comments, to indicate the extent to which the gastronomic needs and tastes of the world have projected themselves into political and diplomatic history, and have affected the destinies of empires, colonies and nations. History can often be interpreted, as the old writers candidly put it, through the belly.

The next chapter takes a closer look at the more particular aspects of gastronomy and the culinary art that are associated with the day-by-day developments of state-craft and diplomacy. From the telescopic view we turn to the microcoscopic view; and sometimes the view through the looking glass. As if approaching one of the many North American roadside restaurants bluntly advertising "EATS," we now pull up and go in.

II

DINING IN POLITICS AND DIPLOMACY

The art of diplomacy may be said to be built largely around the precept given by St. Paul in his twelfth epistle to the Romans: "If thine enemy hunger, feed him; if he thirst, give him drink." This may have been based simply on the ethics or morality of mercy and charity or on customary desert hospitality; but it also carries an undertone of the later adage: "The way to a man's heart is through his stomach," which (though it has come to have a more particular connubial connotation) is equally important in what Machiavelli would have called the Art of Negotiating with Princes.

The maxim has been put into effect since time immemorial. Indeed the fable tells us that Eve won Adam's interest by offering him a certain fruit whereof to eat, although forbidden. Lord Byron in "Don Juan," wrote:

All human history attests
That happiness for man--the hungry sinner--
Since Eve ate apples, much depends on dinner.

On this episode apparently was built up the doctrine of original sin and "salvation." To the Puritans, therefore, feasting and banqueting have always seemed hedonistic and sinful.

Such overtures were customary among the most primitive tribes, including the North American Indians, and such ancient peoples as the Druids, the Egyptians and Assyrians, Greeks and Romans. The banquet, in its various primitive or later sophisticated forms, was as important as the campfire, the forum or the assembly; the refectory or salle à manger, or grand salon was as significant as the Moot, the parlament, or the Senate chamber. The white table was as important as the green baize table for the pursuit of diplomacy. The Round Table was an essential part of King Arthur's Court. Boswell quotes Dr. Johnson: "A dinner lubri-

cates business." Diplomacy is associated with dining and
wining. "The principal functions of an envoy," said François
de Callière, himself an ex-ambassador of Louis XIV, "are
two. The first is to look after the affairs of his own prince;
the second is to discover the affairs of the other." A clever
minister, he maintained, will know how to keep himself informed of all that goes on in the mind of the sovereign in
the counsels of ministers or in the country; and for this end
"good cheer and the warming effect of wine" are excellent allies.

DINNER AND POLITICS

Lin Yutang, the philosopher-essayist, puts the case
from the Chinese viewpoint [The Importance of Living, chap.
iii, iv]:

> Friends that meet at meals meet at peace. A good
> bird's-nest soup or a delicious chow mein has the
> tendency to assuage the heat of our arguments and
> tone down the harshness of our conflicting points of
> view. Put two of the best friends together when they
> are hungry, and they will invariably end up in a quar-
> rel. The effect of a good meal lasts not only a few
> hours, but for weeks and months. It is for this rea-
> son that, with the Chinese deep insight into human
> nature, all quarrels and disputes are settled at dinner
> tables instead of at the court of justice. The pattern
> of Chinese life is such that we not only settle disputes
> at dinner, after they have arisen, but also forestall
> the arising of disputes by the same means. In China,
> we bribe our way into the good will of everybody by
> frequent dinners. It is, in fact, the only safe guide
> to success in politics. Should someone take the
> trouble of compiling statistical figures, he would be
> able to find an absolute correlation between the num-
> ber of dinners a man gives to his friends and the
> rate or speed of his promotion.... I guess there is
> something similar to this Chinese way of life in the
> American political world, since I cannot but believe
> that human nature is very much the same and we are
> all so much alike under the skin.

Among primitive people, it is true, eating was not an
art of the table, but what we might call extremely vulgar.
We are told that in the days of Homer, while convivial repasts were common, they were also somewhat barbaric.

Athenaeus mentions the simplicity of the diet and of the service of it.   No plates, no forks, and knives only incidentally.
They ate, like Charles II, with their fingers, getting themselves in much of a mess, and water poured on their hands
was very necessary.   The common feeding-bowl is still a
custom in the less civilized, or rather less-westernized,
Arab and South Pacific countries; and it also characterized
the Indians of North America.   And the wash-bowl or "fin-
ger-bowl" was doubtless necessary before the adoption of
napkins.

When Sieur de Champlain, and his little French company came to Canada, he had to treat with the "barbarous"
Indian tribes; although he found this a terrible task, he finally succeeded in making friends with the Hurons, rivals of
the Algonquins and the Iroquois.   The Canadian historian
Professor George M. Wrong, who at the University of Toronto first interested me in history, has recorded [The Rise
and Fall of New France, vol. I, p. 221]:

> To a man of refinement one of the most trying exper-
> iences must have been to take a meal with the sav-
> ages.   Champlain was not squeamish, but even he
> drew back sometimes from the ordeal of eating with
> naked men, who defied every decency, who ate out of
> the same plate as their dogs, and gorged themselves
> to disgusting repletion.   On one occasion when Father
> Le Jeune failed to empty his plate his neighbour seized
> it, gulped down its contents in two swallows, and then
> thrust out a tongue 'as long as your hand' to lick
> clean both the bottoms and the sides.

In Ben Jonson's play, The Devil Is an Ass, performed
in 1616, a financial promoter or "projector" named Meer-
craft had a project to introduce into England the Italian custom of using forks, which would "be a mighty saver of linen."
He also hoped to get a monopoly on "serving the whole state
with tooth picks."   But in the Dark Ages there was no
thought either of linen, or of forks, or of finger bowls or
tooth picks.   Indeed, it is recorded that a woman who used
a fork was treated as a witch.

HISTORY OF DINING

The art and diplomacy of dining has gone through
many historical stages, to which only briefest reference need
be made.   There were the transitions from Stoic simplicity

to Roman luxury; from mediaeval coarseness and gluttony
to Italian and French refinement and fastidiousness; from
English good taste and elegance to a more simple taste in
modern times; and there was the passing of the great palaces and houses with their private entertainment, in favor
of more public restaurants and banquet halls.

In Roman history, there was first a period of the
Stoics (ca. 508-202 B.C.). What became known as Epicureanism was a misnomer.   Epicurus (341-270 B.C.) himself
was content with water and a little wine, bread and a little
cheese.   He was essentially a Stoic.   But he was a philosopher and a hedonist who believed in the superiority of pleasure, although pleasure in wise contentment of simple things
--fresh air, the cheapest of plainest food, a modest shelter,
preferably in quiet rural surroundings amid Nature and away
from urban excesses, a few books, and a friend or two.
But some of his disciples perverted this ideal.   Metrodorus
of Lampascus reduced Epicureanism to the proposition that
"all good things have reference to the belly," meaning perhaps bodily satisfaction.   The Gastrology of Archestratus
was labelled by Chrysippus "the metropolis of the Epicurean
philosophy" although it was a wide distortion of Epicurus's
Stoic ideals of bodily contentment through simple but choice
means.   Hedonism, originally emanating from the Greeks,
was a philosophy that holds pleasure to be the chief goal of
man; but it had two forms.   Pleasure may be derived from
the mere satisfaction of sensual desires, as with the Cyre-
naics; or it may be derived from the more lofty belief in
rationally ascetic control of desires, as in the true school
of the Epicureans.

Following the incoming Greek influence (201-146
B.C.), life became more liberated, and changed from stoic
simplicity to reckless hedonism and luxury among the upper
classes.   As physical exertion diminished and wealth expanded, the old simple diet gave way to long and lavish
meals of meat, game, delicacies, and condiments.   Exotic
foods were indispensable to social position or pretence.
There is on record that one magnate paid a thousand sesterces for the oysters served at a meal, another imported
anchovies at 1600 sesterces a cask; another paid 1200 for a
jar of caviar [Livy, XXXIX, 7; Mommsen, 201].   Sumptuary
laws were passed by the Senate limiting expenditure on banquets and clothing, but these were disregarded even by the
Senators themselves.   "The citizens," Cato mourned,   "no
longer listen to good advice, for the belly has no ears."

Later came the period of even greater extravagance and luxury, of millionaires, and conspicuous display.   Lucullus, a
Roman general (110-56 B.C.), was one of the leaders.   He
was a collector of sculpture and art works, learned in languages and philosophy, a builder of palaces and gardens; he
was said to have introduced the cherry tree from Pontus to
Italy, whence it was carried to north Europe and America.
His dinners were the culinary events of the Roman year.
But he had many competitors for these honors.   Eating became the chief occupation of upper-class Rome.   At a certain banquet, it is related, the hors d'oeuvres consisted of
mussels, spondyles, fieldfares with asparagus, fattened
fowls, oyster pastries, sea-nettles, ribs of roe, purple
shellfish, and songbirds.   Then came the dinner--sow's ud-
ders, boar's head, fish, duck, teals, hares, fowl, pastries,
and sweets [Polybius, VI, 17].   Delicacies were imported
from every part of the Empire and beyond: peacocks from
Samos, grouse from Phrygia, cranes from India, tunny-fish
from Chalcedon, muraenas from Gades, oysters from Tar-
entum, sturgeons from Rhodes.   Foods produced in Italy
were considered a bit vulgar, fit only for plebeians.

Such Roman banqueting was not merely for the pleasures of the stomach, or even for purposes of sweet discourse and philosophical or poetical discussion.   It usually
had a political motive--the aim to win friends and influence
people, to impress the Senators or statesmen to gain favor
or rank or position or business privilege.   In modern times
Veblen the iconoclast would have termed it 'conspicuous
waste"; the more recent writer Vance Packard, might have
included it as an example of the "status seekers"; but no
doubt it had a rational purpose.

J. C. Jeaffreson makes a rather extravagant claim
that the Roman occupation of Britain was beneficial to the
conquered people in culinary matters.   The natives had very
coarse and primtive tastes and modes of eating, but the
Romans taught them better.

> Together with his munitions and rules of war, the
> conqueror brought his science and implements of
> cookery.   Cooks completed the work which the tri-
> umphant legions had only begun....   Cookery and
> civilization are not purchased too dearly by barbar-
> ians who acquire them by the sacrifice of a more or
> less imaginary independence.   The more intelligent
> of the Britons thought so, as they sniffed the steam-

ing pottages and sipped the wines of their victors.
Cookery reconciled the islanders to the presence
and sway of the foreigner. No doubt, the older and
less adaptive of the aborigines scorned the allurements of Roman kitchens, and holding to their old no-
tions respecting unclean and sacred meats, disdained
to dip their fingers in a bowl of cocky-leekie. But
the younger islanders, surrendering themselves to
savoury fascinations, learnt to bless the conqueror
who taught them to appreciate the oyster, to stew the
goose, to jug the hare, and cook the pullet in half a
hundred ways. Having accepted the foreigner's government on compulsion, they took his sauces from·
preference, and his ragouts from gastronomic affection [A Book About the Table (1874), vol. I, p. 29].

Even in the Middle Ages, when most dining even
among the knightly classes was crude, eaten off rude planks
or trestles, with stools or benches or perhaps a great table
admirably carved, certain taste was observed, apart from
the food itself. In some mediaeval French homes ingenious
machines raised or lowered into place, from a lower or upper story, a full table ready served, and made it disappear
in a moment when the meal was finished. Servants brought
ewers of water to each diner, who washed the hands there-
in and wiped them on napkins which were then put away.
Each person received a spoon; forks were known in the 13th
century, but were seldom provided since fingers were used,
and the diner used his own knife. Food was abundant, varied, and well-prepared, except that lack of refrigeration
soon made meats high and put a premium upon spices that
could preserve or disguise. Some spices, as we have seen,
were imported from the Orient, but as these were costly,
other spices were grown in domestic gardens--parsley, mus-
tard, sage, savory, anise, garlic, and dill. Cookbooks
were numerous and complex. And in a good establishment
the cook was a man of importance, bearing on his shoulders
the dignity and reputation of the house.

It is interesting to look back on mediaeval food-tastes
if only to see how far we have bridged the historic gap.
Considering Europe only, in the Middle Ages,

...there were no potatoes, coffee or tea; but nearly
all meats and vegetables now used in Europe...were
eaten by mediaeval man. By the time of Charle-
magne the European acclimatization of Asiatic fruits

and nuts was almost complete.... The commonest
meat was pig. Pigs ate the refuse in the streets
and the people ate the pigs. It was widely believed
that pork caused leprosy, but this did not lessen the
taste for it.... Fish was a staple food; herring was
a main recourse of soldiers, sailors, and the poor.
Dairy products were less used than today, but the
cheese of Brie was already renowned. Salads were
unknown and confections were rare. Sugar was still
an import, and had not yet replaced honey for sweet-
ening. Pastries were innumerable; and jolly bakers,
quite unreproved, gave cakes and buns the most in-
teresting--and improper--shapes imaginable [Will
Durant, The Age of Faith, p. 837].

In mediaeval times, perhaps caused by wishful thinking, there was a place known as the Land of Cockaigne--as
Florio described it, "the epicure's or glutton's home, the
land of all delights, so taken in mockerie." If its Italian
form Cocagna is through a Latin word meaning "cake," the
literal sense of this name is "The Land of Cakes." "In
Cockaigne," we are told "the rivers were of wine, the
houses were built of cake and barley-sugar, the streets were
paved with pastry, and the shops supplied goods for nothing.
Roast geese and fowls wandered about inviting folks to eat
them, and buttered larks fell from the skies like man-
na." It was a pleasant fable, evidently reflecting the
Lucullan dreams; we may almost suspect that Alice in
her Looking Glass House was also half-dreaming of
Cockaigne in her repasts with her imaginary King and
Queen.

Throughout the milleniums, until fairly recent times,
the Chinese common people have lived in abject poverty.
Their mainstay was rice; and it was so precious that every
rice-grain was guarded, and skill in chopstick eating was
measured by the preservation of the last or lost or least
grain of rice. When I travelled through China in the 1930's,
hunger was ever a factor among the lower classes; this has
been partly due to a recurring phenomenon, that of vast regional famines, for which China is tragically famous. On
the other hand, the more well-to-do for thousands of years,
have been masters of good eating. From time immemorial,
the Chinese not only excelled in the most refined culinary
arts, but have had a palate for exquisite foods, and a well-
developed skill in gustatory entertainment. The kaleidoscope
and spectrum of their cuisine is enormous, and highly imag-

inative. I myself, while visiting China, experienced some
of their lavish tables of wonderful dishes. At one fabulous
wedding banquet in Shanghai, with a thousand Chinese guests
and four privileged foreign guests, I was confronted with a
150- to 200-dish repast that was an astonishing profusion of
food. I could no more do it full justice by describing it
than I could the full optional menu produced daily on the old
Isle de France or other super deluxe passenger liners which
in recent years have provided the most superb tables and
extensive menus in our Western World.

According to Hugh MacLennan, Chinese food is deca-
dent. Not like the Romans, with their nightingales' tongue
and vomitoria, but it seems obvious that one who enjoys
forty courses at dinner, no matter how much he may actually eat of each, is heading for a fall even though it may
come with grace and little regret. "Chinese cooks," says
MacLennan, "on the grand scale seem to me not cooks at
all, but Toscaninis of food" ["By Their Foods...," Scotch-
man's Return, p. 16].

Compared with the marvels of the Chinese culinary
art, which rivaled, if not surpassed the gourmets of ancient
Rome, and old France, one ordinarily thinks of Japanese
food as simple and spartan. In the past, in private, this
has been so, for the people of Japan were for long poor and
spartan. Even so, the simplest and most elementary local
fare is served with the greatest artistry of design and col-
or-arrangement. The lower Japanese are too poor to provide or consume special food; rice is their basic diet, and
fish. Meat is generally scarce, for there are few grazing
or pasture lands in mountainous Japan. The more well-to-
do are, by nature, loath to display their wealth; their tradition is one of frugal habits. Luxury is everywhere regarded as vulgar. Nevertheless, when they want to entertain distinguished guests, they know how to do so, outside
their own simple and frugal homes. There are beautiful
restaurants and "tea-houses" awaiting them, superb with
gardens, waterfalls, and little pavilions under plum or flow-
ering cherry or wisteria. There are endless numbers of
small restaurants in Tokyo, this one for its notable shark's
fins, that one for its bird's-nest soup, another for its carp.
One can also enjoy French haute cuisine, or sumptuous
Chinese restaurants, or American-style--steak (well-done,
medium or rare), ice water, and shrimp cocktails. But in
Japan, one should try tempura, prawns fried in oil; or sushi,
raw fish and rice; or sukiyaki, fried sliced beef with bam-

boo shoots and other vegetables; or suppon, tortoises cooked
in various ways; or uzura, roast quail; or kabavaki, eels;
or honpen, dog fish; or fugu, a roasted fish that is poisonous if
cooked improperly but which is said to be a powerful aphrodis-
iac.   In Tokyo also are Mongolian, Russian and Italian restaurants with rivers of tomato-purée; one can find Korean,
Formosan, or Indonesian restaurants as well.   One of the
nicest experiences is to eat in one of the vegetarian restaurants (shojin-ryoriya) that are frequently near the big Buddhist temples--such things as airy-light fried chrysanthe-
mums, soups of rare seaweeds, herbs with poetic names.
These are served in frail lacquered cups and delicate porce-
lains.

These certainly seem to match the range of exotic
foods of ancient Rome, or anything produced in more modern
Europe.   Such meals in Japan are still the means of amicable business, or political or diplomatic discourse.   The only
difference is that such entertaining is usually done in the outside restaurants, instead of in the private homes.   During
my sojourn of nearly ten years in the Far East, I had many
experiences with such exotic banquets, in company with diplomatic colleagues as guests of our Chinese and Japanese hosts.

One pauses here to wonder at the development of this
gustatory art; first at the variety of products that have been
found edible, and secondly at the inventiveness of mankind in
making Nature's products into delicacies for the taste and the
digestion of men.   The usually staid and matter-of-fact Encyclopaedia Britannica [11th ed.] ventures the observation
that "Mere hunger, though the best sauce, will not produce
cookery, which is the art of sauces."   Ben Jonson, in his
satire on English newspapers of 1626, The Staple of News,
invented, among other absurdities, news of a humane project sponsored by a colony of cooks, to convert all American
cannibals to the virtue of sauce on sausages so that they will
"forbear the mutual eating of one another."

The English essayist Leigh Hunt, awed by the culinary
arts, over a century ago, exclaimed:

> Think of the enormous multitude of dishes--of the end-
> less varieties of food which nature seems to have
> taken a delight in providing, and of the no less diver-
> sity of tastes and relishes with which she has recom-
> mended them to our palates.   Take the list of eatables
> for mankind alone (if any cook could make one out),

and think of its endless variety of fish, flesh, and
fowl, of fruits and vegetables, and minerals; how
many domestic animals it includes; how many wild
ones; how many creatures out of the sea; how many
trees and shrubs; how many plants and herbs; how
many lands, oceans, airs, climates, countries, besides the combinations producible out of all these results by the art of cookery (for art is also nature's
doing); modification of roast and boiled and broiled;
of pastries, jellies, creams, confections, essences,
preserves.   One would fancy that she intended us to
do nothing but eat; and indeed, a late philosopher (it
was Darwin) said that her great law was 'Eat, or be
eaten' [Table Talk, "Eating"].

As we have seen, the desire for a greater variety of
foods, not home-grown, led to overseas exploration, colonization, and maritime commerce; and introduced to the table
many foreign and even exotic articles of diet.   "The English
table," again to quote Dr. Glover, "recruited by Oriental
spices brought in English ships, by fresh meat fed on Persian clover and Swedish roots, by wheat grown on lands im-
proved by care and science, was further enriched from overseas.   The potato is an American plant, even if it is called
the Irish potato, and in our own day we have seen it reinforced by its more delicate cousin the tomato."   But America had a greater gift for us: the turkey--as Charles Lamb
wrote on Christmas Day 1815, "the savoury grand Norfolci-
an holocaust that smokes all around my nostrils at this moment from a thousand firesides."   "Elia" forgot to thank China
for his tea, but elsewhere, probably in fun, he attributed the
discovery of roast pig to a Chinese peasant.   The historic
results of a taste for pepper and spice, and sugar, have
been mentioned.   And in Canada and the U.S. today, nearly
every table bears foods of imported origins, with romantic
backgrounds--bananas and oranges, marmalades, butter and
cheese and nuts, frozen viands and fish, and wheaten products.   We are indeed, in our common daily life, as well
provided with imported food, staples as well as rare delicacies, as was Lucullus at his splendid exotic banquets. What
would our lives be if, like the Pilgrim Fathers, we had nothing but our inadequate homegrown products to depend on?
And with neither wines nor tobacco to embellish our repasts?

CHRISTMAS DINING

Deriving from the course of the seasons, banqueting

was related to fertility rites, and in Roman days was represented by the Saturnalia, which merged with later Noël
festivities.   This ritualistic banqueting has been continued.
Royal Christmas banqueting in the Middle Ages was the special occasion for some diplomatic demonstrations.   In A.D.
1175 Henry II of England had another King, Henry of Bavaria and Saxony, to dine with him at Windsor Castle.
Neighboring barons were also present, and the tables
groaned beneath a varied array of good things.   The royal
guest brought choice wines from Bavaria.   Nine years later
there was another great Yuletide feast at Windsor, attended
by the brother of the King of Scotland.   The Duke of Saxony,
King Henry's son-in-law, was there too, together with several bishops.   The gathering was also a reconciliation feast,
marking the return to court life of Queen Eleanor, whom
King Henry had imprisoned sixteen years earlier for plotting
against him.

Even political rights of the English people may be
said to have originated in an extravagant banquet.   According to Arthur Turner (Ottawa Citizen, Dec. 24, 1960), King
John put on several huge banquets at Yuletide, but invited
only his erstwhile friends and their followers.   His guests
at Christmas, 1199, managed to account for 300 oxen, 400
pigs, 100 capons, 1000 eels, and nearly 100 peacocks.   The
banquet lasted several days, and at the time it was the most
expensive ever to take place in England.   When news of it
reached the poor people, they began to murmur against such
extravagances.   Barons who had not been invited started to
plot against the king.   This mammoth Christmas feast in
fact did much to increase the disquiet that resulted in the
forcing of King John to sign the Magna Carta at Runnymede
some years later.   Banqueting and politics have always been
connected.

The Christmas season particularly was ever a time
not only of prayer and holy observance of the original miracle of the Nativity and incarnation of the Deity, but also
from pagan origins, of wassail and merrymaking, of feasting instead of fasting, of observing a holiday in place of a
holy day.   Gourmandizing has been a part of Christmas ever
since it was the Feast of the Winter Solstice in the forests
of Northern Europe.   At the Court of King Arthur and his
Knights of the Round Table, the feast of Christmas it is
said lasted for twelve days, during which period the cooks
prepared 30,000 separate dishes!   One English bishop recorded that the people at his manor consumed three complete

carcasses of beef, two whole calves, four deer, 60 chickens, eight partridges, two geese and 4000 eggs.   Even in the more civilized time of Henry VIII, who was himself a very religious man and wrote a defence of the Catholic faith, there is the following telling record from the court accounts of Christmas 1510.   It is part of the gifts made by Henry to his court, and reads: "Paid to the preacher in reward 6s.; Paid to the mynstrel 12s.; Paid to the cook 15s."   The cook outrated them all!   Even though that semi-mediaeval period was one of gourmandizing and gluttony, we only need to regard the present-day "season of holy merchandizing" and of Christmas feasting in private homes to realize that gastronomic interests reach their highest level at this pre-celebration of the New Year; and the culinary experts make their best efforts on these recurring occasions throughout Christendom.   It is noticeable, however, that in public hotels and restaurants, New Year's Eve has become a more important occasion for feasting and carousal in Western countries; it is both a continuation of the Yuletide spirit and an initiatory celebration to welcome in the optimistic New Year.

Among other ceremonial delicacies was the bird of divine plumage, the aristocratic peacock.   The peacock was anciently in demand for stately entertainments.   Sometimes it was made into a pie at one end of which the head appeared above the crust in all its plumage, with the beak richly gilt; at the other end the tail was displayed.   Such pies were served up at the solemn banquets of chivalry, when knights-errant pledged themselves to undertake any perilous enterprise, whence came the ancient oath, used by Justice Shallow, "by cock and pie."   The peacock was also an important dish for the Christmas feast; and Massinger, in his City Madam, gives some idea of the extravagance with which this, as well as other dishes, was prepared for the gorgeous revels of the olden times:

> Men talk of Country Christmas, their thirty pound
> butter'd eggs, their pies of carps' tongues; their
> pheasants drench'd with ambergris, the carcasses
> of three fat wethers bruised for gravy to make sauce
> for a single peacock.

Washington Irving (later the American Minister to Spain) mentions in The Sketch Book such a Christmas banquet which he attended in 1819, at which he beheld "a pie magnificently decorated with peacock's feathers, in imitation of

the tail of that bird. " Unfortunately, as proof that "fine
feathers do not make fine birds, " the peacock has a most
raucous voice, and is no longer in popularity on table-
menus, since the humbler species of pheasant, quail, wood-
cock and domesticated turkey, goose and chicken have taken
the fancy and are more available.

Speaking of Christmas dining, Sir Thomas Hohler,
British Ambassador, relates an incident in Eritrea while he
was posted there as an official. Lord Cromer had gone for
a trip to the Sudan, and was royally received by the Sheikhs
from all over Africa.

> The Sirdar had a large party, and in the afternoon
> [Christmas Day], a lot of them went up the Blue Nile
> in a gunboat; as they turned to come back they ran
> on a rock, and were only just able to push ashore
> before it sank. Luckily they found a man with a
> camel whom they despatched full-speed to Khartoum
> for another steamer; meanwhile foodless, they cast
> lots as to whom they should eat first, while the rest
> of the party in Khartoum ate up the dinner and made
> speeches on the characters of the stranded absentees
> [Sir Thomas Hohler, Diplomatic Petrel, p. 63].

NATIONAL STYLES

In the Middle Ages in Europe, the feasts were as-
semblies of people desperately hungry after long days of
hunting in the forests, or engaged in other violent exercise,
sometimes burdened with armor, and thus capable of seeking relaxation in their tankards and doing justice to prodigi-
ous meals, though crudely served. In the 17th century,
however, the spirit of order, reason and dignity which characterized the formalism of, for example, the literature of
the period, also displayed itself in the elaborate organization and greater refinement of banquets. These, among the
aristocratic and upper classes at least, were conducted according to a regular program involving a whole series of
formal observances, from the ceremonious entry into the
dining room to the regulated order of courses, the wines,
and the toasts.

> In sixteenth century France [says Will Durant], man-
> ners improved while morals declined. Catherine de
> Medici had brought Italian politeness with her, a

sense of beauty, a taste for elegance, a refinement
in appointment and dress. Brantôme thought her court
the finest that had ever been, 'a veritable earthly
paradise,' sparkling with 'at least three hundred ladies and demoiselles' dressed to the height of taxation. Henry III created the office of Grand Master of
Ceremonies of France and issued an edict detailing the
ritual and protocol of court behaviour. Henry III,
timid and finicky, insisted on these rules; Henry IV
violated them freely, Louis XIII ignored them, Louis
XIV expanded them into a liturgy resembling High
Mass.... At last the refinement was carried to excess. The Marquise [de Rambouillet] drew up a code
of correctness of speech and deed; those who practised it too precisely were called précieux or préc-
ieuses; and in 1659, when the Marquise was retired
and solitary, Molière pounced upon these fanciful resi-
dues of her art and finished them off with ridicule
[The Age of Reason Begins].

The 18th century was, generally speaking, somewhat
more witty, volatile, gay, enthusiastic, even robustious. At
the same time there was introduced into cookery more elegance and instinct for pleasure. In both the French Court
and the English Court, which set the example for all the upper classes, gastronomy became a popular indulgence. In
time, about the end of the First Empire, it became an art,
and was renowned by great culinary artists like Brillat-Savarin and Carême.

DINING IN ENGLAND

In the earlier centuries dining amounted almost to
gluttony, and meals were of enormous size. Students of
Pepys' Diary must be astonished to learn of the vast amounts
of food considered necessary in the 17th century for a dinner
of a dozen people. Samuel Pepys describes a good number
of such dinners he hosted: one that he gave to ten people in
1660, he proudly termed "a very fine dinner": "A dish of
marrow-bones; a leg of mutton; a loin of veal; a dish of
fowl; three pullets, and two dozen of larks, all in a dish; a
great tart; a neat's tongue; a dish of anchovies; a dish of
prawns, and cheese." One evening in 1662, with four guests,
Pepys served what he termed "a pretty dinner": "A brace
of stewed carps; six roasted chickens; a jowl of salmon; a
tanzy; two neats' tongues, and cheese." For six distinguished guests in 1663 he gave "a noble dinner": "Oysters;

a hash of rabbits; a lamb, and a rare chine of beef. Next
a great dish of roasted fowl cost me about thirty shillings;
a tart, fruit and cheese. " Pepys notes in his diary his
anxiousness that this was enough! On all three occasions
his guests enjoyed themselves and were "very merry. "
But one wonders how was it possible for them to hold even
a fourth of this quantity of food? These gross excesses of
proffered food marked the higher realms of hospitality
throughout the 18th and 19th centuries. (See Lord Frederic
Hamilton, The Days Before Yesterday.)

Indeed, as Gabriel Tszuchmi, Swiss chef to four
British royal families, tells us in his memoirs, Royal Chef,
that this love of rich and excessive food in the court lasted
until the food restrictions during the 1914-1918 World War.
Up to that time, the upper classes in England were often
landowners or wealthy by inheritance, and could afford to be
the "idle rich"; consequently, their repasts were hours long,
and there was time for leisurely indulgence. But in our
century, the well-to-do are not idle, but as men of business
are pressed for time; and meals are more regulated, shorter,
and thus less luxurious.

Generally speaking and by common repute, English
cuisine is not a competitor with other countries, at least in
modern times, whatever it may have been in the past.
Britain's preeminence in finance and mercantile commerce
has been eclipsed; its vast empire, over which the sun used
never to set, has been dissolved; its imperial sources and
supplies of exotic foods have been reduced; the two great
wars in our century have impoverished the people; and domestic socialism has eroded the aristocratic display of wealth
and extravagance and luxury, including that of the dinner-
table. Gastronomy has been brought to egalitarian propor-
tions. Moreover, the reduction in numbers of domestic
servants, who nowadays prefer other employment, has diminished the formal dinner-giving and the great houses and
salons formed for such hospitality. In place of them, in
London at least, restaurants have developed, and there the
culinary arts still flourish and try to match the Continental
ones. But, after hundreds of years of gluttony, and a century of refined French gastronomy, the taste of England has
apparently declined following two impoverishing wars and
their sad aftermath of austerity.

The Canadian writer Hugh MacLennan claims that the
most fascinating food is English food, because like all things

English, it cannot be considered apart from history, nor
are the reasons or motives for certain foods in any sense
as simple as they may seem. In the years the British Empire was forming, Englishmen ate large quantities of protein
and starch; but after the empire was built, the ruling classes confronted an historic dilemma they knew to be crucial
to their continuance as a nation. If they ate too well and
drank too deep, their empire might slip from them. But on
the other hand, what good was an empire if they were reduced to permanent subsistence on Brussels sprouts?

>The ruling classes of England thereupon came to a
>typically English compromise. Indifferent to the low-
>er classes, themselves accustomed to spending at
>least a month of every year on the Continent where
>they could eat the delicious foods of decadence, they
>decided to outdo Sparta within the home island, nor
>was any law necessary to guarantee the moral salu-
>brity of English restaurant food. By that extrasens-
>ory perception which enables the island to survive,
>English cooks saw their duty and did it. Hence the
>boiled meats and fish, the cabbages and sprouts drip-
>ping with lukewarm water, the incredible gooseberry
>fools, the one all-purpose sauce that looks like
>ground caterpillars and is used to lubricate every-
>thing erroneously called a sweet. But those foreign-
>ers who believe the English drink the kind of coffee
>they do because they lack the wit to make it any
>other way, have [little] understanding of the English
>mentality... [MacLennan, "By Their Foods...,"
>Scotchman's Return, p. 18].

How far the English taste had fallen during the 19th
century and since is shown by the satire lines of William
Makepeace Thackeray, on Cabbages:

>I have seen beef served with radish of horse,
>I have seen beef served with lettuce of cos,
>But it's far nicer, far nicer, I guess,
>As bubble and squeak, beef and cabbages.
>And when the dinner-bell sounds for me--
>I care not how soon that time may be--
>Carrots shall never be served on my cloth,
>They are far too sweet for a boy of my broth;
>But let me have there a mighty mess
>Of smoking hot beef and cabbages.

One remembers the remark made by U.S. Ambassador
Walter H. Page in London in a letter to his brother in 1913:
"In this aquarium in which we live (it rains every day) they
have only three vegetables and two of them are cabbages"
[B. J. Hendrick, Life and Letters of Walter H. Page, vol.
1, p. 158].

Former British diplomat Sir Harold Nicolson regrets
the puddings he was served as a child in Clandeboye or
Shanganagh--"We were offered College Pudding, Bachelor's
Pudding, Hasty Pudding, Tipsy Pudding, Treacle Pudding,
Lemon Sponge, Pancakes, Junket, Coconut Custard, Marma-
lade Pie, Roly Poly, Suet Pudding, Toffee Pudding, Almond
Sponge, Cherry Whirl, Coffee Honeycomb, Apple Charlotte,
Macaroon Hasties, Meringues, Marshmallows, Smyrna
Mould, and all manner of tarts and creams..." but has re-
signed himself to the fact that "the puddings of my childhood have, even as four-wheelers, gone out of circulation"
finding that a range of exotic puddings offered on a voyage
at sea in his later years "were in fact what in British res-
taurant-cars are called 'shape,' being little dabs the size
and form of a child's sand-pie and differing from each other
solely owing to the fact that some contained specks of an-
gelica and some bits of orange or ginger" [Journey to Java].

In the candid reminiscences of Henry Adams, during
his early period in the 1860's, in London, just before becoming an attaché at the American Legation, he expressed
his surprise that the Minister John Lothrop Motley regarded
the London dinner and the English country house as the per-
fections of human society. The youth disagreed: "Motley
could not have thought the dinner itself perfect, since there
was not then--outside of a few bankers and foreigners--a
good cook or a good table in London, and nine out of ten of
the dinners that Motley ate came from Gunter's, and were
all alike. Everyone, especially in young society, complained
bitterly that Englishmen did not know a good dinner when
they ate it, and could not order one if they were given
carte blanche" [Education of Henry Adams, chap. xiii].

If English taste had fallen during the late 19th and
early 20th centuries, and was compulsorily killed by the
austerities enforced by the rationed years of the First World
War, there was also some question as to whether the mixed
peoples of the United States had evolved a European-style
taste for high cuisine.

It is debatable how excellent is American gastronomy. In the first place, North America is a continent of vast extent, its people of many origins; its tastes are regional; secondly, it has such a cosmopolitan people and so many ethnic groups that it resembles Europe, with tastes differing among each group; and thirdly, the criterion is not the historic elegance of high-class European cuisine, but of a certain satisfying nativity in most regions except the cosmopolitan metropolises. This is illustrated, for instance in eloquent language by the New England essayist Robert P. Tristram Coffin.

> The cookery of Maine alone could give proof that here the business of daily living is a fine art.... Whoever has not eaten a pie made of Maine huckleberries taken with the fog on them has not tasted life really; and whoever has not sniffed hot blueberry juice running over in an oven will have to wait till the Last Judgment for completed bliss.... Chicken soup in Maine makes the usual chicken soup a ghostly thing. A spoon will stand alone in it;... The beans that Maine bakes, even in its logging camps, are the hardy ancestors of those degenerate weaklings that have made Boston a name known the world over. And as for fish--well, I must pause for fear I should run out of hyperboles.... Give these Maine cooks [salt] pork [scraps], flour, an onion or two, and a fish just done flopping, and you have the Gates Ajar and all the Delectable Mountains right in your backyard. There are many, remember, who believe that cookery is still, as it always has been, the index of a people's inner harmony and a patent of culture [An Attic Room, p. 178/9].

On the other hand there is some evidence that gastronomy has a slender hold in modern America. In the average home, there is neither time, money, leisure nor sophistication to develop the cooking arts. The so-called "labor-saving" devices demand the skill and patience of professional engineers, which wives are rapidly becoming; children are no longer the domestic servants they once were; neither cook, servant, nor scullery maid has most households--those that exist, according to Clifton Fadiman, "are unteachable, or represent an infinite series of problems in psychiatry." The result has been canned food, the rise of the freezer, the TV dinner, the hamburger. Nevertheless, continues Fadiman,

there is a marked multiplication and apparently successful sale of cookbooks of all kinds; the development of a widespread market in what has come to be
known, rather hideously, as gourmet foods, which include such snobbish nonsense as stuffed larks, grass-
hoppers in honey, and jet-planed fraises des bois;
[and] the refining effect of travel on the taste of
some--as well as its tendency to confirm the barbar-
ism of others, for we have all known patriots who,
after sampling Paris's best, returned home even
more devoted to their steak, potatoes, apple pie and
Scotch ["Party of One," Holiday, Jan. 1966, p. 12-
13].

("I love French cooking: you know--French fries, and all
that!")   Indeed, a recent article describing the exotic attractions of the newer Caribbean resort hotels, mentions Cura-
çao.   "Hotels and restaurants are hopefully expecting the
cruise ships to begin two and three-day layovers, at which
time the food of one restaurant will veer from the rata-
touille niçoise and pêches cardinales to the plain meat and
potatoes that are said to be what tourists want" [Time, Feb.
1, 1963, p. 39].

Yet, even with our new refrigerated and automated
cuisine, there is, it seems, an avalanche of family cookbooks.   To paraphrase Solomon, "of the making of cookbooks there is no end"; publishers report that a good new
cookbook is almost sure to be a steady money-making commodity, if not a best seller.   One such book went so far as
teasing its readers, who are all supposed to be familiar
with the Good and Sacred Book which adorns the parlor of
every simple home.   A remarkable recipe for making a
cake, apparently worked out by some devoted scriptural student, is given in Amy Atkinson's and Grace Holroyd's Practical Cookery:

1.   4-1/2 cups of I Kings IV, 22 v.
2.   1-1/2 cups of Judges V, 25 v.
3.   2 cups of Jeremiah VI, 20 v.
4.   2 cups of I Samuel XXV, 18 v.
5.   2 cups of Nahum III, 12 v.
6.   1 cup of Numbers XVII, 8 v.
7.   2 tablespoonsful I Sam. XIV, 25 v.
8.   Season to taste II Chron. IX, 9 v.
9.   6 cups Jeremiah, XVII, 11 v.
10.   1 pinch Leviticus II, 13 v.

11.   1 cup of Judges IV, 19 last clause.
12.   3 teaspoonsful Amos IV, 5 v.
13.   Follow Solomon's prescription for the making
      of a good boy and you will have a good cake,
      see Proverbs XXIII, 14 v.

Clifton Fadiman continues:

Our psyches have split palates.   On the one hand,
our puritan heritage frowns on 'fancy' foods as somehow immoral, and we embrace the stupidity of steak
as if it were a guarantor of virtue.   On the other
hand, the ladies' magazines swarm with fantastic
recipes related less to gastronomy than to interior
decoration; and we further compensate for our culinary repressions by a voluptuous gorging of will in
the form of commercial candy and doctored pop.
You can buy a hundred kinds of exotic canned soup
--but not many of them taste good, and most of them
taste the same [Ibid.].

But this generalization is perhaps based on the judgment of an American connoisseur and gourmet brought up
or at least influenced by European haute cuisine.   From his
point of view, it may be reasonably true.   But he fails to
mention that, for such fastidious gourmets, there exist in
most American cities innumerable high-class restaurants of
European quality and cuisine, equal to any in the world,
and until very recently the trans-Atlantic super-passenger
liners vied with one another in this matter.   The popular
magazines lead the world in their sections, often succu-
lently illustrated in color, devoted to cookery and restau-
rant-lore.   Nevertheless, the Americans, like Epicurus,
like their own native dishes and forms of cookery, often inherited from the unforgotten simple tastes of Pilgrim fore-
bears.   It is said that President Kennedy's favorite dish
was baked beans; and that Mr. Nixon's preference is meat
loaf.

The taste for plain living was illustrated not long
ago in the Canadian House of Commons.   The Parliamentary
Restaurant is a high-class members' dining room, with an
excellent fare.   In fact so excellent that the socialist squire
of the Kootenay, a Scottish Westerner, H.W. Herridge M.P.,
recently complained that the parliamentary restaurant lacked
good plain Canadian cooking and suggested that the chef
spend his off-time in British Columbia lumber camps pick-

ing up some pointers. Fellow members suggested that Mr.
Herridge may want simple pork and beans, or perhaps flap
jacks which he misses on the menu. The chief chef, Jon
Van Dierendonck, was irate. "Pretty childish," he retorted; "they tell me that there must be variety; I am not allowed to repeat myself.... I must prepare 50 menus a
week and I am not allowed to repeat.... What am I to do?
... and now they also want international dishes...." Only
recently Van Dierendonck had been complimented at a Parliamentary committee, especially for his "smorgasbord." At
the time of Mr. Herridge's complaint, the luncheon menu
offered poached haddock, omelet with chicken livers, Irish
stew with dumplings, roast leg of pork, braised beef paupi-
ettes, julienne of chicken salad, or a cold buffet. And for
dinner the same day, there was offered curried shrimps,
scrambled eggs with ham, Brome Lake duckling, liver,
broiled pepper steak or lobster. Most of these are Canadian dishes. But Mr. Doucett, M.P. said he wasn't too sure
what Mr. Herridge had meant by "good plain Canadian cooking." Perhaps he only wanted pork and beans. Were this
attitude to become widespread, the ancient and even modern
art of good dining would soon collapse.

LUNCHEON

While most dining, wining and banqueting has been a
pastime of the evening, after the chores of daily work are
normally over, an effective alternative has been found in
midday luncheoning. Indeed, many ambassadors and other
diplomats have expressed a preference for this. Sir Bruce
Lockhart complained that while in Russia, since he was invited out almost every evening, he had to do almost all his
own diplomatic entertaining at luncheons. The American
diplomat Charles W. Thayer, wrote:

Foreign politicians, like most businessmen and Washington bureaucrats, overworked and surfeited with social engagements, would shed few tears at the passing of the interminable diplomatic dinner. In my
own experience I have repeatedly found the small
daily lunch meeting with local politicians, with the
emphasis on brevity rather than on food and wine,
far more conductive to accomplishing the business of
diplomacy than the mixed gathering which meanders
leisurely through five courses and as many types of
drinks [C. W. Thayer, Diplomat, p. 221].

While mentioning luncheons, we might note that the American-Canadian nickname "lunch" is misapplied, and is almost a matter of slang. In England, a "lunch" originally meant a fieldworker's refreshment--something which could be eaten out of the hand, such as a lunch of bread and meat. There are people in England to this day who call such a midday meal not a lunch but a "stay-bit." A luncheon was a small stay-bit originally, but came in time to mean a light midday meal. In Victorian days, and still among people who feel that whatever is old is necessarily elegant, it was a social error to call such a meal anything but "luncheon"; it was a word representing gracious living and a leisurely midday repast. Fortune magazine recently dealt with luncheons, or what the Americans abbreviate to "lunches," as applied to big executives. These superior creatures, one learns, do not dawdle over the table, but gobble up their lunches in a mere hour-and-a-half. They eat heartily but not richly. They do not make "big deals" at lunch; they soften up their guests. They do not drink, as it dulls the keen edge of their precision-tooled intellects. A few big executives confine themselves to a couple of walloping big whiskies, and are then as keen as a razor.

But diplomatic luncheons are different. They are slow and leisurely and gracious; they are accompanied with sherries or wines, and serious business talk. In former times, from the days of Pepys, they might last throughout the afternoon, and political problems would be discussed and possibly resolved. Unlike dinners, they were more private and personal, and more informal.

Of course a luncheon period often led to drowsiness and, as they were mostly held in clubs, the club members and perhaps their guests often retired to the lounge or reading-room for a brief siesta.

During war time, departments, sub-departments and special agencies of government multiply in an extremely complex fashion. There is ever a greater strain on coordination. Each section has its official coordinator or liaison, until there comes a time when a coordinator of coordinators is required. The Department of External Affairs in Ottawa is a key department, having connections and inter-relations with almost every other department of the Federal Government. Once the editor of Fortune magazine came up to Ottawa to study the Canadian war organization; he asked Mr. Norman Robertson, the Undersecretary of State for External

Affairs, how all the complex organization was coordinated.
"I think largely in the cafeteria of the Chateau Laurier Hotel," was the reply.

Robertson had long sponsored what came to be nicknamed "cafeteria diplomacy" at the Chateau Laurier. It was
his regular noon-day rendezvous, as the Cheshire Cheese
was for Dr. Johnson. To the Chateau Laurier cafeteria,
providing some of the best food in Ottawa, a few steps from
the East Block and External Affairs department (The "Foreign Office" of Canada), the Undersecretary repaired daily
and was joined either by his own departmental colleagues,
or by other senior civil servants and department heads, or
by diplomats of foreign countries. The politicians and ministers generally preferred the sedate Rideau Club, founded
by Canada's first Prime Minister, Sir John A. MacDonald.

The cafeteria was the equivalent of a coffeehouse
club such as was in vogue in London in the 18th century.
Sometimes this system had its drawbacks. I once was anxious to have an important tête-à-tête with my departmental
chief, concerning problems of the embassy I had just returned from. He suggested that we lunch together at the
cafeteria. After equipping ourselves with trays and food
on the self-service basis, we selected a table in a quiet
corner. But within five minutes, others began to join us,
with their trays, and assemble at the table. It was their
custom; Robertson had the drawing power of Dr. Johnson.
The talk was general; it was "shop"; it was inter-depart-
mental; it was semi-public. There was no privacy; I never
did get to discuss my problems. But on special occasions,
when a private talk with some foreign diplomat or politician
was necessary, Robertson broke his customary ritual and
shared a table alone with his guest either at the Rideau
Club or in the Chateau Laurier main dining room. Cafeteria diplomacy had its limitations, because of its gregari-
ousness. *

---

*In a retrospective editorial on the Chateau Laurier Cafeteria, the Ottawa
Journal (June 21, 1963) remarked: "Where could better rare roast beef
be found? Where else was it carved with the verve of the cafeteria's chefs?
These imposing men might terrify a stranger or a laggard in line, but once
a customer had their confidence and their ear, he was a member of the
cafeteria club. And what a club it has been. Especially before and after
the last war, affairs of state could be discussed by senior civil servants
who turned lunch-hours into intellectual exercises."

The fact remained however, that business was done over a meal, with or without a cocktail.   It was, as the Fortune editor learned, how war-time "coordination" was maintained.   It was how diplomatic problems were usually discussed; not in offices, but at dinner tables.

A dispatch from Brussels in January 1961 noted that the strikes and serious riots of that time seemed always to end at lunch time.   Noon-hour and afternoon were serene. That is striking evidence of the civilizing effect of a European lunch.   A typical midday meal in the New World, as an Ottawa paper remarked, would be more likely to start a riot than to quell one.   A conscientious rioter in the United States or Canada would remain at the melee and gather new fury as he wolfed a prefabricated sandwich held in one hand and brandished his inflammatory placard with the other.   But the morning riots put the meager Continental breakfast in a poor light.   As the Ottawa editorial remarks, had Marie Antoinette promoted bacon and eggs instead of cake she might have changed the history of Europe.

DINNERS IN GENERAL

But evening suppers and dinners, being more leisurely than quick luncheons at cafeterias, will no doubt always prevail.   Ecclesiastes taught us that "a man hath no better thing under the sun than to eat, and to drink, and to be merry...."   Attempting to remedy the extravagances of entertainment (best exemplified later by Lucullus) by a more refined enjoyment of simplicity, Epicurus bade us find an agreeable and intelligent employment for our higher faculties in the pleasures of the table.   La Rochefoucauld wrote that "eating is a necessity, but eating intelligently is an art"; and Vauvenargues averred that "great thoughts come from the stomach."   Here the emphasis is on the intellectual enjoyment of good food, and not mere gluttony or voraciousness. Modern gastronomy is an art, and Molière talked like a Philistine when he made one of his characters say, "we eat to live, we do not live to eat."   The enthusiast writing under "Gastronomy" in the Encyclopaedia Britannica (1957) went so far as to say 'gastronomy is a perfect art, for so wide a range of enjoyment could not be derived from listening to a symphony, hearing a poem read, or gazing at a beautiful building. ... [N]ot merely [is grastronomy] a perfect art, but it is the only art which is perfect."

That the gourmet's palate can be refined to the most

astonishing tasks for rare, exotic or esoteric foods is illustrated even in our own times--indulgent, effete, or not--by
an advertisement in a current American magazine, which
lists a number of strange (but edible and apparently salable)
rarities for the experimental connoisseur:

Gourmets Wanted!

Whole sparrow on skewer	2 oz. tin
Whole baby octopus	6 1/2 oz.
Broiled octopus on skewer	5 1/4 oz.
Cocktail smoked rabbits	3 2/3 oz.
Boiled quail eggs	4 2/3 oz.
Fried Baby Bumble-bees (in soy oil)	1 2/3 oz.
Fried Grasshoppers (in soy oil)	1 1/5 oz.
Fried Silkworms (in soy oil)	1 1/2 oz.
Chocolate-covered Grasshoppers	3 1/2 oz.
Chocolate-covered Caterpillars	3 1/2 oz.
Chocolate-covered Baby Bees	3 1/2 oz.
Chocolate-covered Ants	3 1/2 oz.
Chocolate Assortment, Bees, Ants, Caterpillars	2 1/2 oz.

Frederick's Fabulous Foods*

Since that advertisement appeared in 1961, many of these
exotic delicacies are now regularly offered for sale in Canadian, American and European "delicatessen" stores, gro-
cery stores, and supermarkets.

But I have not noticed outside the Orient that such
exotic dishes appear on the diplomatic tables, as they might
have in the days of Lucullus, when their rarity and value
was so much greater and when there was a more courageous
and tolerant connoisseurship.

One illustration of the role of food in the entertainment of an important head of state was related in an A. P.
news dispatch of April 2, 1960, concerning Premier Khrushchev's visit to France. "For 10 days and nights Nikita
Khrushchev has run a gastronomic gauntlet of rich French
foods and heady wines. He looks fine. In fact, the Soviet

---

*On reading this list, I was reminded of my early school days when I first
learned of the Reformation and puzzled over Martin Luther and his Diet of
Worms.

Premier looks better than when he arrived on March 23 as a guest of the French Government. That was right after a siege of the flu. Unquestionably, this is a testament to both his hosts' cooking and his own liver. Khrushchev has cancelled certain side trips and minor visits--but not once has he ducked an official meal. Early in his stay, however, he sent an emergency order to Moscow. He asked for a large shipment of Narzan, the famed mineral water of his native land. Well stocked with this, Khrushchev has eaten his way through some memorable menus.

"Before coming to France he politely suggested to his hosts that he would appreciate the lunches and dinners being held to two main courses, and two wines. Reluctantly, the French agreed to hold the meals to two courses, but they wouldn't yield on wine. They have consistently put three wines before Khrushchev, explaining with French logic that, as one was a dessert wine, it didn't count.

"The score card shows that Khrushchev has eaten: chicken four times; steak, twice; lamb, three times; salmon, smoked and grilled, twice; lobster, three times; veal, once; spiced pork, once; guinea hen, once; duck, once; roast beef, once; mixed spice sausages, once. As warmups he has been served pâté and caviar and delectable goodies of various regions he has visited. Twenty-eight of France's choicest wines have been put before him and 19 of her most splendid champagnes. His hosts have also poured him some of the finest and oldest cognacs in the nation's cellars. This groaning array of food and wines includes only official banquets and luncheons. Additionally, Khrushchev has enjoyed some private meals with De Gaulle, details of which have not been announced. If he has put on any weight, he's keeping it secret."

While this is merely a peep-hole view of the feeding by diplomatic circles in France of the representative of the Russian bear, it would seem to emphasize the importance placed on food during a diplomatic mission, or visit of a Head of State--especially by a country which for centuries has rightly claimed the highest renown in matters concerning the gastronomic arts.

In the days when Lord Lansdowne was the Governor-General of Canada, he gave every year two evening skating and tobogganing parties at Rideau Hall, in Ottawa. Here is Lord Frederic Hamilton reminiscing on the dining at these parties:

Supper was served in the long, covered curling-rink,
where the temperature was the same as that of the
open air outside, so there was a long table elaborate-
ly set out with silver branched candlesticks and all
the Governor General's fine collection of plate, but
the servants waited in heavy fur coats and caps.
Of course no flowers could be used in that temperature, so the silver vases held branches of spruce,
hemlock, and other Canadian firs.   The French cook
had to be very careful as to what dishes he prepared,
for anything with moisture in it would freeze at once;
meringues, for instance, would be frozen into uneat-
able cricket-balls, and tea, coffee, and soup had to
simmer perpetually over lamps.   One so seldom has
a ball-supper with North Pole surroundings [The Days
Before Yesterday].

Time magazine reported, on September 7, 1962, the
completion of an alliance or "semi-union" between Saudi
Arabia and Jordan.   The pact between the two dynasties,
headed by King Saud and by King Hussein, was announced in
Saud's summer capital of Taif "after the monarchs and their
retainers had polished off a barbecued camel."   Thus the
old custom, oriental as well as western, of the negotiations
of princes being accompanied by feasts, is once more illustrated.

DINING AND POLITICS

The role of dining in politics has always had an importance not often enough emphasized.   It was summed up
nearly a hundred years ago by a gastronomical writer, the
Marquis de Cussy, Prefect of the Palace under the Empire,
in a book L'Art Culinaire.   He studied eating as a department of political science, and insisted that history should be
written from the gastronomic point of view.   To know the
peoples, he held, it was necessary to know their dishes.
England should be criticized with continual reference to
roast-beef, beefsteak, pudding and porter.   Holland could be
understood only by a connoisseur of cheese and salt beef.
The genius of Germany lurked in sauerkraut and sausages.
Caviar afforded the clue to the mysteries of Russian policy.
The "pilau" of Turkey, the "macaroni" of Italy, and the
"olla-podrida" of Spain revealed the respective instincts and
tendencies of the three nations.   According to De Cussy,
dynasties rose or fell through sympathetic devotion or sullen

indifference to culinary ideas. The disasters of history were referable to dinners; and the student, who would account for the successes of statesmen, should pay more attention to the records of the kitchen than to their labors in the cabinet. The free institutions of England were the result of her liberal (though rather oppressive) fare; her supremacy was the work of statesmen and thinkers who, in addressing the minds, had never forgotten to humor the stomachs of their followers. Walpole governed by corruption and cookery, so nicely blended that it was impossible at times to separate the one from the other. Holland, Chatham, North and Addington were all statesmen of the table. Locke, Addison, Clarke, Hume and Gibbon were not more eminent as philosophers than as diners. To readers who have never taken the gastronomic view of history, De Cussy's statement of the influence of hospitality on our public affairs may appear altogether fanciful, but it has an element of truth.

Though he was no gourmet, and was disastrously neglectful of his personal interest in good cheer, Napoleon had a proper respect for cookery as an instrument of government. On dispatching the Abbé de Pradt to Poland, he observed impressively, "Tenez bonne table et soignez les femmes"; and the supreme duty of his famous arch-chancellor Cambacérès was to maintain a kitchen and table for the furtherance of state affairs. On dismissing high plenipotentiaries, after a satisfactory conference, he would say in his most gracious manner, "Go and dine with Cambacérès." In illustration of prodigal expenditure for the arch-chancellor's table, a story is told of a trout sent to it from Geneva, for which the municipal authorities of that city charged 300 francs. Thinking this an extortionate price for a single trout, the Imperial Cour des Comptes disallowed the payment; the immediate result of which interference was a sharp reproof from the Emperor, who bade his officers of the Cours to forbear for the future from vexatious economy in matters pertaining to his chancellor's table.

I think it was Thackeray who said: "I would have a great deal more hospitality practiced than is common among us--more hospitality and less show. Properly considered, the quality of dinner is twice blest; it blesses him that gives, and him that takes; a dinner with friendliness is the best of all friendly meetings--a pompous entertainment, where no love is, the least satisfactory."

As has been remarked diplomatic dinners are gatherings not solely for pleasant colloquy and discourse. Nor are
official banquets solely ceremonial obligations embellished
with forms of protocol, like military reviews, parades, or
other routine ceremonies. In theory there is a deeper purpose, which was well understood in all the 18th- and 19th-
century salons of Europe. There was of course the first
underlying motive: If you wish to charm and win over your
adversary, feed him. But there was another broader motive,
that of bringing statesmen, politicians, or diplomats together, especially in the after-dinner period, over coffee, liqueurs (brandy or port) and cigars, for intimate discussions
or exchange of views in a cosy, friendly and informal atmosphere following a charming dinner and with the glowing
feeling of a well-filled stomach. It was this after-hour
which was important, and often the raison-d'être of political
and diplomatic dinners.

To one writer, this art of gastronomic politics was,
between the two wars, nicknamed "spa diplomacy." An international lawyer, Genêt, wrote: "There is an after-dinner sweetness from which sentiments of international tender-
ness spring. The most savage hearts are softened then, the
most severe countenances are relaxed in the smoke-laden
beatitude of laborious digestion; the narcotic of generous
wines reduces all asperities. M. Briand is aware of this,
and loves to foregather with a companion in the quietitude
of Thoiry, or to regale Europe round the tables of the [Ho-
tel des] Bergues [in Geneva, where Briand habitually stayed"]
[Traité de Diplomatie, I, p. 112].

During the 1920's, when plans for peace and security in Europe were constantly being discussed by various
European statesmen at Geneva, Paris, Locarno, and elsewhere, diplomatic meals played an incalculably important
role. If Briand became famous for trout dinners at Thoiry,
where he settled agreements with Herr Streseman, Lloyd
George became distinguished for his "breakfasts." When
the American Willard Straight was a member of Sir Robert
Hart's Inspectorate General of the Imperial Maritime Customs of China, and posted in Peking in 1901 at the age of
21, he wrote in his diary of September 30, 1902, "Peking
is a place of many dinners, not ordinary dinners that one
eats daily with a clear conscience and a good digestion, but
formal dinners that are haunted by thoughts of having to re-
pay the hospitality and made lurid by visions of liver and
dyspepsia as one goes through dish after dish and absorbs

wine after wine.   There are diplomatic dinners where one
legation tries to even off scores opened by various others.
There are mess dinners given by officers of different legations and by the Customs assistants.   There are home-like
little gatherings in the American barracks, where the officers' wives have a few well selected people in for dinner
and music afterwards.   Then there are awful affairs given
by misguided hostesses, where the guests are all mixed,
where no one cares for his neighbor, and where, when the
meal is finished, everyone adjourns to the parlor and sits
in a circle.   The most interesting functions in Peking society are the dinners given once or twice a week by 'Sir
Robert Hart.   Here one sees a truly characteristic show,
for it is absolutely international.   There may be four ladies,
there may be six, or when he has visitors, as he frequently does, there may be even eight.   But there are men ga-
lore and men of all sorts and conditions, ministers, chargés
d'Affaires, officers of the Legation Guards, Customs people,
Consular officials, with an occasional engineer or globe-
trotter or two thrown into the whirl of officialdom.   At the
table everything is arranged according to rule, and a rule
that is unbending and unbreakable.   Sir Robert takes out
the first lady.   The senior Minister sits opposite to him
with the second lady.   Then to right and left people are arranged according to their respective positions in life, Secretaries of Legations, officers, with the juniors, generally a
sub-lieutenant, a junior assistant in the Customs or a British Consular student, seated at the ends of a long table"
[Herbert Croly, Willard Straight (1924), p. 88].

        But, Straight implied, all these exchanges of dinners
in Peking had a general purpose, besides that of obligation:
that of making friends, and close political contacts, and exchange of news, information, and ideas--even creating an
amenable climate for political relations.   A glimpse of this
is given us by Sir Ronald Storrs, who was returning through
Paris in 1918 to resume his post as Governor of Palestine.
In his diary he records:

        14.IX.19.   Breakfast 9.15 with Mr. Lloyd George in
        the Rue Nitol.   President [sic] Paderewski; Bonar
        Law and Miss B.L.; Maurice Hankey, and later Win-
        ston Churchill and Seely.   Of course Paderewski
        knocked out any talk of Jerusalem and Palestine by
        the urgency of the Polish-Bolshevist situation.   At
        first L. G. by talking round and over sooner than at
        a subject, seemed to me a less practical man than

the Slav pianist on his right.   At the same time fire,
and great good humor.   Paderewski's thesis was that
instead of arming Letts, Finns and Boches against the
Bolshevists the Allies might well help the Poles, who
were quite prepared to take it on.   All then started
against him, but when he had talked for two hours
most seemed to think his proposals should be exam-
ined--a great feat in my opinion. ... The party
broke up about 11.30 [Memoirs of Ronald Storrs, p.
342].

On a more practical level, even in the highly important business of lobbying for votes on resolutions before the
United Nations, the business of dining also plays its role.
Mr. Henry Cabot Lodge, United States Ambassador to the
United Nations, pleaded with the U.S. Senate for a dining-
room table with forty seats because "that is where I try to
line up the votes.   Under United Nations rules, an important question must receive a two-thirds vote," he went on
to explain to the Senators, "and you know how hard that is.
If you get a man up and give him a good dinner and get him
into a good frame of mind, you can get a good deal more
done!" the ambassador added.

Who has not heard of the luncheon or tea-terrace of
the Parliament Buildings of Westminster, where Ministers
entertained other politicians, important visitors, or visiting
foreign statesmen.   And that wonderful dining terrace at the
Palais des Nations overlooking Lake Geneva, which has been
the center of critical diplomatic negotiations.   I have shared
meals at both.

The United Nations headquarters in New York has to
a considerable degree recognized this factor of diplomacy.
The Delegates' Restaurant is as important as the Delegates'
Lounge-Bar.   Between formal sessions and Committee meet-
ings, delegates from various countries invite their colleagues
to lunch or supper in the beautiful roof-terrace restaurant
overlooking the East River, and over their meal discuss international and diplomatic business in a spirit of intimacy,
amity, affability, and no doubt gastronomic euphoria.   At
least that used to be my experience.   A white tablecloth often is more effective than the green baize of a Committee
Room roundtable or of a conference hall, or in the lobbies
and corridors.

A correspondent at the United Nations, Tom Hoge,

has described this business of diplomatic dining.

> The envoy first must stand in line up to half an hour
> to pay his respects to the host ambassador. Then
> he is free to battle his way through the packed room
> in search of a cocktail tray. If the drink gives him
> courage to try the buffet, the guest attaches himself
> to another long line inching past the food tables.
> Then he has the problem of finding a place to sit.
> After a three-week round of U.N. receptions and
> banquets during his 1960 visit to the Assembly, Sovi-
> et Premier Khrushchev told a reporter: 'This life
> would make a stone sick' [Ottawa Journal, Dec.
> 1962].

In the early years of the U.N., with many fewer members,
there were perhaps two rather small gatherings every week
during the time the U.N. was in session. Nowadays a delegate might feel it necessary to visit two or three parties in
one night. When the session is over, he will have "gone to
more than 80 such functions and consumed enough spiced
food to turn the ordinary stomach to suede" [Hoge, Ibid.],
in his diplomatic rounds gleaning tit-bits of information from
and socializing with fellow delegates. Those nations that
have vast guest lists often use New York's big mid-town
hotel/motels to hold their lavish affairs; the main dining
room of the U.N. itself can contain "only" 750 persons.

This only goes to confirm that diplomacy, as practiced at the United Nations, includes the first principle,
enunciated in Ecclesiastes, and asserted by Callières, that
the emollient, lubricant and solvent of gastronomy is an essential factor; and that dining and wining break down many
barriers to intercourse and amity.

Lt. Gen. Maurice A. Pope, while he was Canadian
Ambassador to Belgium and to Luxembourg, notes:

> Diplomatic life is marked by a never-ending succes-
> sion of luncheons, receptions, and dinner parties,
> which, while often fatiguing, are nevertheless essen-
> tial. For it is at such gatherings that the diplomatic
> agent meets his colleagues, and with them he is able
> to trade gossip regarding the ever changing scene.
> Many an interesting tip is picked up in this way....
> There are those, of course, who contemptuously dis-
> miss diplomatic life as mere 'cookie-pushing' and

claim that those who serve their country abroad in a
representative capacity live only fat and lazy lives.
In this they are wrong. Social functions at the end
of a busy day are often exhausting; they demand the
expenditure of much nervous energy, since one must
always be on the alert, as well as the physical effort involved in standing about for hours at a time.
I think some of these critics would be surprised if
they knew with what relish members of the foreign
service, certainly the older ones, look forward to the
prospect of 'a night in bed' [Soldiers and Politicians,
p. 400].

There are "courses" both of the academic curriculum,
and of the meal table. It is well-known that in the older
British universities, dining in hall is a part of the academic ritual; that in order to qualify for a law degree or even
a Master's degree, one has to "eat a certain number of dinners." Every major tradesmen's guild has its gastronomic
obligations and most of the "Halls," like the Goldsmiths',
the Silversmiths', and the Stationers', had great banquet facilities, where many important political and commercial contacts have been made. The Inns of Court have their historic chambers where dining and wining have ever formed a
part of the legal life of London. And every palace and
nobleman's mansion in Britain and Europe was in past days
the setting for grand banquets of state. The political and
the social history of those countries cannot ignore the importance of this side aspect. In fact, all political annals
and developments are associated with dinners or banquets;
not only as garnishes or fringe-benefits accompanying the
more serious affairs of state, but even as powerful agencies in politics or diplomacy.

Tradition has many quirks, which still survive. The
barristers who are members of the Middle Temple partake
each week of a pudding prepared by Queen Elizabeth I.
About 350 years ago the Queen made a pudding for her favorite Middle Templars; and ever since, every week, a new
pudding has been made into which a portion of the previous
week's pudding is incorporated. So today they are still eating Queen Elizabeth's pudding.

At the hospital of St. Cross at Winchester, you can
go up to a grating and receive free bread and beer--a perfectly natural consequence of the fact that in 1136 the
church's founder, Henry of Blois, the grandson of William

the Conqueror, commanded that this be done. In 1847 Emer-
son and Carlyle stopped off and got their bread and beer;
and Carlyle afterwards cussed out the charitable priest on
the ground that the people were paying him a salary to the
tune of £2000 per annum. (But of course Carlyle was a
Scotsman and had stomach ulcers.)

A Bachelor of Oxford has only to enroll himself for
another year and entertain his faculty members by giving
"three dinners" to enable him to acquire the degree of Master of Arts.

What this lengthy survey of political and diplomatic
gastronomy shows is two-fold. In the first place, it is seen
that dining and wining are essential if not major components
of the profession of "negotiating with princes," though even
Machiavelli seems to have overlooked this aspect; or to have
taken it for granted. The appeal to the satisfied stomach is
as powerful as the appeal to the mind. Indeed, while the
conditioned mind and intellect may be able to resist the allurements of argument, the stomach rarely can resist the
allurements of the table and the intriguing cup and glass. In
Elizabethan language, the belly is paramount.

In the second place, the history of this gustatory and
gastronomical approach forms an important aspect of sociological, as well as political history. Human feeding and
drinking habits, while basically unchanged, vary in particular form from epoch to epoch; the tastes in liquid attractions
move from coffee-clubs to gin-palaces to tea-salons to cocktail receptions in direct progression. Banqueting scarcely
changes, but the menus offered now become more uniform
and standardized; since what were once exotic, rare and expensive are now so universally available, and individualistic
and artistic chefs are now replaced more and more by commercial caterers. This throws a greater burden on hosts
who wish to retain originality and piquancy in their formal
dinners. One remembers the exceptional productions; but
they become exceptional. The sociological forces of uniform-
ity and merging civilizations make for less frequent uniqueness. What was once national has become international;
Western Civilization, permeating all areas of the world, is
the great leveller, so that diplomatic banquets and drinking
parties are more or less the same in every corner of the
world, and the uniqueness of native styles, at least in foreign gatherings, is lessening. All over the world, menus
are in the traditional French--however bastard; and plates

are universal; "pudding à la diplomat" (or "pudin" or "poudang") has become a universal dessert. The social historian will mark this levelling tendency, which tends to offset the otherwise extending movement toward Nationalism and Separatism. Native gastronomic styles are now meretriciously maintained mainly for the tourists, who wish to taste Chinese "chop suey," "tempura" or "sukiyaki" in Japan, "poi" in Hawaii, and "asados" in South America-- though even these are mainly Western or American innovations in the first place, transferred to their native habitats. One does not even have to visit France to taste French cuisine. The world has contracted, trade (under refrigeration) has become universal, and national uniqueness has lost its former glamour. The social history of gastronomy therefore becomes progressively uniform.

Nevertheless, without dinners there would be no diplomacy. This is an axiom, but one which is often overlooked in histories of diplomacy.

III

THE ARTISTS OF HIGH CUISINE

Since cuisine is the basis of good dinner tables, and one of the factors in diplomatic success, the onus of quality lies mainly upon the managers of the kitchen, the chefs and cuisiniers. Lord Lytton, who wrote under the nom-de-plume of "Owen Meredith," and who was a British Ambassador in Paris, summed up the importance of dining and cookery in these well-known verses:

> We may live without poetry, music and art;
> We may live without conscience, and live without
> heart;
> We may live without friends; we may live without
> books;
> But civilized man cannot live without cooks.
> He may live without books, --what is knowledge but
> grieving?
> He may live without hope, --what is hope but deceiv-
> ing?
> He may live without love, --what is passion but
> pining?
> But where is the man who can live without dining?
> [Lucile, Pt. I, Canto iii, st. 19]

The art of cookery was of so great importance that often it was pursued not only by professional cooks, but by gentlemen of rank, even the host himself. Montaigne wrote: "To give a good dinner requires no slight skill and gives no small pleasure; neither the great commanders nor the great philosophers have disdained to learn and practice the art" [Essays, iii, 13]. Robert Burton, who died in 1640, said in Democritus to the Reader: "Cookery has become an art, a noble science; cooks are gentlemen." If, at least, cooks became gentlemen with conferred rank, often times gentlemen were also cooks.

71

In 1789 Thomas Jefferson sent his secretary to Italy
to learn how to make macaroni.   In Vienna in 1815 Talley-
rand, seeing Metternich and the Czar of Russia conversing
privately in a corner, sneaked behind a pillar and heard
Metternich giving the Czar a recipe for plum-pudding.

The famed Cambacérès, of whose dinners many stories are told, was Napoleon's chancellor; the even more
famous Anthelme Brillat-Savarin (1755-1826) was a French
judge.   They knew, from their official positions, the political and diplomatic importance of fine cuisine, and personally took a hand in it, and even wrote books on their art.
In the amazing period of Louis XIV, the unfortunate Vatel,
the maitre-d'hotel of the Prince of Conde, threw himself on
his sword because the fish he had ordered for a dinner given
in honor of the King had failed to arrive on time; his successor, the Chevalier de Bechamel, became the superintendent of King Louis' household.

So it was, also, in Japan in the Emperor's court in
Kyoto and the Shogunate Court in Yedo (Tokyo) in the 17th
century.   Shijo taught the courtiers the art of dressing dinners, and cooking, which was considered the art of a gentleman.   When a culinary artist prepared a dinner and laid it
out, it was common for the public to admire it as a work of
art--after paying an admission fee (Murdoch, History of Japan, iii, p. 170/1).

Even kings in olden times were addicted to cookery.
One need not mention King Alfred, who marred instead of
made the bannocks of the neatherd's angry wife, for he was
thinking of other things than cake-baking.   Charles II took
an interest in culinary things.   On one occasion, while the
King lay in hiding, Colonel Carlis went in to the sheepcote
of a farmer residing near Bocobel, and with his dagger
killed one of the best sheep, and then had the carcass
brought home.   The next morning was a Sunday morning,
and Charles, having muttered his prayers, went eagerly to
the parlor to look after the stolen mutton.   "It was hardly
cold, but Will Pendersell brought a leg of it into the parlor;
his majesty called for a knife and a trencher, and cut some
of it into collops, and pricked them with the knife-point,
then called for a frying-pan and butter, and fried the collops
himself, of which he ate heartily.   Colonel Carlis, the while,
being but under-cook (and that honor enough) made the fire
and turned the collops in the pan. " When the colonel afterwards attended his majesty in France, his majesty was

pleased to propose as a problematical question, whether himself or the colonel were the master cook at Bocobel; "the
supremacy was of right adjudged to his majesty." Circumstances which made the royal adventurer a King were the
spoiling of an excellent cook. When he was secretly so-
journing at Trent, his meat was, for the most part--to prevent the danger of discovery--dressed in his own chamber;
"the cookery whereof served him for some divertisement of
the time" [Doran, "English Kings at the Table," Table Traits
(1859)].

Princess Marie Louise of Schleswig-Holstein, grand-
daughter of Queen Victoria, relates in her My Memoirs of
Six Reigns that in her early years she was rather unfamiliar
with cooking. When she was a new bride, living in Berlin
in 1891, she relates:

> I knew nothing of household duties. But I had a mar-
> velous Hungarian cook, Frau Herlein. I own I was
> very frightened of her, and it was somewhat of an
> ordeal to criticize her cooking, as her invariable an-
> swer was: 'Der Frau Prinzessin versteht das nicht'
> ('The Princess does not understand it'). I was, how-
> ever, determined to understand the mysteries of cook-
> ing, so I descended into the kitchen and requested
> her to teach me. She was so keen on her culinary
> art that she was delighted to impart her knowledge,
> and it was a proud day when a dinner was served
> which I had prepared and cooked myself, and my
> guests found no fault with what I had provided for
> their entertainment.

In due course Princess Marie-Louise became a competent
cook; and used to pass on her recipes to her friends. In
her last year before her death in 1956, she wrote in her
recollections: "If I once embark on my culinary hobby,
these memoirs will not only be a guidebook, but end up as
a cookery-book!"

Many more examples might be given of princes and
noblemen who indulged themselves in the art of cookery, as
a predilection or a pastime. Queens, and even kings, have
not disdained to enter their kitchens and take a hand in the
preparation of food. Even ambassadors have made a hobby
of cooking.

One of my own ministers, the late Jean Désy--later

Ambassador to Italy and to France--was a gifted amateur of
cooking; and privately at home used to don a white coat and
chef's cap, perform his culinary skill and craftsmanship in
his own kitchen, and produce exquisite dishes for his wife
and myself or other guest.   On one occasion, when we were
travelling together on a Moore-McCormick luxury liner from
New York to Rio de Janeiro, he invited some other diplomats to a special dinner, and went into the galley to personally instruct the chef as to how the exotic meal was to
be prepared.   Alas, however, the sea-weather that evening
proved inclement, and most of his guests left most of the
superb repast barely eaten.   I have known one or two other
diplomats who exercised "kitchen diplomacy" by their private
hobby of personal cookery.

    Hugh Wilson, later U.S. Ambassador to Germany,
relates that while he was posted in Berne in 1916, the chief
of the French Embassy's Press Section was Professor Hag-
uenin, a professor of French literature in the Berlin University until the war.

> In culinary matters, Haguenin was outstanding. When
> he invited you to lunch he met you at the door wear-
> ing an apron and hurried back to the kitchen to su-
> pervise the completion of the sauce that could only
> be put on the stove after the guests had arrived.
> Once a number of us were discussing the best way of
> spending a vacation.   One loved to climb mountains,
> one to bathe in the Mediterranean.   When it came to
> Haguenin to express his opinion, he was in no doubt
> at all.   'I always do the same thing the month of
> August, and it is what I prefer in all the world. My
> old father lives on a farm in Normandy....   We pre-
> pare a list of guests for the midday dinner.   Then
> my father and I make out the menu, divide the dishes
> between us, tie aprons around our middles, proceed
> to the kitchen and get to work.   About four o'clock
> the guests arrive, we serve them our dinner in a
> sort of competition, allowing the jury of guests to de-
> cide which are the best dishes [The Education of a
> Diplomat, p. 214].

    Besides the princely or other noble chefs, there were
the princely or noble attendants and waiters in the dining
hall.   They, also, formerly held distinguished rank.   Dr.
Doran, the 19th century commentator of dining, states:

The old emperors of Germany, on state occasions,
were waited on at dinner by the two happy feudatory
princes of the empire. [On] one of these occasions,
we are told that old General Dalzell, the terrible
enemy of the Scottish Covenanters, was invited to
dine with the Kaiser, and the prince-waiter nearest
to him in attendance was no less a personage than
the Prince of Modena, head of the house of Este.
Some years afterwards, the Duke of York (James II)
invited Dalzell to dine with himself and Mary of Modena. That proud lady, however, made some show
of reluctance to sit down en famille with the old general; but the latter lowered his pride by telling her
that he was not unacquainted with the greatness of
the Princes of Modena, and that the last time he had
sat at the table with the Emperor of Germany, a
prince of that house was standing in attendance behind the emperor's chair [Table Traits, p. 436].

A good and not infrequent English surname is that of
Carver. This goes back to mediaeval times. In the days
when the offices of footmen and other male menials were
filled by gentlemen servingmen, the carver was always a
gentleman of good lineage, and not seldom a person of noble
degree, though of a rank inferior to that of his employer.
The four carvers and cup-bearers of Edward IV's special
table were "bannerets" or 'bachelor knights"; and at the
banquets attending Archbishop Neville's "inthronization," the
chief carver was Lord Willoughby, the Earl of Warwick was
steward, Lord Buckingham was cup-bearer, and other noblemen had other official positions of service.

To bring these examples down to the present day,
we learn from a press report that President John Kennedy
often dismissed the servants early when Mrs. Kennedy was
away, and invited old friends to share dinner left in warming containers. Sometimes he went even further. One
couple, invited on short notice, arrived in black-tie attire,
ready for a candlelight supper in the elegance of Mrs. Kennedy's early 19th-century dining room. Instead of a butler,
they were served by the President who ladled out the soup
while in shirtsleeves with a tea-towel wrapped around his
waist. But even a President, if youthful and seeking relaxation and fun among his intimate friends, might enjoy a
few hours of informality when occasion offers. It is a modern American custom for a host in a private occasion--
whether he is the President or other high official--to revert

to the simple informal life. In Ottawa I have attended diplomatic parties given by a chef du protocol who gave out-
door "barbecue" parties at which he presided both as cook
and serviteur. But these are exceptions to the more general customs of formality.

But then there are the professional chefs, whose sole
business is in managing the kitchen staff or preparing or inventing the dishes. In early times, the mess tables were
laid out in a great hall in which a huge open fireplace provided the place for cooking the food, roasting on the turn-
ing-spit, and heating or boiling the food to be served. But
in due course, this culinary function was divorced by sepa-
ration into a special room, the kitchen. All the delights of
the table depended on the operations in the kitchen, which
thus became one of the most important centers of an official establishment, from palace and castle and monastery to
the smaller aristocratic home. In consequence, the master
of the kitchen, or the principal chef, was a personage of
highest importance and was therefore highly rewarded.

The menage of the castles in the Middle Ages was
extraordinary. Olivier de la Marche, master of ceremonies,
wrote a treatise L'Etat de la Maison du Duc Charles de
Bourgogne, composed at the request of Edward IV, King of
England, to serve him for a model. In this work he ex-
pounds the complicated service of breadmasters, carvers,
cup-bearers, cooks, and the ordered course of the banquet,
which was crowded by all the noblemen filing past the duke,
who was still seated at the table, "pour lui donner gloire."
"The kitchen regulations," says Huizinga, writing about La
Marche's work, "are truly Pantagrualistic." Huizinga describes kitchens of heroic dimensions, with seven huge chim-
neys. Overlooking it all is the chief cook, seated on a
raised chair and holding a large wooden ladle. With this he
both tastes soup and broth and chases or strikes idling
kitchen workers.

La Marche speaks of the ceremonies ... as if he were
treating of sacred mysteries. He submits to his
readers grave questions of precedence and of service,
and answers them most knowingly. Why is the chief-
cook present at the meals of his lord and not the
'ecuyer de la cuisine'? How does one proceed to
nominate the chief-cook? ... When the office of chief-
cook falls vacant at the court of the prince, the
'maitres d'hôtel' call the 'ecuyers' and all the kitchen

servants to them one by one. Each one solemnly
gives his vote, attested by an oath, and in this way
the chief-cook is selected. Who is to take the chief-
cook's place in case he is absent: the 'spit-master'
or the 'soup-master'? Answer: Neither; the substitute will be designated by election. Why do the pane-
tiers and cup-bearers form the first and second
ranks, above the carvers and cooks? Because they
are in charge of bread and wine, to which the sanc-
tity of the sacrament gives a holy character [The
Waning of the Middle Ages, chap. ii].

Huizinga comments further that the etiquettes involved
in high dining can be understood only in the context of their
ritualistic, almost religious significance. He says, "All
forms of etiquette are elaborated so as to constitute a noble
game, which, although artificial, has not yet degenerated altogether into a vain parade."

As far back as Roman times an expert cook was not
without honor. There is the familiar record of the emperor
Elagabalus, or Heliogabalus, who, as Gibbon points out, was
a gross indulger in women, wines and dishes, and revived
his appetite with sauces. The invention of a new sauce was
liberally rewarded; but if it was not relished, the inventor
was confined to eating nothing else until he had discovered
another, more agreeable to the Imperial palate. He is said
to have offered a Consulship or a Kingdom to the cook who
invented a new sauce gratifying to his taste. Roman chefs
were crowned with flowers by the guests who ate largely
and well, and the inventor of a new sauce had a patent for
its exclusive preparation for a year. One cook recorded in
history was the happy mortal to whom his master, Antony,
gave a city, because he had cooked a repast which had
called forth encomium from Cleopatra.

The old cooks were a special, almost priestly class,
whose heirs took up the mission of their sires. This mission was so far triumphant that, at the period of Charle-
magne, the imperial kitchen recognized in its chef the representative of the Emperor. Later French kings granted
corporate rights to the different trades connected with the
kitchen and the table; and one of the most valued privileges
was that conceded by Charles IX to the pastry cooks, who
alone were permitted to make bread for the service of the
Mass. In proportion as he was likely to be bribed to poison his lord, the cook was paid lavishly. The sovereign

in Norman England placed over his household a courtier who
had a strong, selfish interest in keeping him alive. Usually a man of noble lineage, the Steward of the Royal household was gratified with princely bounties, and encouraged
with princely promises. He was thus taught to feel that under any circumstances he would be a great loser by his
chief's death. The steward's subordinate officers, especially those who held chief places in the kitchen or approached
the royal person at festal moments, were appointed from
the same consideration, and paid with the same prudent
prodigality. The chef, a man of noble ancestry and of science, according to the scientific light and darkness of the
time, seldom retired from the office of "Coquus Dominicae
Conquinae" without a grant of lands that fixed him and his
heirs amongst the territorial magnates of a shire. Thus
the Norman Conqueror William bestowed several portions of
land on these highly favored domestics, the "Coquorum
Praepositus" and the "Coquus Regius."

Domesday Book records that a manor was bestowed
on Robert Argyllon, the "Grand Queux" to be held by the
service of making one mess in an earthen pot in the kitchen
of the King on the day of his coronation, called "De la
Groute"--i. e., a kind of plum porridge, or water-gruel
with plums in it. This dish is still served up at the Royal
Table at coronation by the Lord of the same manor, called
Addington. At the Coronation of George IV, the petition of
the Archbishop of Canterbury, which was presented by Sir
G. Nayler, at the Court of Claims on July 12, 1820, claim-
ing to perform the service of presenting a dish, "De la
Groute," to the king at the banquet was considered by the
Court, and allowed. The explanation of the curious tenures
requiring the holders of certain lands to perform, or be
ready to perform, culinary service for the sovereign's comfort, must be sought in the usages of the time when the
cooks at court were gentlemen who rose to wealth and dig-
nities in the ordinary course of professional service. Another version is as follows:

> Cooks in England may boast of a noblesse de cuisine,
> which dates from the Norman Conquest. When Wil-
> liam, who wooed his wife Matilda by knocking her
> down, had established himself in England, he gave a
> great banquet, at which his cook, Tezelin, served a
> new white soup of such excellent flavor, that William
> sent for the artist, and inquired its name. 'I call it
> Dillegrout' said Tezelin. 'A scurvy name for so

good a soup,' said the Conqueror, 'but let that pass.
We make you Lord of the Manor of Addington!'
[Doran, Table Traits (1859), p. 98].

Proudly did Dr. Pegge, author of Forms of Curry
(1780), say: "We have some good families in England of
the name of Cook or Coke.... Depend upon it, they all
originally sprang from real professional cooks, and they
need not be ashamed of their extraction any more than
Porters, Buttlers, &c."

It is related that Madame du Barry, piqued at the
King's opinion that only a man could cook to perfection, had
a dinner prepared for him by a cuisinière with such success
that the delighted monarch demanded that the artist should
be named, in order that so precious a cuisinier might be
engaged for the royal household. "Allons donc, la France!,"
retorted the ex-grisette, "have I caught you at last? It is
no cuisinier at all but a cuisinière, and I demand a recom-
pense for her worthy both of her and of your Majesty"
[Britannica (11th ed.), "Cookery"].

One can sympathize with poor little Alice, who was
not allowed to explain to the Red Queen how bread was
made. The Queen had proposed the question as an intelligence test; but then the White Queen only tried to destroy
Alice's earnest answer. "Can you answer useful questions?"
she said. "How is bread made?" "I know that!" Alice
cried eagerly. "You take some flour--" "Where do you
pick the flower?" the White Queen asked. "In a garden or
in the hedges?"

"Well, it isn't picked at all," Alice explained, "it's
ground--" "How many acres of ground?" said the White
Queen. "You musn't leave out so many things." "Fan her
head!" the Red Queen anxiously interrupted. "She'll be feverish after so much thinking."

There are various accounts of cooks who were also
artists in other media. Many of them were men of high culture and versatility. William Hazlitt (1778-1830), in his essay "On Coffee House Politicians," refers to one of the attendants he knew: "William, our waiter, is dressed neatly
in black, takes in the Tickler (which many of the gentlemen
like to look into), wears, I am told, a diamond pin in his
shirt-collar, has a music-master to teach him to play on
the flageolet two hours before the maid is up, complains of

confinement and a delicate constitution, and is a complete
Master Stephen in his way." P. G. Wodehouse's famous
Jeeves, butler-valet and factotum to several gentlemen, is
of course a legendary name.

Cookery became the grand passion with the upper
classes in the France of Louis XV. At that time the culinary art flourished and its professors became a recognized
and esteemed class in society, whose spoiled children they
were. They have left many great names in social history,
such as Brillat-Savarin and Carême, who were honored in
their day. It is said that the best cookery in France was
originally imported from Sicily and Italy. Then it became
so good in France that French cookery was later imported
into England. According to Boswell, Mrs. Thrale told Dr.
Johnson in 1775 that in England the cookery of the French
was forced upon them by necessity; for they could not eat
their meat unless they added some taste to it. But the con-
sensus of opinion is that all these benefits drawn from the
fastidious Continent somehow vanished in modern England,
until today the cuisine in England is deplorable, unimagina-
tive and tasteless. The Englishman perhaps vindicates himself with some classical and Stoic version of "plain living
and high thinking."

Of France's living culinary prodigies, few enjoy
greater fame and fortune than a burly, black-bearded, flam-
boyant Gascon named Raymond Olivier. The owner and on
special occasions the chef of the ancient Paris restaurant,
Le Grand Véfour, Olivier is privileged to wear, among
twenty-three assorted decorations, the red ribbon of the Le-
gion of Honour, the green rosette of Agricultural Merit, and
the vermilion medal of Arts, Sciences and Letters. The
French Academy created him an officer (not to be confused
with a full-fledged member); the Ministry of Education created him a Commander of Educational Merit. As "Ambassador of French Cuisine," an honorific bestowed by the Government Tourist Bureau, Olivier travels with a visa de
service, similar to a diplomatic passport. (See John Kob-
ler, "Master of Cookery," Sat. Eve. Post, Jan. 21, 1961.)

One of Mrs. Kennedy's first acts after moving into
the White House was the acquisition of a superb chef, René
Verdon, well-known in France as chef of the fashionable
Normandy resort-hotel at Deauville. At the palatial Peruvi-
an Embassy in Washington, Ambassador and Mrs. Fernando
Berckemeyer had in their service a French-trained chef,

Stanley Baudon, whose father was once chef in Buckingham
Palace.   There is always a competition among statesmen
and diplomats in the acquisition of a superior cook, which
of course enhances the latter's prestige and market value,
in the same way as rival football or hockey teams, or even
universities, will compete to "purchase" the best players.

"The art of dealing with one's chef is one of the
most delicate facets of diplomacy," said one ambassador in
Washington.   "You must pay him royally, let him have ab-
solute sovereignty in the kitchen, praise him often and gently criticize him on fine points--just enough to make him try
harder" [P. Cahn, "Diplomatic Delicacies," Sat. Eve. Post,
May 26, 1962].

In olden times, cooks had a crucial position in the
household.   He could be the trusted chef who would safeguard his master from poisoning by scrupulous care and
watchfulness; or he could also have his master at his mercy
by invisible poisoning of the food.   With this opportunity at
his command, he could be susceptible to bribes from his
master's enemies.   But besides this vulnerability and test
of his honor and fidelity, the kitchen and the serving staff
in any great political household could and sometimes did
harbor spies and eavesdroppers, or even careless gossips.
Without the greatest precautions and attention to secrecy,
state secrets of importance have been leaked out by casual
gossip of servants, as paid spies or otherwise, without even
the necessity of surreptitious eavesdropping or listening at
the keyhole.   In Lederer and Burdick's The Ugly American,
several cases are cited.   When Czar Nicholas II and Kaiser
Wilhelm arranged a private yachting rendezvous to sign a
secret German-Russian alliance--the abortive Bjorkoe treaty
of 1905--the French speedily realized that some sort of intrigue was going on when their intelligence agents in Russia
learned from a French chef employed by the Imperial kitchens that on July 20 orders had been handed down to rush
the gala table service, only used in entertaining royalty, to
the Czar's yacht.   (Edmond Taylor, The Fall of the Dynasties, p. 42.)

In passing, it may be mentioned that the famed and
notorious Janissaries of Turkey--a sort of praetorian guard,
reactionary and frightening to an extreme degree, and especially powerful during the reign of Sultan Abdul Hamid--
seemed to have adopted the Imperial Kitchens as their
symbol.

Their titles all derived from the kitchen--the chief
was called the Chorbaji-Bashi, or Head Soup Dis-
tributor; next came the Head Cook, and so on. Their
standard displayed a vast cauldron or kettle. ...
When the Janissaries were in camp, their kettles
were piled before the tent doors in the manner of
regimental drums. ... Each week, their rations were
fetched from the Seraglio kitchens in these kettles.
If they were dissatisfied, they would reverse the kettles and begin drumming on them ominously with the
long ladel-like spoons each man wore fixed into his
cap. So terrible were their uprisings that the whole
Seraglio, the Sultan too, would listen for the dreaded
sound [L. Blanch, "Aimée Dubucq de Rivery," The
Wilder Shores of Love].

Cooks in the ancient great ducal houses and palaces
were not merely kitchen menials or artisans in tall white
caps. They had to be artists and inventors. They were
great innovators. Jonathan Swift remarked that "He was a
bold man who first eat an oyster." Who was it, asks A. G.
Gardiner in one of his "Alpha of the Plough" essays, who
discovered that two such curiously diverse things as mutton
and red-currant jelly make a perfect gastronomic chord?
"By what stroke of inspiration or luck did some unknown
cook first see that applesauce was just the thing to make
roast pork sublime? Who was the Prometheus who brought
to earth the tidings that a clove was the lover for whom the
apple-pudding had pined through the ages?" Some of these
things, of course, were doubtless accidental, like the legendary discovery of roast pork as described by Charles Lamb.
But others were the results of informed or imaginative ex-
perimentation or intuition by expert culinary artists. The
results of their concoctions were honored either by the inventors' name, or by special names, usually in French, often the names of their illustrious appreciative patrons. A
chef who became distinguished for original masterpieces that
proved acceptable to gourmets' palates, was renowned
throughout the social milieu, and was honored by his master with title and rank; special dishes were given his name.

We sometimes partake of our viands with a grain of
salt. Are we also to take Old Elia also cum grano salis?
According to Lamb's famous dissertation upon roast pig,
"Mankind, says a Chinese manuscript, ... for the first seventy thousand ages ate their meat raw, or biting it from the
living animal, just as they do in Abyssinia to this day.

This period is not obscurely hinted at by their great Con-
fucius in the second chapter of his Mundane Mutations,
where he designates a kind of golden age by the term Cho-
fang, literally the Cooks' holiday." He then presents, as
from the Chinese manuscript, the imaginary account of the
discovery of roast pig through the accidental, and afterwards
the deliberate, burning down of the pig stable.

The Marquis or Chevalier de Bechamel was immortalized, in the reign of Louis XIV, by his invention of cream
sauce, for turbot and cod. Madame de Maintenon conceived
the "cutlets in curl-papers" which go by her name, and
which her ingenuity created in order to guard the sacred
stomach of the Grand Monarque from the grease which he
could not digest.

It is said that Henri Charpentier, the famed French
chef who died in January 1962 in California at the age of 81,
invented in 1894 crêpes suzette by putting together a "sweet
never before served to anyone" for the delectation of the
then Prince of Wales, later Edward VII.

Indeed it was expected that cooks should be inventors
of culinary "creations." Marie-Antoine Carême was pastry
innovator-extraordinary and private chef successively to Tal-
leyrand, King George IV, and Czar Alexander I. Auguste
Escoffier of the Ritz was the inventor of the peach Melba.
Anthelme Brillat-Savarin, (born in 1755 in a town named
Belley!), whose aphorisms his compatriots never weary of
repeating, said "The discovery of a new dish does more for
the happiness of mankind than the discovery of a star."
The present-day high priest of cookery in France, Mr. Raymond Olivier, is quoted as saying: "Like the painter with
colors, like the poet with words, I select, I blend, I har-
monize aromas, flavors, and textures. Ah, but yes, in
every true cook there lies an artist."

Ude, with magniloquence, maintained that to compose
an oratorio or opera was an easier feat than to invent a new
entree, and that a man of the requisite natural endowments
could sooner qualify himself to compete with the Royal Aca-
demicians than with the chief operators in cookery. Ude observes, "Music, painting, and mechanics in general possess
professors under twenty years of age, whereas in the first
line of cooking pre-eminence never occurs under thirty. We
see daily at the concerts and academies young men and wom-
en who display the greatest abilities; but in our line, nothing

but the most consummate experience can elevate a man to
the rank of Chief-Professor."

Up till the 1870's, entertainment for the rich and
aristocratic in London was more or less limited to private
homes and governed by conventions of the most inhibited
Victorianism.   Hotels were a matter of necessity for foreigners or country families without town houses, while visiting royalties were put up at the several palaces available to
the British Crown.   In 1884 D'Oyly Carte was seized with
the idea of a hotel which should outdo in convenience and
elegance anything the world had ever seen.   Richard D'Oyly
Carte created the Savoy.   He was the original producer of
Gilbert and Sullivan operettas which were the mainstay of
his Savoy Theatre to such an extent that they became known
as the Savoyard operas.   D'Oyly Carte was taking the cure
at Baden-Baden when he encountered César Ritz of Paris
and he persuaded this famous Swiss to help open the Savoy
Hotel in 1889.   With him he brought another great expert,
George Auguste Escoffier.   Soon the wonderful hotel and cuisine attracted the royalty and nobility of the Edwardian epoch, the great Jewish bankers, courtiers of fashion, diamond millionaires from Kimberley, champagne salesmen,
and the greatest actors, actresses, prima donnas, and
painters.   Escoffier rose to the occasion.   For the Prince
of Wales he dreamed up Cuisses de Nymphes à L'Aurora--
frogs' legs served cold in a jelly of cream and Moselle
tinctured with paprika.   For Mme. Nellie Melba, Australian-
born prima donna, he created Pêches Melba--fresh peaches
poached in vanilla syrup served in a timbale on a layer of
vanilla ice cream coated with raspberry purée.   The initial
presentation took place one evening after the diva had sung
Elsa in Lohengrin and it was Escofier's happy conceit to
bring the new creation to the table in a magnificent swan
carved from a huge block of ice borne by four tottering footmen in knee-breeches, to the applause of the entire restaurant.   Escoffier's les Suprêmes de Volailles Jeannette,
breasts of cold chicken in jelly, with foie gras, had an interesting origin.   In 1881 the Arctic exploration vessel Jean-
ette, preparing for a voyage of discovery to the North Pole,
became icebound, and its entire crew, save only a handful
of surviving sailors, perished off the Siberian coast.   Fifteen years later Escoffier unveiled a monument to their
memory when he first introduced Suprême Jeannette at a
Sunday evening dinner for 300 in the Main Restaurant of the
Savoy, the individual portions being served amid barriers of
crushed ice reminiscent of the floes which had spelled the
doom of the ship's company.

Alice was impressed with the White Knight, who told her "I keep inventing new things. Now the cleverest thing of the sort that I ever did was inventing a new pudding during the meat-course.... I don't believe that pudding ever will be cooked! And yet it was a very clever pudding to invent."

Charles Lamb, in "Grace Before Meat," refers to a passage of Milton's Paradise Regained, describing a banquet given by Satan; and says that "the whole banquet was too civic and culinary, and the accompaniments altogether a profanation of that deep, abstracted, holy scene. The mighty artillery of sauces, which the cook-fiend conjures up, is out of proportion to the simple wants and plain hunger of the guest."

To the French is attributed the art of the making of sauces, which are incorporated in their cookery. This results in the fact that most French cooking is "saucily" tasty. It is noticeable however, that most English cooking as well as American cooking, devoid of this sauciness, is relatively tasteless; and thus there is the vogue of applying extraneous manufactured sauces, like Worcestershire Sauce and H.P. and, especially in the United States, catsup, Chile sauces and relishes.

Oscar Wilde, in his first play Vera, had this to say:

Prince Paul: To make a good salad is to be a brilliant diplomatist--the problem is entirely the same in both cases. To know exactly how much oil one must put with one's vinegar.
Baron Raff: A cook and a diplomatist! An excellent parallel. If I had a son who was a fool I'd make him one or the other.
Prince Paul: I see your father did not hold the same opinion, Baron.... For myself, the only immortality I desire is to invent a new sauce....

As regards sauces, there is an anecdote that Sir Walter Scott, one day in spring, was walking around Abbotsford with Lady Scott. Passing a field where there were a number of ewes and rollicking lambs, Sir Walter said: "Ah, 'tis no wonder that poets, from earliest ages, have made the lamb the emblem of peace and innocence." "Delightful animals, indeed," rejoined Lady Scott, "especially with mint sauce."

Besides sauces, salt has ever been an important condiment. I once knew a kindly old Englishman who eschewed salt in his diet, because it was a mineral. "Man," he explained, "is a meat-eater; and meat comes from grazing. Thus he is a vegetarian, even though an intermediate stage. Any mineral salts his body may require must come from vegetation, either directly, or predigested in grazing animals. It is unnatural for man to eat directly pure minerals, such as table salt." He was not convinced when I argued that most grazing animals love mineral salt, or gather at the salt-licks, or even lap salt water; and that it is a common thing to replace the loss of saline content in the body's lymph, through perspiration, by remedial absorption of salt, raw or in solution--a well-known practice in tropical countries. Salt is a popular condiment. Cicero said: "It is a true saying that we must eat many measures of salt together to be able to discharge the functions of friendship" [De Amicitia, xix, 67].

Salt was, from ancient times, habitually associated with offerings. This practice is found alike among the Greeks and the Romans and among the Semitic peoples (Lev. ii, 13). Homer called salt "divine"; Plato names it "a substance dear to the gods." As covenants (i.e., treaties) were ordinarily made over a sacrificial meal, in which salt was a necessary element, a "covenant of salt" (Numb. XVIII, 19) can easily be understood. It is probable, however, that the preservative qualities of salt were held to make it a peculiarly fitting symbol of an enduring compact, and influenced the choice of this particular element of the covenant meal as that which was regarded as sealing an obligation to fidelity. Among the ancients, as among Orientals down to the present day, every meal that included salt had a certain sacred character and created a bond of piety and quest friendship between the participants. Hence the Arab phrase: "there is salt between us" and the expression: "to eat the salt of the palace" (Ezra. IV 14, R.V.). Early in the history of the Roman army and in later times an allowance of salt was made to officers and men, or its later equivalent in money, from which is derived our word "salary."

An Arab custom, based on desert practice, is that he who has partaken of salt in his host's tent, is, whether a friend or an enemy, an inviolable guest, to be entertained with fullest consideration so long as he is under the host's roof. If the salt is offered, it is a pledge of hospitality.

Kipling knew that when he wrote: "I have eaten your salt."
I have also heard it said that in Eastern countries if a guest
is served tea with a rose-petal floating on top, it is a token
of confidence and welcome; if tea is served without the
flower, it is an intimation that he is tolerated so long as he
is a guest, but is not welcome, and may look to himself as
soon as he leaves the sheikh's hospitable tent or roof. A
foreign visitor or diplomat must be well-versed in these local customs and practices.

We have stressed the importance of the cook and the
chef in the business and art of dining. Times have changed
and the role of the private cuisinier has diminished; there
are fewer masters of high cuisine than there used to be;
and fewer awards and titles are accorded them. But before
we pass from them to the guests, we may mention a few of
the hazards that sometimes confront cooks even in the best-
regulated palaces and houses. Accidents are bound to happen from time to time, although it is astonishing that they
occur so seldom. If the management of a dinner is likened
to the conducting of an orchestra, a few sour notes are not
unknown.

Even the most excellent chefs have their tribulations
and misfortunes. Once I had an excellent Japanese cook,
who on short notice could, like a magician producing a rabbit out of a silk hat, produce a chicken dinner for unexpected guests out of an empty larder, by borrowing his
neighbor's dinner supplies. But even he was crestfallen
when I once came home to dinner and he said: "Danna-San:
Very sorry. No dinner tonight." I asked him what he
meant. He said he had a chicken preparing on the stove,
and while his back was turned, a neighborhood dog slipped
in, smelt the delicacy, grabbed it off the stove and ran off.
What an ignominy for a conscientious cook. A not dissimilar episode is recounted by Sir Francis Colchester-Wemyss
in India, a dozen miles from Jubbulpore where his battalion
was stationed.

> I and two companions had arranged a party of six on
> a hot weather night "au clair de la lune" and had
> taken out with us a sumptuous meal. This was laid
> on a table just outside the bungalow some ten yards
> from the veranda, where the party of six was sitting.
> The servants were just announcing that everything
> was ready when there was a terrible commotion. A
> mob of fifty or sixty langoors--the big grey and white

and black Indian monkey--came leaping from the
rocks, overran the plateau, upset the table, scattered
the glasses and bottles and cutlery, and disappeared
as quickly as they had come with every morsel of our
beautiful dinner. All that remained was to drive
home twelve miles and scratch up some beer and
sandwiches [Food and Drink, p. 29].

There was once a hen intended for the cooking pot
which was destined to survive into old age as a family pet.
The British Ambassador Sir Esmé Howard, later Lord Howard of Penrith, tells how, as a boy, he went to Paris to
study, and knew his cousin Alan Herbert, an old bachelor
and doctor, who looked after a Children's Hospital. The
cousin recounted tales of the siege of Paris and the Paris
Commune in 1870. Lord Howard wrote of him: "During
the siege his cook had brought a white hen, intending to fat-
ten it up so that her beloved M. le Docteur would have a
good dinner once at least, instead of eating rats and other
things which were then common. But the hen had become
so attached to him and he to it, that it used to wander
about in his dining-room, sit on the back of his chair, and
share his scraps of food. It was, I believe, the only hen
that lived through the siege of Paris and the days of the
Commune" [Theatre of Life, vol. 1, p. 43].

Other mistakes not infrequently happen. There is a
story concerning the cinema mogul Louis B. Mayer.
He was crazy about chicken soup and had it served almost
daily in the MGM commissary, recalls Beth Day in This
Was Hollywood. Once a Chinese dignitary told Mayer's
brother Jerry (who had been his host during a visit) that he
was going to send a token of his gratitude from China.

A few weeks later, Jerry received the exciting news
that his friend had shipped a crate of rare and beautiful birds from the Orient. Weeks went by and
Jerry heard nothing further. On a worried hunch,
he visited the studio loading-dock and asked if anyone
had seen any trace of his birds. 'Why, yes,' one
laborer scratched his head, 'I do remember a crate
of mighty pretty chickens came in a few days ago.
We sent them to the commissary.' Jerry rushed
frantically to the commissary kitchen. 'Sorry' the
chef told him. 'We butchered the last one yesterday,
and put it in Mr. Mayer's chicken soup!'

There is also the classic story of the rare tulip bulb which the great botanist Linnaeus brought home and placed on his table for later examination, and which his cook, mistaking it for an onion, cooked in his soup.

Just after Mr. Edward Page, Jr. (later Ambassador to Bulgaria), and his newly-married wife Terry, were posted to the United States Embassy in Moscow in 1935, Mrs. Page had the proverbial cook problem. While she was worrying away with unpacking furniture and wedding presents at their first post she left her new cook unsupervised with an array of canned goods newly arranged on pantry shelves. Mrs. Page relates, "Later, beginning to feel the pangs of hunger, I ran to the kitchen to see how the cook and lunch were progressing. On the stove in a big open kettle--madly boiling--were half a dozen tennis balls! These had been packed in sealed tins, and were on the shelves with the other canned goods. The cook thought they looked filling and substantial!" [Foreign Service Journal, November 1960]. *

With such episodes as have been recounted, one can appreciate the comments of Thackeray in The Snobs of England, in which he refers to the dinner hostess. "The hostess is smiling resolutely through all the courses, smiling through her agony; though her heart is in the kitchen, and she is speculating with terror lest there be any disaster there. If the soufflé should collapse, or if Wiggins does

---

*This is apparently the authentic story told by Mrs. Page herself to Mr. James B. Stewart of the American Foreign Service in Budapest in 1936. But it was such an amusing story that it found its way, with variations, into other versions. For example it appeared again in an article by Kay Halle in Coronet, September 1960, p. 47. In Holiday, February 1961, p. 93, Nathaniel Benchley embroidered the story considerably and attributed the episode to U.S. Ambassador the late Joseph E. Davies. Charles W. Thayer gave his version, as a colleague of the Pages, in his book Bears in the Caviar (1950), p. 87. "Another Foreign Service Officer, Eddy Page, who had been studying with Chip [Bohlen] in Paris, arrived in Moscow with his bride Terry. Terry, by then, had heard a good deal of what to expect in Moscow and was well on her guard against mishaps. We'd arranged everything in their new apartment as best we could, in advance, including a local cook straight off a collective farm.... The Pages had hardly unpacked before they hurried down to the [Embassy] commissary.... Terry bought the spices and the canned foods. Eddy got the cocktail fixings and some tennis balls. Within an hour or so they were sitting down for their first meal in their new home. Some canned soup was produced and eaten. Then there was a long pause. While the Pages waited for their next course, they could hear the cook muttering away in the kitchen. Eventually she burst into the dining room.... 'They won't cook, I tell you, these darned American potatoes won't cook!' She poked the saucepan under Terry's nose and stabbed at the 'potatoes' with the fork. Bobbing about in the boiling water were a couple of Eddy's tennis balls."

not send the ices in time--she feels as if she would commit suicide--that smiling, jolly woman!"

Waiters, no less than cooks, have their misadven-
tures.   Mrs. Beatrice Russell, describing her first steps
as a junior American Foreign Service Officer's wife in Ad-
dis Ababa had occasional difficulties with her native cook
and houseboy.

> Debobie could usually be counted on to come through,
> although I do remember one time when he mistaken-
> ly used baking powder, instead of confectionery sugar,
> in the whipped cream, with mouth-puckering results.
> But the error only served to break the ice, and
> transformed what might have been a stiff dinner party
> into an enjoyable evening.   Tesfay, on the other
> hand, had to be rehearsed before each dinner.   Once,
> when I neglected this dress rehearsal, I was horri-
> fied to see Tesfay serve the entire table of twelve
> first, leaving our guest of honour, the Egyptian Am-
> bassador, for last.   When I managed, not entirely
> covertly, to call his attention to his oversight, he
> became so flustered that he forgot to give us dessert
> plates, and proceeded to serve the pie to the ambas-
> sador, who hesitated, reluctant to place the cream
> pie on the lace place setting [Living in State (paper
> ed.), p. 41].

Frederic Morton, author of The Rothschilds, reminds us that the great international banker Alfred Rothschild was an incomparable host who anticipated every wish
of his guests.   The footmen, butlers, and waiters were im-
peccably trained.   A visitor who stayed overnight was
greeted in the morning by the footman, wheeling in the
breakfast cart.   There was an infinite variety of foods from
which to choose.   The well-trained footman would ask:
"Shall it be tea, or coffee, or chocolate, sir?"   If the guest
chose tea, the next query would be: "China, Indian or Ceylon tea?"   The guest would then indicate his choice.   Then
the footman would ask: "Lemon, milk, or cream, sir?"
If the guest preferred milk, the footman would enquire so-
licitously: "Jersey, Hereford or Shorthorn, sir?"   (See
Ottawa Journal, Feb. 16, 1963.)

There are other stories concerning the mishaps of
waiters.   Lord Redesdale's Memories (page 129) includes
a curious episode at a dinner for men given by Sir Anthony

de Rothschild in honor of royalty. "Sir William Middleton,
who was famous for his wigs, was sitting next to Mr. Bernard Osborne, who was as bald as a billiard ball. In handing round some dish one of the gorgeously-liveried footmen
caught Sir William's wig in his aiguillette or a button: off
came the wig. The unhappy footman lost his wits and seeing two bald heads, crammed down the wig on the wrong
one. B. O. , as he was affectionately called, was delighted
and roared with laughter. To Sir William it was a tragedy. " (This would have made a wonderful scene for one of
Charlie Chaplin's films, along with the scene where the butler spills some ice cream down a lady's décolletage. It
also seems as absurd as Alice's tea party with the King,
Red Queen and White Queen.)

Accidents happen at dinners even in the best families. Mrs. Eleanor Roosevelt tells of a Hyde Park dinner
given with White House butlers, in honor of King George
VI and Queen Elizabeth during their visit to the U. S.
in 1939, and at which Prime Minister W. L. MacKenzie
King of Canada was one of the guests. The President's
mother, the matriarchal Sarah Roosevelt, had had extra
china put on a side table that wasn't used very often.

> ...[S]uddenly in the middle of dinner the serving
> table collapsed and the dishes clattered to the floor.
> Mama tried in the best-bred tradition to ignore it,
> but her step daughter-in-law, Mrs. James Roose-
> velt, from whom she had borrowed some plates for
> the occasion, was heard to say: 'I hope none of my
> dishes were among those broken!' ... One would
> think that one mishap of this kind would be enough
> for one evening, but just as we had gone down to the
> big library after dinner, there was a most terrible
> crash, as the butler, carrying a tray of decanters,
> glasses, bowls of ice, and so on, fell down the two
> steps leading from the hall and slid right into the
> library, scattering the contents of the tray over the
> floor and leaving a large lake of water and ice cubes
> at the bottom of the steps. I am sure that Mama
> wished that her English butler had stayed [This I Re-
> member, p. 196].

Princess Marie-Louise of Schleswig-Holstein, tells
of a dinner party she gave in Calvi, Corsica, to commem-
orate her birthday. She and the mayor, newly arrived,
greeted each other and repaired to the courtyard for coffee

and liqueur. "Here a disaster occurred, for François, the waiter, was so agitated that he upset the entire tray of liqueurs over me. I had put on my best pale blue chiffon evening dress, and the sticky liqueurs so stuck to it that I had to retire to my room and have the dress cut off me. But, of course, with a sweet smile I had to say 'It really doesn't matter'!" ["Travels," My Memoirs of Six Reigns].

Among the other contretemps at diplomatic dinners was the story told by Sir Thomas Hohler about his colleague in Mexico, the American Minister Mr. Stronge, "a charming gentleman, well-read, writer of excellent despatches," but an untidy and dishevelled man who possessed a pet parrot. Stronge, the possibly apocryphal story goes, was giving a large dinner party to important persons in Chile during a visit there: "...as usual the parrot was introduced and placed on the table; something frightened it, it fluttered, and lighted on the nearest object, which happened to be the head of the richest and most influential old lady present; she uttered a piercing shriek and everyone dashed to her assistance, whereupon the bird in fright flew off again, carrying with it the lady's hair and scattering diamonds" [Diplomatic Petrel].

Sometimes other things go wrong at a table. Lawrence Durrell, in his satirical skit "The Unspeakable Attaché," (from Stiff Upper Lip, p. 30) tells a comic tale. "The Assistant Military Attaché's office was always full of meccano and string. He read Popular Mechanics in secret. He was always tampering with electrical circuits, fuses, and using that beastly sticky stuff and so on. He was in league with the Devil on one side and De Mandeville, First Secretary, on the other.... They invented an electric train for serving food and sold the idea to Drage as a labor saving device. The train ran on to the dining-table and stopped before the diners with a plate on each carriage. On the face of it, it seemed ingenious. It was worked by buttons from [Ambassador] Polk-Mowbray's place. Mind you, I had my doubts. But as there was an Electrical Trades Union Conference and we had some of its members to lunch, Polk-Mowbray (who had a childish streak) thought he would impress them with his little toy. You have guessed? It was not until the Bombe Surprise was loaded that the machinery went wrong. There was a frightful accident, the train was derailed into our laps, and the Bombe (a marvelous creation on which Drage had spent all night) lived up to its name.... De Mandeville got Number One

Field Punishment. He had to feed goldfish in the Residence for a month."

Speaking of the role of the kitchen in diplomatic life, it is perhaps worth remembering the episode of 1960, when, during the American election campaign, Vice-President Nixon visited Moscow and met Soviet Premier Nikita Khrushchev face-to-face in the famed American "Miracle Kitchen" at the American Fair in Moscow. In what a reporter called "one of the great historic debates between East and West," Mr. Nixon and Mr. Khrushchev shouted at each other about their respective political systems, and while nothing much came of the debate, the Miracle Kitchen did offer a convenient and novel setting for international talks.

A friend the other day at a private supper observed that outside of classy restaurants, the elegant art of dining seems in our own time to have somewhat faded; and there are no longer the spectacular courses of rare exotic dishes and intriguing strange concoctions of inventive culinary artists. One reply is that, as Gabriel Tszuchmi, the Royal Chef has remarked in his Memoirs, the two wars brought about food restrictions and severe austerity, which broke old habits and left an aftermath of stoicism or simplicity, especially in England; a whole rising generation have not known their forefathers' epicureanism, and have not missed it. Another cause is the extending egalitarianism among social classes, by which the extravagances of the upper classes, and their expensive connoisseur tastes, have become unpopular displays of conspicuous luxury. Industrial and Hollywood millionares still are numerous in America, and even in some other countries, and form an upper class of nouveau riche; with some exceptions their earlier simple background and culture do not include an inherited connoiseurship and hereditary refinement of palate. Another major factor seems to lie in the fact that nothing is rare, exotic and supremely expensive now. Where in olden times exotic foods were brought to banquets from remote regions over long distances at vast expense, like fresh caviar brought in packed ice over deserts and mountains to a host's Lucullan table, nowadays anything from any of the four corners of the world can be bought in preserved, canned, or refrigerated form, in any super market, and be served at any breakfast, luncheon or dinner table at a moment's notice, at moderate expense. Nothing is strange, precious, or unusual any longer. Even at the simplest breakfast in Europe or America, the fruit-juice comes from Florida or California, oranges from Israel or Lebanon

or Sunkist Valley, apples from Okanagen, coffee from South
America, tea from Ceylon, Burma, etc., bread or toast
from Canadian wheat fields; and it is all taken for granted.
There is little excitement or "kudos" in embellishing a dinner table with former rarities which are now commonplace
items in the stores and shops. Rare or singular sauces are
no longer a cook's special chef d'oeuvre if they can be pur-
chased at any time around the corner. Thus the glorious
old-fashioned "culinary art" has suffered a severe if not
mortal blow, except, in a sort of rear-guard action in still
surviving restaurants renowned for their originality of cooking. Diplomatic dinners in particular have suffered from
this falling-off of individual distinction, since professional
caterers are so frequently used in place of private master-
chefs; and they produce almost the same standardized menus
and meals for every Embassy. In earlier years, I looked
forward to every visit to a Russian Embassy for a taste of
my favorite Black Sea caviar; today I serve it most naturally in my own buffet-parties. It has not lost its savor, but
it has lost its uniqueness. We have entered an age when
dining is not a highly individualist art of cookery and gastronomy, but a commercialized and almost standardized routine.

Alas! After all the wonderful history of gastronomy,
are we to be reduced to a form of regimentation attributable
to our much-vaunted scientific progress? Shall we eat syn-
thetics in which refrigeration, canning and chemical pre-
servatives obliterate the romance of the Spice Trade, or the
delectable art of culinary invention? Are artistic chefs to
become mere artisan cooks? and magnanimous hosts to become merely chairmen of routine banquets? and are dinners
to be provided by catering firms?

The age of the kitchen, the vast staff, the maître
d'hôtel, the chef and all his under-cooks and minions, has
declined with the introduction of automatic electric cooking
devices, prepared foods and sauces and a scarcity of that
social class, cuisiniers, as professional artists. Thus the
art of dining is affected by the dearth of cooks and by the
mechanization of cooking. Synthetic foods are not unknown,
and were often used as food-substitutes during the war.
There is the well-known story of the German Jew who, under the Nazi regime, felt that life was not worth living, and
decided to end it. He bought himself a length of rope, and
attempted to hang himself; but the rope was ersatz, it broke,
and he survived. He then procured a revolver, loaded it,

and fired it at his head; but the bullets were ersatz, they
didn't explode, and he survived.   He then bought some poison, and drank it, but the poison was ersatz and he survived.   After these three attempts he decided that God did
not want him to die, and that his life was being divinely
protected.   Thereupon, he reflected, if I am meant to live,
I shall live handsomely; I shall first give myself a splendid
dinner.   He went to the best restaurant, ordered the best
food and the best wine, and set himself to enjoy them.   But
the dinner, also, was erstaz, and he died....

IV

PROTOCOL

When we come to consider the behavior of guests at formal dinners, we encounter an even greater incidence of problems, errors, and recriminations, than with the kitchen staff and the chefs. The regulation of the kitchen, or in Army terms, the "commissariat," is, with certain exceptions already noted, generally well managed and controlled. But the behavior of guests is obviously not under any such managerial control, since each guest is an independent individual of rank and quality who is under no command, other than the unwritten laws of custom, politeness, good conduct, and--what has in modern times come to be accepted as a regulating factor--etiquette.

Among hosts and their guests, there are the problems of superstitions, of absences, of uninvited guests, of late arrivals, and of rank and placement. Some of these difficulties have been partially solved by a universally acceptable code of conduct, formalized in diplomatic "etiquette" and-- as regards recognition of rank, in "protocol."

NUMBERS

Let us refer first to the eccentricity exhibited in matters of superstition concerning numbers of guests. Superstition has followed a long trail from primitive and tribal times to our own day and society. It accounts for taboos and rites of a myriad of kinds. In our so-called Age of Enlightenment, many ancient taboos and superstitions, based on ignorance or groundless fears, or on pagan worship, have been discarded. But even so, we still inherit and preserve some superstitions. For instance, we still "keep our fingers crossed" and "knock on wood"; sometimes we exclaim "God Bless!" when someone sneezes; we cover our mouths with our hands when we yawn to keep spirits from sailing forth; we look askance at black cats crossing our path, drop salt

over our left shoulder if it is spilled at table, occasionally
wish on first seeing a new moon, avoid walking under a lad-
der, and take note of "unlucky" numbers.   Indeed, many hotels are obliged to respect this superstition.

That renowned gentleman of candor, Michel de Montaigne, erstwhile Mayor of Bordeaux like his father before
him, confessed that "it seems to me excusable if I accept
an odd number rather than even, Thursday in preference to
Wednesday; if I had rather make a twelfth or fourteenth than
be thirteenth at table...." *

On the other hand, the French philosopher Auguste
Comte could not liberate himself from the fascination of
numbers.   Thirteen had a peculiar charm for him as the
seventh prime member--i.e., the seventh number that has
no multipliable parts.   He experienced an animating sense
of good fortune whenever he found himself at table with
twelve other companions.   In nothing was he more eccentric
than in this preference for a number that has for centuries
been regarded as the number of evil omen.

The dismal incidents which followed the Last Supper
occasioned the ancient opinion that whenever thirteen--and
no more--persons broke bread together, death would in the
following year take at least one of the party.   Writing in the
earlier half of the 17th century, Peter du Moulin (pedanti-
cally self-styled Petrus Molineus) observed: "If there are
thirteen guests at a feast, it is believed that one of them
will die within a year; for just so many persons reclined at
table when Christ celebrated the Eucharist on the day before
he died."   (It is said that this superstition apparently goes
much further back than the Last Supper.   Twelve of the
Norse gods were dining at Valhalla, when Loki intruded,
making a thirteenth--and Balder was slain.)   In 1874 J. C.
Jeaffreson commented:

> The prejudice against 'thirteen' still endures.   It af-
> fects even vigorous minds, who are nonetheless

---

*Dean Swift, in his satirical A Tale of a Tub (Section 1), claimed, prob-
ably with tongue in cheek, that "the profound number THREE is that which
has most employed my sublimest speculations, nor even without wonderful
delight."   He proposed to write and publish an essay, "wherein I have, by
most convincing proofs, not only reduced the senses and the elements under
[THREE'S] banner, but brought over several deserters from its two great
rivals, SEVEN and NINE; the two climacteries."

troubled by it because they are aware that an average mortality removes yearly from the world at least
one out of every thirteen persons of middle or old
age.   Lord Chancellor Erskine could never be in-
duced to seat himself at a table with only twelve other people; and the same nervous dislike to be one of
thirteen at a social meeting is felt by a considerable
proportion of educated Englishmen, who are secretly
ashamed of their weakness in yielding to a superstition [A Book about the Table (1874), p. 304].

It is said that in Poland, at the traditional Christmas Eve Dinner, it is important that there is an even number of diners.   An uneven number means death for one of
the company within a year.   So strongly is this believed
that a special small table is customarily laid for chance
guests.   Many hotels that boast every modern convenience
omit a thirteenth floor and have no rooms numbering 13.
Some theatres even omit row "M" because it is the thirteenth letter of the alphabet.

Diplomats or their wives are no less free from superstition than other persons.   I remember a luncheon once
given by the Canadian Minister to Japan at the Legation, at
which one of the principal guests was the British Ambassa-
dress, Lady Clive.   Just as we were about to be called into the dining room, she discovered, or was told with apologies, that there would be thirteen seated guests.   She immediately exclaimed her horror.   In an apologetic way, she
said that she was obsessed with this superstition and would
not dare sit down at a table of thirteen.   The host and
hostess were consternated at this last-moment contretemps.
I, a mere junior secretary, promptly offered to absent myself from the luncheon, thus leaving a company of twelve.
But this was not acceptable.   Could I obtain a fourteenth
guest?   Were any of our secretaries available at the office
across the compound?   I said I thought that by this hour
they had already lunched or gone out for lunch; but I would
run across and see.   In the office I found one of the female staff, just returned after completing her lunch.   I
said: "Quickly, there is an emergency at the Legation.
Have you got a hat to put on?   Whether you've already eaten
or not, you've got to come to the Minister's luncheon to
make a fourteenth guest.   Otherwise the British Ambassa-
dress is prepared to leave.   Quickly!"   And nobly, she
came to the rescue of the luncheon; and had to sit before
a second repast, and pretend to partake of it.

A peculiar aspect of "etiquette" concerned the right of a guest to criticize his host after a dinner. This must have been a relic of the age of chivalry, for it sounds somewhat quaint to our modern age. Monsieur Aze, in his Gastronomic Code, forbade a guest to slander his host until a certain time had elapsed since the regalment of a dinner-- the length of forbearance from defamatory speech varying in proportion to the goodness of the repast. By a fairly good dinner, a host could purchase security for eight clear days from the slanderous proclivities of the guests at his table. By a meal of superlative excellence, he could extend the period of safety from lying tongues to six months. But no dinner, however costly and complete, could oblige a guest to refrain for more than half a year from the pleasure of calumniating its giver. Thus by entertaining all his friends once in every six months, a competent and lavish host could maintain a blameless character in the circle of his private acquaintances.

FORGETFULNESS

In a survey of the peccadillos of men in the art of dining, we may note that sometimes dinners go awry be- cause of a secretary's forgetfulness or absent-mindedness in advising his ambassador. When Mr. W. Cameron- Forbes was U.S. Ambassador in Japan, he on one occasion planned to give a diplomatic men's luncheon; he instructed his third secretary, Walter Washington, to sound them out separately to find a mutually acceptable date, and to inform the ambassador as to the date chosen. The secretary car- ried out the enquiries, found a suitable date, but forgot to inform his chief. One by one the guests began to arrive, but the ambassador was slow to realize the reason. When the first colleague arrived, Mr. Forbes, who had been rest- ing in dishabille, thought that this was just a friendly person- al call and, making himself presentable, affably received his visitor. Then another, and another, arrived. Mr. Forbes began to realize that something was up, but asked the rea- son of this concerted visit. "We thought you were expecting us for lunch," was the reply. Mr. Forbes, being quite un- prepared, murmured some excuse, and said that refresh- ments were being prepared; and quickly ordered the kitchen staff to arrange an impromptu and rather improvised lunch- eon as quickly as possible. He had been completely "caught out." After the guests had all left, more or less satisfied with the amicable picnic-style luncheon, the ambassador sent for his secretary. "Come in, Mr. Washington. Sit

down; take the armchair. A glass of sherry? A cigar?"
Finally turning his glinting eyes on his secretary, he paused
a few moments, and then simply said to his ashamed secretary: "My God, it was awful!..." Then, after a further
pause, he said: "Alright, Mr. Washington, you may go.
That's all!" Mr. Forbes was an elderly Southern gentleman with the greatest Southern courtesy and politeness.
Not long after this episode, Mr. Walter Washington was
transferred to another post--first to Stamboul and then suddenly, when he and his family were halfway en route, to
Bogota, Colombia.

A similar episode happened in Shanghai while Colonel
Moore Cosgrave was senior Canadian Trade Commissioner
there. He had gone home to the outskirts of the city for
his family lunch. Suddenly a group of visiting Canadian
businessmen arrived at the Shanghai Club but could not find
him. The Assistant Trade Commissioner, Mr. Bruce Macdonald, was located and was asked where Colonel Cosgrave's
luncheon was. Macdonald knew nothing about it, and telephoned his chief, who was already halfway through his lunch
at home. The Colonel then remembered that he had extended an invitation to the visiting Canadians, but had forgotten
all about it. He asked Macdonald to keep the guests happy
at the bar--then boasting to be the longest in the world--
for half an hour until he could get back into town. When he
arrived at the Club, he preemptorily ordered an ex tempore
luncheon; then went among his pals in the main dining room,
already at their own lunch, and taking advantage of his
great popularity, "shanghaied" them from their tables, told
them he had some important visitors whom he wished them
to meet, and managed somehow to round up a party and provide them all a pleasant impromptu luncheon. Few of his
Canadian guests were aware of the near-fiasco and their
host's absent-mindedness.

Charles W. Thayer relates an episode in Berlin in
1939, "when Hitler was using his guns, and butter was not
the only food missing from Berlin tables." At that time
Alexander Kirk was in charge of the U.S. Embassy, and
George Kennan was his counsellor. Kirk had been in the
habit of having a huge luncheon spread out buffet-style every
Sunday as a solution to the problem of entertaining. One
Saturday Kirk was summoned to Paris for a consultation;
before he left that day he called in Kennan to cancel the
luncheon. " 'Please take the necessary steps to call it off, '
he told Kennan. A few days later he returned from Paris

and called Kennan into his office. 'You did a pretty good
job cancelling the Sunday lunch,' he told him. 'There were
only two people you forgot to tell.' 'Who were they?'
George asked. 'The chef and the Japanese Ambassador,'
Kirk replied" [Bears in the Caviar, p. 167].

Then there is the matter of the invited guests' forgetfulness. Monsieur Aze decreed that to fail to keep an
engagement for dinner was an offense for which the delin-
quent should forfeit five hundred francs to the disappointed
host. By giving forty-eight hours' notice of his inability to
fulfil his engagement, the offender might, however, reduce
the penalty of his breach of promise to three hundred francs.

When I was a young diplomatic secretary, I was repeatedly adjured by one of my seniors that once a dinner
engagement had been accepted no excuse "except death"
would justify its last minute cancellation or defection. An
unforewarned absence--unless notified in plenty of time--
would disconcert the host and hostess, upset the carefully
arranged seating plans, and would be unforgivable. Once I
was at a dinner given by my minister in Japan, which was
delayed by the non-arrival of a high Foreign Ministry official. After ten minutes or so, a butler was instructed to
telephone the official's home to find out whether he had left,
or was on his way, or had got lost. The official himself
sleepily answered that he had completely forgotten the engagement and had gone to bed; he suggested, with fullest
apologies, that the dinner, already delayed, proceed without
his presence. More apologies were sent the following day,
and he was ultimately forgiven. I myself barely escaped a
similar faux pas, when having supped early at home and settled down to an evening of relaxation, my cook intruded to
tell me that the servant of the Norwegian chargé d'affaires
had just called to say that his other guests were awaiting
my arrival for dinner. I had mistaken the date. As the
Norwegian house was only one street away, I sent back word
that I was coming immediately; hastily dressed for the formal occasion, and arrived while the party was finishing its
last round of cocktails, whereupon I ate a second dinner
with nothing seemingly amiss. On another occasion I was
invited to a dinner given by the United States military attaché in Warsaw, in a house very difficult to find in a remote outlying suburb. I had been given detailed instructions
as to how to find it, and gave these to my chauffeur. It
was a stormy and very black night; he mistook a turning,
and lost his way, and I was an hour late in my arrival.

I gave my driver a thorough rating, saying that the British
Ambassador would not tolerate his driver making a stupid
mistake and bringing him late to dinner. When I finally arrived, expressing apologies, the party was just finishing its
cocktails, and I was just in time to take my place at the
dinner table. In answer to my apologies, my host said:
"Oh that's all right, we never expect our guests to find our
place or to arrive on time. At my last dinner, the British
Ambassador arrived an hour late." But formal dinners are
not so easy-going or lenient; they are punctual and punctilious; and lateness on the part of a guest is a venal sin.

So too is premature arrival. Once, through a mistake in dates, I turned up at a host's home for dinner only
to be informed by the servant that the "Master" was out of
town, that day, but was giving a dinner the following night!

UNEXPECTED GUESTS

There is also the occasional problem of uninvited or
unexpected guests arriving at a diplomatic dinner--mostly
due to a mistake as to the address or date; and this of
course is bound to cause confusion to the host and hostess
and the seating plan, as well as to the kitchen and serving
staff.

Once my minister in Japan, Sir Herbert Marler, was
giving a formal dinner, and suddenly discovered a strange
lady in the company--a Japanese Princess. Nonplussed, he
had a place set for her near the top of the table, and carried on with perfect courtesy. As the dessert was being
served, a flunkey came up behind the minister and whispered in his ear: "Is the Princess here? The -- Embassy
has enquired. They are awaiting her presence at their dinner." The minister whispered back, 'Tell them that she
has arrived here by mistake: she has almost finished dinner here. She will go to the -- Embassy for coffee. Tell
them not to wait for her." He then had to tell her tactful-
ly that the -- Embassy would be pleased to welcome her
presence after dinner.

Paul S. Reinsch, American Minister to China, relates a similar story. He and his wife were giving a dinner party for a departing friend who worked with the Y.M.
C.A. The thirty guests were all American missionaries in
Peking. Suddenly a prince, Pu Lun, was shown in to the
reception room, evidently mistaking an invitation. Says
Reinsch:

...as there appeared to be no other dinner given at
the Legation I made no effort to clear up the error
and tried to make him thoroughly welcome.   I had
the table re-arranged so as to seat the Prince between two ladies both of whom spoke Chinese very
well.   He appeared to be surprised at the composition of the company and the absence of wines, but
was apparently well entertained by his neighbours.
When the dinner was about half way through, Kao,
the head boy, came to the back of my chair and
whispered to me: 'Mrs. Lee's boy outside.   Say
Prince belong Mrs. Lee's dinner.'   So after dinner
I felt in duty bound to tell the Prince that Mrs. Lee
had sent word she would be very happy if he could
come to her house in the course of the evening.
After a short conversation...the Prince departed, to
recoup himself at the house of the navy doctor for
the abstinences laid upon him at the minister's dinner [An American Diplomat in China, p. 118].

On one occasion I was invited to a large luncheon
given by the Japanese Foreign Ministry for a visiting dele-
gation.   I accepted, and at the proper time, arrived.   On
looking at the seating plan, I found that my name was missing.   I thought that the best idea was therefore to disappear.
As I was stealthily leaving the hall, the Japanese Protocol
Officer, whom I knew well, noticed me.   "Where are you
going?" he asked.   I explained that I had been overlooked
in the arrangements and was disappearing to save trouble.
Perhaps the acceptance had gone astray.   "Nonsense," he
said.   "There had been a technical mistake.   I remember
receiving your acceptance.   We shall immediately make a
place for you.   You must stay."

But in Rio de Janeiro, where acceptances to invitations are most casual or irregular (and often have to be confirmed by telegram instead of the unreliable post), the Para-
guayan Ambassador had formally declined an invitation to a
dinner being given by my minister.   As cocktails were being served, he suddenly appeared; and of course did not
find his name on the seating plan, which offended him.   He
complained to the host; and my minister, much concerned,
interrogated me.   I replied that he had definitely declined.
"Well, anyhow," said the minister, "here he is; and is in
a very bad temper.   Fix a place for him; and make sure
that it is his rightful place of rank."   I replied that I
could arrange for an extra place, but I could not guarantee

his position, as I had not a diplomatic list to show what
precedence he was entitled to.   I made a random guess,
and a seat and name card were prepared.   He stole out to
the dining room to see where he was seated; and apparently was satisfied; my rough guess had been close enough.
After we sat down, my minister made much of him, toasted
him, chatted effusively with him, and flattered him, until
he was thoroughly placated; and after the dinner the ambassador and my minister were exchanging abrazos as the
best of friends.

      Lieutenant General Maurice Pope, Canadian Ambassa-
dor to Belgium and later to Spain, describes a state dinner
given by the Commonwealth representatives on the occasion
of Queen Elizabeth's Coronation.   As doyen, General Pope
was responsible for arranging and giving the dinner, which
King Baudouin attended.   Everything went well as it turned
out but the occasion did cause a good deal of last minute
"scurrying around."   Word had arrived while the guests
were arriving that one of the ambassadors and his wife
would not be able to come.   Alterations in the seating plan
were ordered instantly.   "Great then was my astonishment
a few moments later," wrote Pope, "to see this couple coming in.   Springing from my place, I sought out Arnold Smith
(later ambassador in Cairo, and Moscow) and told him that
it was a matter of urgency to restore the original seating
arrangement.   Soon afterwards, Jim Langley, one of the
Canadian secretaries and a master of ceremonies for the
evening, passed by and whispered that we had duly crisis'd
and uncrisis'd in a matter of minutes" [Soldiers and Politicians, p. 407].

      In a small diplomatic circle it is not rare to find
oneself entering the wrong house for a dinner, especially
when diplomatic dinners are given in almost every house on
almost every evening.   I remember once turning up at the
German Embassy in Tokyo.   The police waved my car up
to the front door.   I entered and even handed my coat and
top hat to the butler.   I had been invited to the German
counsellor's dinner, and understanding that the ambassador
was out of town, I surmised that the counsellor, as chargé
d'affaires, might be using the embassy residence for his
dinner.   On the threshold, I asked a flunkey--"Is this
Count ---'s dinner?"   With surprise, he said 'Oh, no, Sir;
this is the Ambassador's dinner!   Count ---'s dinner is in
the house behind."   Thus I just saved myself from an im-
proper intrusion, and hastily made my way to my proper
host's residence.

On another occasion a friend in the British Embassy
in Tokyo invited me for dinner. Most of the British secretaries had identical houses within the compound. I entered
one, doffed my coat and hat, and entered the salon where
cocktails were going on. Suddenly the Embassy host, also
a good friend, came up and said, "Whose party do you think
you're at? You weren't invited here." I said the name of
my host. "Oh," he said, "he's in the other house, next
door." So I made my apologies for crashing into his own
dinner party, and proceeded to my host's next door. I only suggested that the embassy might arrange for better
identification or numbering of their identical houses, to
avoid such mistakes and embarrassments.

One of my awkward moments while in Buenos Aires
was when a certain lady telephoned me, in Spanish, to invite me for dinner on a specified evening. I imagined that
I half-understood her; she said she had met me previously
at a recent dinner of the Turkish Ambassador. She gave
me vaguely her name and her address. Afterwards I failed
to be able to check the address to verify her name, or to
check her doubtful name by the vaguely given address. I
was completely non-plussed. I made private enquiries of
my friends in the Argentine protocol division of the Ministry, but without success. Finally on the evening indicated,
I dressed up and had my chauffeur drive me to the address
I thought she had given me. It turned out to be a shop,
closed and barricaded for the night. I was thus quite sty-
mied. The address was wrong; I had not caught her name.

Suddenly I saw, passing me, a car with a diplomatic
licence plate. "Follow that car," I urged my chauffeur. A
block beyond, it stopped. I waited to see who stepped out.
It was, I recognized with relief, the Turkish Ambassador
and his wife. I thought: "she said she had met me at the
Turkish Ambassador's dinner. Now he is going in here.
Perhaps this is a reciprocal dinner. Perhaps this is where
I, too, am expected. I shall go in and follow them, and
see." So I went in. There was quite a crowd assembled.
A young man in black-tie was playing at a piano. The
Turkish Ambassador and his wife were being introduced.
Then some bejewelled lady met me and vaguely began introducing me--to almost all strangers except the Turkish pair
and a chargé whom I recognized. Then we went in to the
dining room. The young man at the piano who had not been
introduced, played on in the empty drawing room; it turned
out that he was a hired entertainer and not a guest. The

dinner table was large, and circular; I finally found a place-
card, with "Canada" on it but not my recognizable name.
I sat down; and tried to assess and identify the company--
mostly strangers.   General conversation crisscrossed the
table throughout the well-served meal.

When the gentlemen retired to the smoking room for
coffee, brandy and cigars, I greeted the Turkish Ambassador and the Honduran chargé d'affaires, and said to the latter: "Tell me, please--I'm quite confused--whose party is
this?   Who is the hostess?   I have been trying to guess.
Is she the blonde lady who was seated opposite me?"   "Oh,
no," he rplied, "that is my wife!"   I hastily apologized,
saying that I had not been aware that he had a wife.   "The
hostess," he said, "was sitting three seats from you around
the table to your right, near the Turkish Ambassador."   I
thanked him, and explained that, while I was somewhat
doubtful if she knew my name, I was equally in doubt as to
hers, as I didn't hear it clearly on the telephone.   He told
me her name.   I asked him who she was.   He said that
she was a wealthy Argentine widow, who liked to give din-
ner-parties--graced as often as possible with diplomats.
She had no other connections or official position.   She hired
a musician to give entertainment, in the next room, during
the repast.   It was just a pastime or hobby of hers.   I
thanked him for this information, later met his wife, and
ultimately identified and bade goodnight to my hostess.   After this peculiar "blind date," with an unknown hostess at
an unknown address (revealed only by the fortunate arrival
of the Turkish Ambassador's car a block ahead of me), I
never saw her again.   She probably invited the next diplomat on the diplomatic list to her next private dinner, to
lend lustre to her confusing round table!

LATENESS

Then there are the inconveniences resulting from
late arrivals at dinners or similar functions.   These throw
out of order all the perfectly timed programs, the carefully calculated kitchen preparations, and the quality of the
warm repast.   Because a formal dinner is constructed like
a concert program or a symphony, the smallest obstruction
is calamitous to its success.

In Spain and in the Spanish-American countries, very
late dinners are customary.   Sometimes the guests do not
sit down at table until 10 or 11 o'clock p.m.   This is ac-

cepted practice for those who are accustomed to it; especially since few ambassadors of those countries turn up early
the next morning at their embassies or chancelleries.   But
it is very unpopular among the Anglo-Saxons, who normally
dine reasonably early (8 p. m. is their customary diplomatic
dinner-hour), who go to bed reasonably early, and keep
early Anglo-Saxon office hours in the mornings.   I remember the American Ambassador to Chile, Mr. Claude Bowers
--who held his post there for over ten years, telling me
that he never ceased to resent these late Spanish hours; and
that often, in silent protest, he had his own dinner at home
at the normal hour of eight, and then proceeded to the late
diplomatic dinners, refused to eat anything, and explained,
if necessary, that he had already had his dinner at a "respectable" hour.

Prince Bernhard of the Netherlands is pictured by
his biographer Alden Hatch, as a man who takes seriously
the saying that promptness is the courtesy of kings.   "If a
luncheon invitation says 12:30, you can count on Prince
Bernhard arrived at 12:29 and a half."   Washington, D.C.,
according to Mr. John Elliot, Jr., former social secretary
to John Foster Dulles, is the most punctual of U.S. cities.
The tone is set by the diplomatic corps.   "Often, before a
dinner," Mr. Elliot says, 'I have seen diplomats being
driven round and round the block in their limousines, to
avoid being a minute too early or a second too late."   If
this is true of Washington and other diplomatic capitals, it
was certainly true of Tokyo.   The Japanese are normally
punctilious and punctual; even their railway services are so
precise that the locomotive driver is fined for each unjusti-
fied minute he is overdue at a station.   Likewise the diplomats in Tokyo ran their formal dinners like clockwork.   If
a guest was more than five minutes late, telephone enquiries were made, and the dinner itself rarely waited for a
late-comer more than a few minutes.   There was also a
precise hour, normally 10:30 p. m. when the guests were
expected to take their departure, in order of precedence,
and rarely did any of them linger afterwards.

When President Theodore Roosevelt and his wife visited Paris in 1914, a state dinner was given by the President of the Senate, at the Luxembourg Palace.   A chief
guest was the short-lived French Premier Ribot.   The
American Ambassador, Mr. Myron T. Herrick, relates that
"the dinner was for about 150--many ambassadors were
there, and we were all kept waiting until long past the hour.

After three-quarters of an hour, I enquired whom they were
waiting for, and was told for 'one of the members of the
Cabinet.' I remarked that he was taking great chances of
losing his seat at the table because the Cabinet might fall
before he arrived. I had not observed Madame Ribot sitting
near by. She did not seem to enjoy the joke quite as much
as the others who were less interested. The prophecy was
not far wrong, for the cabinet fell the next morning..."
[T. Bentley Mott, Myron T. Herrick, Friend of France,
p. 105].

Somewhat similar was the case of the Canadian Minister in Buenos Aires, Justice W. A. F. Turgeon, who had
succeeded in inviting to dinner a prominent Argentine Army
leader, General Rawson. On the afternoon of the dinner,
an aide telephoned my minister to express regret that General Rawson would not be able to be present. The dinner,
perforce, had to go on. The next morning it was revealed
that during the night the Young Officers group, with Colonel
Perón a secret agitator, had staged a coup d'état, and over-
thrown the Castillio civilian government, and had declared
a Revolutionary Government, with General Rawson as the
front-man and temporary president. A few days later he
was replaced by General Ramírez, followed by General Far-
rell, until Colonel Juan Domingo Perón had intrigued his
way to the vice-presidency and presidency. General Rawson's sudden absence was at least excusable.

Sir Bruce Lockhart tells of one grand official dinner,
a banquet of 100 guests, at which the newly arrived British
Ambassador Sir George Clark attempted to include the entire
Czechoslovak cabinet, legislative leaders, and party heads,
and their wives, and the important nobility; in other words,
the leaders of the new-proletarian Czechoslovaia of 1920,
together with members of the Old Regime aristocracy. "The
nobility had replied to the invitations with exemplary prompt-
itude and in the prescribed manner," but the government
officials had replied in a variety of manners, or not at all,
some with mention of their wives, some without.

> Dinner was at eight-thirty.... Between twenty-five
> and half-past eight, all the nobility had arrived; at
> half-past there was not a Czech in the room. Be-
> tween half-past eight and nine o'clock odd assort-
> ments made their appearance.... I realized that my
> table-plan would have to undergo an eleventh hour
> operation. Czechs who had refused or not answered,

had arrived. Some, who had accepted for their
wives, had left them at home. Others, who had refused, had brought them with them. Between nine
and a quarter-past a few more stragglers put in their
appearance. For myself, I was in a sweat. I had
been dashing backwards and forwards between the re-
ception-rooms and the dining room in a feverish effort to bring some order into my wretched table-
plan. I now rushed off to the telephone [to call the
last two] missing ministers. While I was ringing up
the exchange, one minister arrived with his wife who
had not accepted. I could not get on to the other
minister. At twenty-five past nine he came in very
sheepishly, his face red with nervousness and his
new shoes creaking loudly on the parquetted floor....
We sat down to dinner just after nine-thirty. It went
off better than I expected. The food, it is true, was
spoilt. The soup was cold [but] Sir George's remedy
was champagne and more champagne. Fortunately
neither the Czechs nor the 'Blacks' were teetotalers,
and after a silent beginning tongues flowed freely.
But the two groups did not mix, and the experiment
was not repeated [Retreat from Glory, p. 68-69].

I have a recollection of a great state banquet being
arranged at the Jockey Club of Buenos Aires with President
Perón as the guest of honor. Preparations had been meticu-
lously made; the guest-list acceptances had been checked and
rechecked, and finally a seating-plan had been elaborated, in-
scribed, and mounted in the lobby outside the dining room.
There was constant delay; there were worried protocol officers; there were repeated deletions or amendments made in
the table-plan, with consequent rearrangements of places and
place-cards at the tables themselves. An hour passed; rumors flew; the President would not be able to attend. Everyone was nervous. But at last he and his retinue arrived,
and we entered the salle-à-manger, and found our places,
and the dinner was served, although the chefs must have
been frantic and the culinary arts were badly impaired. Had
the fish been late in arriving, a Vatel would have killed himself; but when a guest is late, the host, hostess and culinary establishment can hold no responsibility, and therefore
have to tolerate the inconvenience.

Queen Alexandra was extremely unpunctual and had
no sense of time. She was frequently five or ten minutes
late for meals. This lateness for meals inconvenienced a

good many people, both the guests, who could not be seated
until the Queen had arrived, and the kitchen staff, who had
prepared meals.   It was the custom for the dining room
staff to begin serving at the top of the table, and after the
King and Queen had been served their portions, to carry on
round the table, ending up with the last few guests.   When
everyone had finished, a bell was rung and the plates were
cleared for the next course.   Once a shooting-party of
about thirty people was being entertained at Windsor, and
the King, irritated with the delay, decided that the sooner
they took advantage of the weather to set out, the better.
So, hardly saying a word, he hurried through the first
course, and as soon as he had finished eating he rang the
bell for the next course to be brought on.   This was a little hard on the last guests to be served for they had only
just begun to tackle the meal when the footmen cleared away
their plates.   The same thing occurred with the following
seven or eight courses.   As soon as King Edward had finished, the footmen were summoned, and when the roast was
reached the guests were beginning to give up hope of managing more than a few mouthfuls during the whole meal.
All of them had hearty appetites, and there were downcast
expressions by the time the dessert course was reached.
As the King had expected, Queen Alexandra was aware of
their plight, but she could do nothing to help them, for it
was to some extent her fault that the meal had to be so
hurried.   (See Gabriel Tschumi, Royal Chef, p. 104-106.)

It is said of Francis Joseph, monarch of the Austro-
Hungarian Empire, that he had the knack of splendor but no
taste for the artificial glitter of court life.   The state banquets he gave were true ordeals for his guests.   The opu-
lence of the appointments, the perfection and splendor of the
servants, the beautiful and historic table setting, fine great
wines and so on "made even the haughtiest royal visitors
feel like parvenus.   Since Francis Joseph did not believe in
wasting time over his food, and detested small talk, he had
trained the palace staff to serve and clear away a twelve-
course dinner in less than an hour.   A new course was
served the moment the Emperor finished his plate, and
guests at the bottom of the table were likely to have theirs
whisked away before they had taken a mouthful" [Edmond
Taylor, The Fall of the Dynasties, p. 92-93].

John Buchan, Lord Tweedsmuir, while Governor General of Canada, was in delicate health, which he endured
with great fortitude and courage until his final fatal stroke.

His aide-de-camp, Colonel Willis O'Connor, records that he
had a very serious stomach ailment necessitating a strict
diet. "All his meals were weighed, and he ate something
every two hours. At the Government House dinner parties
he had a different menu, and sometimes a spot of awkward-
ness developed, because of the custom of removing guests'
plates as soon as his Excellency had finished the course.
We used to cling to our plates with one hand and gobble as
fast as we could, for Lord Tweedsmuir--having eaten a
poached egg, for example--always finished first!" [Madge
Macbeth, and O'Connor, Inside Government House, p. 81].

> The Red Queen began. "You've missed the
> soup and fish," she said. "Put on the joint!"
> And the waiters set a leg of mutton before Alice,
> who looked at it rather anxiously, as she had never
> had to carve a joint before.
> "You look a little shy: let me introduce you to
> that leg of mutton," said the Red Queen. "Alice
> --Mutton, Mutton--Alice." The leg of mutton got
> up in the dish and made a little bow to Alice; and
> Alice returned the bow, not knowing whether to be
> frightened or amused.
> "May I give you a slice?" she said, taking up
> the knife and fork, and looking from one Queen to
> the other.
> "Certainly not," the Red Queen said, very de-
> cidedly: "it isn't etiquette to cut anyone you've
> been introduced to. Remove the joint!" And the
> waiters carried it off, and brought a large plum-
> pudding in its place.
> "I won't be introduced to the pudding, please,"
> Alice said rather hastily, "or we shall get no din-
> ner at all. May I give you some?"
> "But the Red Queen looked sulky, and growled
> "Pudding--Alice, Alice--Pudding. Remove the pud-
> ding!" and the waiters took it away so quickly that
> Alice couldn't return its bow.
> However she didn't see why the Red Queen
> should be the only one to give orders; so, as an
> experiment, she called out "Waiter! Bring back
> the pudding!" And there it was again in a mo-
> ment, like a conjuring trick. It was so large that
> she couldn't help feeling a little shy with it, as
> she had been with the mutton: however, she con-
> quered her shyness by a great effort, and cut a
> slice and handed it to the Red Queen.

"What impertinence!" said the Pudding.   "I
wonder how you'd like it, if I were to cut a slice
out of you, you creature!"
      It spoke in a thick, suety sort of voice and
Alice hadn't a word to say in reply: she could only sit and look at it and gasp.
      "Make a remark," said the Red Queen: "it's
ridiculous to leave all the conversation to the pudding."

      Sometimes a dinner can be the reverse of hurried.
The first United States Ambassador to the Argentine, Mr.
Frederic Stimson, was a great talker.   He would load his
plate at the commencement of dinner--he loved fine food--
but then begin to discourse most engagingly or interesting-
ly or both.   The other guests would listen, but they would
also finish their dishes.   Mr. Stimson would end his remarks in leisurely fashion, pick up his fork and begin his
food with equal leisure.   The guests waited patiently, the
hostess waited in anxiety, the cook waited in fury--and
the soufflé didn't wait at all--it collapsed" [Hugh Wilson, The
Education of a Diplomat, p. 120].

SEATING

      The matter of proper seating, according to status
or rank, has always been a problem of formal dining.
"Honor to whom honor is due" is an honored tradition and
precept.   Even among the most primitive tribes, the tribal
chief, the medicine man, the magus or sage, the white-
haired elder, was usually given his proper recognition and
precedence.   It is interesting to notice that in the mediaeval
ages, salt was served at table in a fine ornamental covered
salt-cellar, which later became one of the most important
pieces of household plate.   Principal guests were seated
"above the salt"; inferior guests were placed "below the
salt."   It was but natural that on regal occasions the King
should have the highest place of honor; in pre-war Japan,
the Emperor, still having some vestigial attributes of divinity, never sat with his guests, but sat at a separate table
apart.   The gradation and ranking of guests, and accordingly their placement at a formal dinner-table, is a serious
matter, full of dangerous pitfalls.

      Rank within a certain circle has become established
and recognized; even the relative gradations of rank in Army
and Navy and Air Force are fixed and clear.   The hier-

archy of the Church is clear.   Problems began however
when different organizations met at dinners together.   Who
was to decide the relative ranks of royalty, foreign princes,
presidents, ambassadors, field marshals and generals, ad-
mirals and archbishops, and unofficial but world-renowned
savants.   The rules of protocol do not clearly regulate these
matters, although the official Orders of Precedence of some
countries do lay down local rules as to the royal, senior political, and senior ecclesiastical priority of their own nationals and of certain foreign ambassadorial representatives.
The place of visiting potentates and high officials, however,
is more or less empirical.

In early days ambassadors and ministers regarded
themselves, and were generally so regarded, as to the personal representatives or alter egos of their sovereigns; and
the relative rank of sovereigns was based on the status of
their kingdoms as Great Powers and the accepted half-dozen
or so Lesser Powers.   Between these Great Powers themselves there was acute rivalry for preëminence; and this
was reflected in the relative ranking of their diplomatic representatives in foreign capitals.

In the chaotic confusion before the Vienna rules, there
were apt to be violent clashes.   In the 1760's, at a Court
ball in London, the Russian ambassador, arriving early, sat
down in the place of honor at the right of the Austrian ambassador of the Holy Roman Emperor.   The Frenchman, arriving a few minutes later and finding what he considered his
place taken by the Russian, leaped over the back of the
bench on which the Austrian and the Russian were seated
and managed to squeeze between them.   The brawl that followed led eventually to a duel between the Frenchman and
the Russian in which the Russian was wounded.

Finally, to overcome this kind of uncertainty as to
relative status, rank and position, an important and salutary
innovation was adopted at the Congress of Vienna in 1815,
and added to at the Congress of Aix-la-Chapelle in 1818.
According to this code of protocol, there were to be inter-
nationally recognized grades of diplomats: ambassadors
(representing the sovereigns of the Great Powers); legates,
nuncios, ministers plenipotentiary and ministers resident
(representing the Lesser Powers); and chargés d'affaires en
titre (of lower grade than the two former) or ad interim
(acting only in the temporary absence or gap in replace-
ment of ambassadors or ministers); and within each of these

categories, rivalry was avoided by making relative precedence dependent on the seniority of presentation of creden-
tials of each incumbent of office in the particular local post.
This simplified protocol and partially obviated the acrimoni-
ous contentiousness of national representatives at a post
abroad.   As between such diplomatic representatives on the
one hand, neatly categorized, and other branches of officialdom, such as prelates and ecclesiastical office-bearers, government ministers, senior officers of armed services, and
other parallel ranks, the adjustment of relative or corresponding grades had to be determined by each national government's schematization, or in the local foreign capital, by
its office of protocol.   Wives normally shared the rank of
their husbands.   But single ladies offered greater difficulties.

The history and scandals in the Days of the Empire
in France are filled with the problems of presentation and
recognition of the King's mistresses, whether they were
"morganatic wives" or mere concubines.   One need only
read the Court annals of Madame de Pompadour and Madame
du Barry and their ilk, to see what political consequences
were involved in these ceremonial problems.

Sometimes protocol incidents result from ignorance
of local customs.   For example, during a 1959 visit by
President Sékou Touré of Guinea to Washington, he called
the incumbent Protocol Chief, Wiley Buchanan, a few minutes before a White House dinner in Touré's honor was to
begin, and "demanded that his girl stenographer accompany
him to the dinner.   Buchanan remonstrated that stenogra-
phers were not normally invited to official White House affairs.   Unimpressed, President Touré retorted haughtily:
'If it's a matter of title, I hereby make her Secretary of
State.'   Informed of the crisis, Christian Herter, who then
headed the department, remarked ruefully: 'The young lady
must have something I don't have.   It took the President
much longer to appoint me to that post' " [E. Weintal, New
York Times Magazine, May 13, 1962, p. 59].

Shortly after he became President, Thomas Jefferson gave a dinner for the British Minister, who was dean
of the diplomatic corps.   As the guests were about to file
into the dining room, Jefferson unthinkingly offered his arm
to Dolly Madison, wife of the Secretary of State and unofficial First Lady.   This was a breach of diplomatic etiquette,
as he should have escorted the Minister's wife.   The latter

was furious, and insisted that her husband report the incident to the British Foreign Office. Officials there were equally indignant, but little could be done about the matter. However, they could and did prevent a recurrence of such an incident. For years thereafter, they sent only bachelor ambassadors to the United States.

The story of Mrs. Gann, sister and social hostess of Vice-President Charles Curtis, will not be forgotten by Washington diplomats. She had insisted on taking a rank and place corresponding to what would normally be the place of a Vice President's wife. Her claim was not tenable, and the Protocol Section of the State Department was very embarrassed when she claimed a position above that of ambassadors and their wives at diplomatic dinners. The matter was finally put up to the diplomatic corps, which had the position to recognize, or not recognize, her tenuous claim to seniority. The diplomatic corps, on grounds solely of courtesy, as might have been expected, sardonically agreed to concede her claim, and to accept not only her position as "hostess" of the White House, but her anomalous position as "senior lady" at diplomatic dinners, which was more an act of diplomatic courtesy than of entitlement.

But even among the official diplomats themselves, with all the Vienna rules before them, there were sometimes difficulties. These generally came to the fore in arranging the seating at dinner tables. Even the usually accepted practice that the host may designate whomever he chooses as his principal guest of honor, to sit "above" all the other guests, is sometimes disputed.

In 1960 at a luncheon given by a distinguished member of the United States Senate, French Ambassador Hervé Alphand had been given second place to the guest of honor, who sat on the host's right; and the French Ambassador refused to sit down until the seats were switched. While the somewhat embarrassed guests waited for the reshuffling of place cards, the Ambassador explained, "As Hervé Alphand," he said, "I can sit under the table. But as the Ambassador of France I must insist on the proper place for the country I represent" [Weintal, N.Y. Times Magazine, May 13, 1962, p. 62].

One ambassador in Washington on a certain occasion invited his good friend Arturo Toscanini, the conductor, to dinner at the embassy. It was to be a white-tie

affair attended by the cream of the diplomatic corps. The
ambassador had hoped to seat the famous maestro near the
head of the table, but protocol dictated otherwise. As each
dignitary on the invitation list sent word that he would attend, the host was obliged to move the conductor's place
one seat further away. When Toscanini arrived, he discovered that his seat was at the lower end of the table, next
to the kitchen. He was kept so busy dodging the swinging
doors that most of the food that was placed before him
went untasted.

In February 1963 there was organized a "Mona Lisa"
preview dinner in Manhattan's Metropolitan Museum of Art.
Invitations sent out included the U.N. Secretary General U
Thant, the Under-Secretary General Dr. Ralph Bunche and
other U.N. officials. French Ambassador Hervé Alphand
balked when he discovered this. He felt that it should have
been a strictly Franco-American affair. The harassed Metropolitan Museum officials endeavored to find a compromise
by proposing two head tables, with Ambassador Alphand and
Mr. Adlai Stevenson, U.S. Ambassador to the United Nations, at one and Madame Alphand at the other with U Thant.
M. Alphand agreed to this, but stipulated that the Secretary
General should not have his picture taken either with Madame Alphand or the "Mona Lisa." The Secretary General
coldly refused to attend, along with a half-dozen other U.N.
officials including Dr. Bunche.

Once, I recall, our minister in Tokyo wished to seat
a South American Ambassador one chair lower than his entitlement, because this would give him a pleasanter opportunity of conversing with one of his lady neighbors in his
own language. The proposed special arrangement was explained to him on his arrival but unfortunately without an
actual prior request for his assent. He took great umbrage;
barely ate the dishes put before him; and when the dinner
guests rose to retire to another room for coffee and liqueurs, he said to his host that he was suffering from a
severe headache, and made his immediate departure.

On another occasion, my minister wished to shift a
colleague, for special reasons, to a place one degree dep-
low his rightful position. I, as junior secretary, was dep-
uted to call on him to explain this detail and gain his con-
sent. He was a most gentlemanly old-school European diplomat. He received me gracefully, and even offered me a
glass of sherry and a cigar. When I explained the problem,

he replied: "Sir, I have risen in the diplomatic ranks, and I know the pleasure of the younger generation. The juniors, with their ladies, at the lower end of the table, are always gayer and livelier company than some of the stuffed-shirt senior diplomats at the head of the table. If this were an informal dinner, I should be delighted to sit as far down the table as I could, for sheer pleasure. But this is a formal dinner, where protocol applies. I am the representative there of my august sovereign. I am very sorry, but I cannot yield my rank and position, as the King's representative, to a subordinate position, even one seat lower than that to which I am officially entitled." He said it in a very sympathetic and gracious way, but his attitude had to be respected, and he was accordingly given his rightful place.

Dr. Paul S. Reinsch, former United States Minister to China, noted, "At a very formal dinner, it is of course always safer to follow rank and let the conversation take care of itself. Any enjoyment people get out of such dinners they set down as pure profit, anyhow" [An American Diplomat in China, p. 234]. Colonel O'Connor, aide-de-camp to the Governor General of Canada, related a story about a dinner given one night at Government House in Ottawa at which a senior Canadian official--"a touchy, peppery little man"--had inadvertently been placed at the table one seat below his due, through O'Connor's error. The official was furious. He not only gave me a good raking over the coals that night after dinner, but wrote bitterly to the Governor General. 'Tommy' (Lascelles), who opened His Excellency's mail, got the letter first and brought it in to me. Of course I was upset, and Tommy saw it. 'What the hell is he making such a stink about?' he cried. 'This place! That place! Doesn't he realize that he has only one behind to sit on?' I laughed. That was what he wanted. When he left my office I felt much better" [Inside Government House, p. 75].

A much more difficult situation occurred in Tokyo when my minister, who had been elected a vice president of the International Red Cross Society, wished to give a formal diplomatic dinner in honor of the President, the Duke of Saxe-Coburg Gotha, an elderly man, during an international conference then being held in Tokyo. The German duke was a first cousin of the reigning British King. I was asked to consult the British Embassy as to the propriety of giving him the seat of honor on the host's right. The British counsellor was a little non-plussed and suggested that I consult the ambassador, Sir Robert Clive. I saw the ambassador, who had also been invited to the dinner, and explained the dilemma. He answered that this was a most difficult situation. The ambassador was the "personal representative" of his sovereign--i.e., was in alter ego, the King himself; the duke was only a cousin. The ambassador, therefore, could not yield his rightful place of seniority at the dinner table. He told me that such dilemmas sometimes occurred. One solution was to have two round tables, separating the two diplomatic rivals. I said that in our legation dining-room, that could not be arranged. He insisted that, in that case, as the King's person, he could not yield to a subordinate place. I then went to the German Embassy and explained the dilemma; but they too were adamant. The duke was of blood-royal; he was the principal guest-of-honor; he was entitled to the superior position. There was no reasonable solution. My minister decided to exercise his prerogative of placing his guest-of-honor, the duke, on his right, and the British Ambassador on his left.

All the guests arrived, and the senior guest, who normally arrives last, came with his German Embassy entourage of invited guests, at the last minute. I was at the front door to receive them and lead them to the cloak-room. But the British Ambassador was smarter. He waited in his car outside the gate until the Duke had arrived, and then entered, to show that he, as the last to come, was the senior guest.

After the dinner and the coffee and liqueurs, a German secretary hinted to the royal duke that it was time for him to make his farewells. The old man began to do so, but the British Ambassador was smarter; he jumped up, expressed his thanks and farewells to the host, and was on his way out before the Duke, thus displaying his seniority. The diplomatic cars lined up in the driveway outside the front entrance had the Duke's car in the lead. A general reshuffle had to be made to get the British Ambassador's car out of the line to be at the forefront in the driveway. Naturally this little game of protocol rivalry was not too well taken by the entourage of the German duke.

Catherine A. Galbraith, the wife of the recent U.S. Ambassador to India, has related some of her diplomatic experiences:

One noon we were having a luncheon for some gen-

erals.   The number of acceptances had risen during
the last hour before lunch from fourteen to sixteen.
Fourteen was all our regular dining-room table would
hold, and so at that point we had to shift to two
round tables each seating eight.   The guests started
arriving at one fifteen; at one twenty I found myself
meeting a general and his wife who were not on the
guest-list, and the total number was obviously now
eighteen.   What to do?   There was no time to change
from two tables of eight to three of six, so I told
the bearer to remove the butter-plates, this way we
could fit in nine at each table.   I thought we had
concealed the error, but I heard later that our unexpected guests had noticed that the handwriting on
their place-cards was different from that on the
rest ["Mother Doesn't Do Too Much," Atlantic, May
1963, p. 48].

"Protocol" is supposed to eliminate most of the
trouble over proper placement.   But it can, on occasion,
even when correctly applied, create problems it was designed to avert.   I remember during the war days, while
Chile was still neutral, the Chilean Foreign Ministry once
gave a vast state banquet on the occasion of the inaugura-
tion of the new President Rios.   By following the order of
rank, seniority and precedence set forth by protocol, the
German Ambassador and the British Ambassador, representing enemy countries, were placed side by side, separated only by a lady who was the wife of the Swiss Minister.   Both ambassadors lavished conversation on her,
passed dishes to her, tried to light her cigarette, and gave
her their attention.   After dinner, in speaking with her, I
congratulated her on being such a successful neutral buffer-
state, although I expressed my sympathy for her embarrassing situation.   The two ambassadors, of course, did not
even bow to one another.

SERVING

Next to seating and placement, and the escorting of
guests to the table, is the question of serving.   During the
first days in the White House, for example, former President
dent Eisenhower came to realize that his established ideas
about chivalry would have to be revamped.   On one occasion not long after the Eisenhowers had been in the White
House they were having old friends in for supper.   When it
came time for food to be served, the President bade his

friends to take note of what happened.

> The butler approached the group, served the President first, then Mrs. Eisenhower, then the wife and husband who were their guests. 'The first night we were in the White House,' said Mr. Eisenhower, 'this happened and I told the boy: "Look, in my house, the ladies are served first." The next day and the day after that, they sent in a different waiter each time we were served and I had to give the same instructions again. Finally I sent for the head man and explained the new procedure for what I thought would be the last time. When the traditional practice continued, it finally dawned on me. These boys are teaching me how to be President' [R. K. Gray, Eighteen Acres Under Glass].

An odd adherence to strict protocol is recorded by Major-General Maurice Pope, when he was Canadian Ambassador to Belgium and Luxembourg. In giving an official Commonwealth dinner celebrating the coronation of Queen Elizabeth II, he had invited as one of his guests King Baudouin of Belgium, who accepted.

> His Majesty, of course, arrived with truly royal punctuality on the dot of 8 o'clock. It fell to me, as the senior Commonwealth Ambassador, to present our guests to the King. In due time, the maître d'hôtel approached the little salon to which the King had momentarily retired, and in a stentorian voice announced 'Le Roi est servi.' No doubt this was correct traditional protocol, although it strikes one as a little odd that the chief of the Embassy servants should not announce to the host or hostess 'Dinner is served!' in the usual manner, but should instead address the principal guest of honour,...a crowned head of State [Soldiers and Politicians, p. 407].

DEPARTURE

Then there is the matter of order of departure after a dinner. It also has its rules of protocol, which is concerned with rank. It is customary for the guest of honor, or the guest of superior rank, not only to be the last one to arrive at a dinner, but also to be allowed to be the first to depart. Other guests wait for the ranking guest to make his farewell and leave first.

More than once I have seen a diplomat, usually new
in his role or promoted status, forget that he is the senior
guest present at a dinner and therefore must make the first
move to withdraw. I have done it myself, forgetting, in the
enjoyment of the postprandial society, that I was the senior
member present.

When Mrs. Clare Boothe Luce was newly arrived in
Rome as American Ambassador, the first state dinner she
attended was at the Spanish Embassy. In a city of late dining the Spaniards sit down later than most others. Dinner
began at ten, ended at eleven-thirty. As the guests gathered in the drawing-room, Mrs. Luce wondered how soon
she could leave. She had been instructed that no one leaves
before the guest of honor. So she watched the British Ambassador, Sir Victor Mallet, who was the doyen of the diplomatic corps. Time passed. Sir Victor chatted endlessly
on. Twelve-thirty. One, one-thirty. Mrs. Luce was growing sleepy. Finally she whispered desperately to the wife
of the Spanish Ambassador: "What time does Sir Victor
usually go home?" "When the guest of honor leaves," was
the frigid reply. 'But who is the guest of honor?" The
Señora's eyes were like black ice as she answered "You
are!" It took the Luces forty-five seconds flat to make
their adieux and depart. Afterwards Mrs. Luce learned
that, as the only woman Ambassador in Rome, she often automatically sat on her host's right and when this happened
she was therefore considered the guest of honor. (See Alden Hatch, Ambassador Extraordinary, p. 213.)

There is also a protocol of departure in front of the
door, as the guests leave the scene. Willard Straight, when
at the age of 22 he was attached to Sir Robert Hart's Inspectorate General of the Imperial Maritime Customs of China,
describes in his diary (September 30, 1902) a rather bliss-
ful form of the ending of a diplomatic dinner.

As the music stops and the musicians scuffle away,
the older men who have been smoking and gossiping
in the billiard room--the Commander of the Italian
legation Guard, the Austrian Chargé d'Affaires, the
French Military Attaché, pull themselves together
and go out to find their wives or to make their bows.
One by one the people file past and vanish through
the door, out into the garden beyond. There is no
last strain of music, as one goes away, no yelling
for carriages, no rattling of cabs on the pavement,

no chattering of many voices as the people pass
through a great door; nothing but the pat, pat, pat-
ting on the gravel path--an occasional laugh, and
finally, as one comes to the gate, the crying of the
rickshaw coolies as they look for their fares...
[Herbert Croly, Willard Straight, p. 90].

Every diplomat in foreign countries is familiar with
this little drama of departure after a dinner; but times have
changed, and there is usually a line of sleek automobiles,
in place of rickshaws or carriages, lined up outside the
door; and often an announcer at the door calling by loud-
speaker for the car of His Excellency So-and-So, or the
name of the representative's country, or a number denoting
each guest's car.   Usually the cars are already lined up according to the rank or precedence of the guests; but if a
guest exits out of order, the whole line-up is disarranged
to allow the called-for car to reach the door.   Unless there
is the strictest protocol in order of their going, there is a
general confusion in the departure.

I recall one occasion when two guests of honor at a
diplomatic dinner each considered himself to rank above the
other.   At the appropriate moment, the supposedly senior
guest, an elderly European prince, rose in the drawing room
with the intention of making his farewells, as the ranking
guest is supposed to do.   His rival, an ambassador, a
younger man, sprang up and got in first with his farewells,
collected his coat and hat from the cloakroom attendant, and
was outside the front door first.   Unfortunately the prince's
car was at the door, waiting ahead of the ambassador's.
This car had to be driven forward, to let the ambassador's
car come up; and it had great difficulty in getting back into
its foremost position ahead of the procession of all the other waiting cars lined up in order of guests' ranking.

My most embarrassing moment in this connection was
after attending a levée given by the Emperor and Empress
of Japan in the Imperial Palace in Tokyo.   A moment after
my hired limousine picked me up at the Palace door, and
was driving off, it suffered an ignominious puncture; I had
to remain seated, top hat and all, while many of the other
departing diplomats drove past.   Fortunately the Japanese
chauffeur was skillful; and, timing him, I found that he took
exactly four and a half minutes to replace the punctured tire
with a spare wheel, and to drive off to my home.

While on this subject of protocol at dinners, I may
mention that while sovereigns can entertain sovereigns in the
usual way of giving one another the respective seats of hon-
or at the same table, there was one exception during my
diplomatic career. I have sat at a banquet table where
kings, emperors, princes or presidents have been seated as
guest of honor with other sovereigns or presidents or ambassadors, acting as their hosts. (Indeed, I am in sympathy with that excited ten-year-old Alice, in her Looking-
Glass House: "Now take a good look at me! I am one that
has spoken to a King, I am: mayhap you'll never see such
another; and to show you I'm not proud, you may shake
hands with me!") But in Japan, in my day, the Emperor
was still the traditional divinity. Therefore, at all his own
state banquets, he did not sit with the other guests. He
had a table to himself, on a slightly raised platform. This
was not invariably the case when he was entertaining in the
Imperial marquée at his formal garden-parties, nor in the
rare event that he was ever entertained by another sovereign or ambassador. What the practice is now, since his
"divinity" has been repudiated, I do not know. And it is
the case that while he could not accept the hand of a Japanese subject, even his highest ministers, he did democrati-
cally shake hands with foreign diplomats, an anomalous and
almost paradoxical compromise and concession to Western
usage in salutation. But in his own palace, even as host,
he could not, prior to World War II, sit at the same table
as his guests.

All these foregoing comments on the business and art of
dining are prompted by the recognition that dinner-giving,
or dinner-eating, is an essential part of the profession of
diplomacy. Dinners and teas bothered Alice in her Wonderland World; and the Diplomat Through the Looking Glass
finds himself confronted with similar duties and problems.
They are generally regarded as incidental to the main business of information-gathering, reporting, and negotiating;
but in very fact dining is the basic means by which this
business can effectively be accomplished; and thus they hold
a paramount place in diplomatic life. History provides
some background; yet history is continuous, even into the
present and future; and the contemporaneity of today is history tomorrow, and becomes one more of a succession of
yesterdays. Diplomatic dining may change shape; but it
goes on, and will go on.

Every professional diplomat finds his social life harassed by these very grave problems of "protocol," even at dinners which should be occasions of joyousness and informality and amicableness.   Generally speaking, diplomatic dinners go off gracefully and pleasantly, in thousands of customary gatherings.   He is a happy diplomat who escapes the trickiness of nervous protocol, and can maintain a popular record of undisturbed hospitality.   But most of this can be achieved only by a meticulous respect for the sensitivities of other diplomats or of his lenient guests, and by a careful observance of established rules of protocol.   Senior diplomatic representatives sometimes are as proud and temperamental as prima donnas, and their claims of rank, status, or seniority must always unostentatiously be given respect and consideration.   Dinners themselves must be soothing and emollient; but the details of dinner-arrangements must also run smoothly and be acceptable.

In general, the established rules of etiquette and official protocol serve to achieve their object of averting errors or irregularities, avoiding "incidents," and rendering the business or pastime of dining pleasant, agreeable and happy.

V

DRINKING AND THE "DIPS"

Ambassador:
You sent us, envoys to the Great King's Court ...
And weary work we found it, sauntering on,
Supinely stretched in our luxurious litters
With awnings o'er us, through Caystrian plains
'Twas a bad time....

And oft they feted us, and we perforce
Out of their gold and crystal cups must drink
The pure sweet wine....
For only those were there accounted men
Who drink the hardest, and who eat the most.

--Aristophanes, "Acharnians"

There is nothing better for a man that he
should eat and drink, and make his
soul enjoy good in his labour.

Ecclesiastes I

While the French verbs diner and boire are quite dissimilar, and the English words dinner and wine, or dinner and drinks, are also dissimilar, there is such a natural and poetic similarity in the words "dining" and "wining" that they invariably go together, both in rhyme and orthographic texture, and in the real facts of life. They form a natural ensemble: they trip off the tongue as a single phrase; there is an affinity both in the sound and the sense.

Having just written some observations on diplomatic dining, I must include some on diplomatic wining, in its various forms and manners. It might be justifiably said

125

that apart from man's being both herbivorous and carnivor-
ous--i. e. omnivorous--he is the only species in nature that
indulges in fermented or distilled liquors, a trait which, like
the capacity of laughter, distinguishes him from other mam-
mals or beasts.   Despite what the theologians of Original
Sin may say, despite what the Puritans and Abstentionists
may have upheld through the centuries, man is incorrigibly
addicted to the "cup that cheers"--to beer since pre-Egyp-
tian days if not since Noah, and to wine from the proto-
historic days of the mythic Gods.

Alcohol, in various of its hundreds of forms as a
beverage, has been such a universal solvent in the political
and diplomatic problems of world history, that it merits
greater attention than it has generally received by conven-
tional historians.   History cannot avoid being sociological,
as has already been noticed in reference to the influence of
food and diet on world history.

In European social history the drinking habits of
courts and diplomats covered a wide range: from the vogue
of coffee-drinking, and tea-drinking, to ales and beers,
wines and spirits, and even the universal elixir, water.

> The vast ambrosias of drinks;
> Tea, that domestic mandarin;
> Bucolic cider; loose-lipped-gin;
> Coffee, extract of common sense,
> Purgative of the night's pretense;
> Cocoa's prim nursery; the male
> Companionship of crusty ale;
> Cognac oily as a ferret;
> The faintly iron thrust of claret;
> Episcopal port, aged and austere;
> Rebellious must of grape; the clear
> Bluff confraternity of beer--
>
> All these are good, all are a part
> Of man's imperative needs that start
> Not in the palate but the heart.
>
> --Louis Untermeyer

Diplomats are frequently nicknamed the "dips." How
old the cognomen is cannot be said, but Ambassador Sir
Maurice de Bunsen referred to "the Dips" in a letter written in 1893.   In 1904 Sir Cecil Spring-Rice, at St. Peters-

burg, wrote of "the foreign dips" in a letter to his friend, Mrs. Theodore Roosevelt. The term unfortunately has a certain dual connotation; this abbreviated word is also sometimes applied to excessive drinkers. With only a few exceptions known to me during my varied career of three decades, there have been few diplomats who were dipsomaniacs. Because of general background, education, breeding and sense of official responsibility and public obligation, such individuals are scarce in the professional service. Possession of confidences and state secrets makes any diplomatic or governmental agent who might become loose-tongued a dangerous security risk and unreliable, and he is quickly removed. In former centuries, however, it seems to have been more normal for gentlemen to be heavy drinkers of port, claret, brandy or wine, frequently to drink themselves or their guests under the table, or to be victims of liver or gout.

In some countries, the privileged license-plate of a diplomat's motor-car is preceded by the identifying letters "DIP," which evokes laughter; but mostly, to avoid this embarrassment, the letters "C.D." are used, signifying the Corps Diplomatique. But in Lisbon, which it seems is no longer a very onerous post for most diplomats, it is said that wise-cracking Portuguese interpret the letters "C.D." as standing for "Cavaleiros Desocupados," or "unemployed gentlemen"; while the French sometimes interpret the letters as "Contrabandistes Distingués." In the United States diplomats' automobiles carry the letters "DP" on their license plates.

Apart from the humorous ambiguity of "DIP," all but a few diplomats are, by the nature of their profession, unavoidably spirit or wine tasters and this merits some attention, since it is a diplomatic quality not included in the training manuals or the qualifying examinations.

The fact cannot be gainsaid that from most ancient history the horn of mead, the tankard of ale, the stein of beer, the flask of spirits, the flagon of wine and "beaker of the warm south" have been a social appurtenance, an easer of tensions, a broacher of confidences, a token of amity, and thus, in all diplomatic connections, have been a part of hospitality and friendly relations. The cup that cheers but not inebriates--whatever its original application by the poet Cowper to tea or, as some claim, to coffee-- is the cup of amity, except when it is perversely abused for ulterior or nefarious ends.

Kings presented the rarest wines as diplomatic gifts
to one another and among lessers it became an English custom, from the days of Chaucer and Ben Jonson, to reward
the chief court poet, or Poet Laureate, with an annual
award of a cask of canary wine from the Whitehall cellars.
Jonson's copy of Chaucer's poetry carried the information
that his great predecessor had been given a similar grant
of wine, and what had been suitable for Chaucer was clearly right for Jonson also. When there was a delay in the
delivery of the cask, Jonson wrote a brisk epigram on the
subject: "What can the cause be, when the King hath given
          His poet sack, the household will not pay?"

WINE-TASTERS

Incidentally, the poisoning of food and drinks is an
ancient story. Cases recorded in history could be cited interminably. Even today, in the purlieus of the demi-world,
the drugging of customer's drinks is a well-known practice
among harlots in league with thieves and "rollers," attached
to what are known as clip-joints. In certain barbaric countries it was used in political and diplomatic circles; and
was notoriously practiced by the unscrupulous Borgias of
Renaissance Italy. From his earliest childhood, the harem-
raised Abdul Hamid, who became the great autocratic ruler
of the Ottoman Turkish Empire, had lived in fear. He was
morbidly afraid of disease, electricity, crowds, and assas-
sins. After he ascended the throne, he built a new fortified palace, the Yildiz Kiosk, overlooking the Bosporus; he
felt so insecure that he kept shifting from one bed to another. The kitchens where the sultan's meals were cooked
had barred windows, and the food arrived on his table in
sealed containers; even so, the chief chamberlain had to
taste each dish before the Sultan did. The very cows in
the model farm at Yildiz were kept under guard, to make
sure that no one tampered with the ruler's milk. (See Edmond Taylor, The Fall of the Dynasties, p. 109-10.)

Certain statesmen, even in our own day, seem to
live in perpetual fear, distrust and precaution, especially
when they know that they are, as tyrants, unpopular everywhere. As in ancient times, they retain their own cup-
bearers and food-tasters, who were to take the first risk
in testing or demonstrating the safety of the food or beverage offered to their masters; some unpopular and fearful

leaders still retain this custom. Even Stalin, who was a
callous murderer himself, took such precaution lest he himself be poisoned.   Lord Beaverbrook, in an address to the
students of the University of New Brunswick in 1960, told
of a Churchill-Stalin dinner which he attended.

> When the wine was brought, it was very good. It
> was Russian champagne. I prefer French myself,
> but there it was. It was worth drinking anyhow.
> And as the champagne was brought, I saw the waiter,
> a soldier, come with a bottle, uncork it in the pres-
> ence of Stalin, set it down in front of him. And
> Stalin at once put a tumbler over the neck of the
> bottle. I wondered why. So through an interpreter
> I asked him: 'Why do you put a tumbler on the top
> of your bottle?' And he said to me: 'To keep the
> bubbles in.' But I knew very well that it was to
> keep something else out. He was a bit suspicious
> of some of the Russians, who might have liked to
> change the dynasty [quoted in the Atlantic Advocate
> and the Ottawa Journal, Nov. 26, 1960].

But these are the exceptions to the general rule, that
social and diplomatic amenities are normally fostered by the
amicable sharing of wines and spirits. As Iago said "good
wine is a familiar creature if it be well used."

THE WINE TRADE

It should not go unnoticed, in passing, that there has
been a certain inter-relationship between diplomats and the
wine or liquor business. The first great English poet Geoffrey Chaucer was of a vintner's pedigree. His grandfather
had been a vintner; his step-brother Thomas Heyroun and
his father John Chaucer were vintners; Geoffrey's son Thomas was for thirty years the "King's Butler." Geoffrey
Chaucer, a diplomat on occasions, himself was for twelve
years a customs official, comptroller of customs, which duties included wine inspection and control. A vintner was a
merchant, an exporter or importer of wines. He was not
a retailer, a tavern keeper, or a bartender. He was an
honorable and dignified merchant, and normally a member
of the Vintners' Guild.

Samuel Adams, "Father of the Revolution" and organizer of the Boston Tea Party, happened to be a brewer.
John Ruskin was the son of a wealthy wine merchant. One

of the greatest sherry firms in Jerez de la Frontiera is
that of Domecq, founded by Pedro Domecq in 1730. It is
interesting to note that John Ruskin's father was this firm's
agent in England and thus a vintner; and it is said that the
wealth which he thus acquired enabled his celebrated son to
take up with ease his career of art and literature. The
American Ambassador to Czechoslovakia in 1962, Mr. Out-
erbridge Horsey, is the grandson of the founder of the "Old
Horsey" rye distillery in Maryland. Jean Monnet, the
French statesman, is a French brandy merchant. Some fif-
ty-five years ago he made the rounds as a brandy salesman
of such western Canadian cities as Medicine Hat, Moose
Jaw and Calgary. "If young Monnet could not get cash for
his brandy he would trade for a horse or anything else and
this readiness to try new methods pleased Western Canada,
and decades later, Western Europe" [Ottawa Journal, April
26, 1962]. Then there was the well known German who
was a champagne salesman and who married the daughter of
Germany's leading producer of champagne; he too had been
known as a salesman in Halifax. He became a politician,
ambassador to London, and Chancellor Adolf Hitler's foreign minister; his name was Joachim von Ribbentrop, (he
became "von" through adoption by an aunt). The contro-
versial first Premier of the independent Congo, the late
Patrice Lumumba, has been frequently described as a former beer salesman.

I used to know, as a young secretarial colleague in
Washington, a certain German diplomat whom I later met
when we both held senior positions in The Hague. Because,
on the outbreak of war, he was anti-Hitler, he fled to England and thence to the United States where he found asylum.
A few years later I learned that he had been seen by
friends serving as a barman in a distinguished New York
night club. No doubt various exiled Russian princes may
be found in somewhat similar circumstances, some are
maîtres d'hôtel in famous restaurants, and others have found
a temporary occupation as barmen in night clubs. The long-
time foreign minister of Luxembourg, M. Joseph Bech, was
also the minister of wine growing, though these duties took
very little of his time. According to former Canadian Ambassador Maurice Pope, "He must have had a magic touch,
for over the years he had brought about a remarkable improvement in the quality of the wines of his country which
are produced on the Luxembourg bank of the famous river
Moselle" [Soldiers and Politicians, p. 399]. A Polish ex-
diplomat of great respect, after retirement in exile, cre-

ated a private business as importer of wines and spirits for
the diplomatic corps in Ottawa where he had his adopted
residence. Many other examples may be found.

The Worshipful Company of Vintners, originating in
England in 1364, was the offspring of what might be called
a diplomatic royal banquet. In 1363, four distinguished visitors, the kings David of Scotland, John of France, Walde-
mar of Denmark and Amadeus of Cyprus, sat down to a
banquet in the City of London, at a place where the Vintners' Hall now stands, along with that warlike and chronical-
ly hard-up monarch, Edward III of England, and the actual
purveyor of the feast, Sir Henry Picard, Master of the
Vintners' Company of merchants. The dinner consisted of
twenty-one kinds of fish and thirteen kinds of bird, and included beakers and goblets of Muscatel and Malmsey, Ver-
nage and Osey, Cute, Crete, and Bastard. Although John,
King of France, died before he could return to his own
country, the dinner was good enough to earn at any rate the
English King's eupeptic gratitude, for he immediately relaxed a vexatious regulation that forbade the vintners of London to travel to Bordeaux with English currency to buy
wines, and followed this signal mark of royal approval with
the charter of the following year, giving to the Worshipful
Company of Vintners certain privileges to sell wine whole-
sale, retail or by the glass without an excise license, in
certain specified cities and towns in England.

FOREIGN POLICY

Before describing in more detail the diplomatic characteristics of certain alcoholic potables, and experiences
relating thereto, a few other general remarks may be made.
There is an interesting relationship between wines and spirits and foreign policy which should not go unnoticed. The
great scholar and promoter of navigation and exploration,
Prince Henry, younger son of the King of Portugal, sponsored many great expeditions at sea. The Canary Islands
were already known to the Spaniards, but the Portuguese
discovered Porto Santo and Madeira. According to Win-
woode Reade, a vicar, explorer and historian, an emigrant
ship sent to Porto Santo had on board a pregnant rabbit.
She was set ashore "and, there being no checks to rabbit
population, [her young ones] increased with such rapidity
that they devoured every green thing, and drove the colonists across into Madeira. In that island the colonists were
more fortunate; instead of importing rabbits they introduced

the vine from Cyprus, and the sugar-cane from Sicily; and
soon Madeira wine and sugar were articles of export from
Lisbon to London and other ports" [The Martyrdom of Man,
chapter iii].   Thus a commerce of wine for wool was established between the ports of the Tagus and the Thames.
Partly in consequence of that complementary trade, a diplomatic friendship arose between Portugal and England that
has continued for centuries.

The introduction of gin into England as the national
drink in the 18th century, is related to the wars in the
Netherlands, the accession of the Dutch prince William of
Orange to the throne of England, and the return of British
troops from the Netherlands.   Also, the import restrictions
and onerous taxation of French wines, as a political act,
led to the growth of distilleries in England and the popularity of gin, and of port.

Of port, it has been said that "never was there a
wine more political, not only because it is, exceptionally,
a wine over which our British Government has a treaty with
a foreign power, but because it has repeatedly excited political pamphleteers and political lyrists" [T. Earle Welby,
The Dinner Knell.].   For two hundred years English firms
dominated the Portuguese wine industry, so that an English
writer could say: "We are entitled to boast of port almost
as if it had been produced under the British flag."

During the Anglo-French wars, French wines were
almost prohibited in England; one writer complained of "the
caprice of British statesmen, who were more concerned to
make gestures of political hostility or friendship than to en-
sure a supply of wholesome and pleasant wine to the nation."   Enactments passed during the Duke of Wellington's
premiership gave monopolies to British beer and ale brewers, incidentally producing reprehensible beer-houses.   The
import taxes levied by the British Government on the importation of rum from the West Indies into the British colonies
of America, notably New England, were said to be a factor
contributing to the "Boston Tea Party" and the ultimate secession of the American colonies.

Prohibition in the United States during the period
1919-1933 led to a vast network of liquor smuggling, which
strained relations between the United States, and Britain
and Canada.   The consequent cocktail vogue in the United
States penetrated into England, reviving the languishing gin

industry there.   The international trade in wines and spirits
forms a very significant proportion of total trade between
certain countries, especially noticeable in respect to Scotland (whisky), the West Indies (rum), and Spain and Portugal (port).   The internal economy of these countries might
well collapse were this international trade disturbed, as is
illustrated in Cuba with respect to its sugar trade, which
has now involved Russian intrusion.

THE BAR

With the characteristic of the English language to
make one work represent a multiplicity of meanings, one
may look at the word "bar."   The dictionary will indicate
its connection with a variety of things, the legal, the heral-
dic, the marine, the gastronomic, and even chess.   In any
one of these connotations, we may apply the words found in
Through the Looking Glass: "Alice watched the White King
as he slowly struggled up from bar to bar, till at last she
said: 'Why, you'll be hours and hours getting to the table,
at this rate.' "

The bar, in its beverage application, used to be an
adjunct to a tavern, i.e., a "public house"--republican in
spirit, often rough and rowdy, operated by a "publican"
(who in scriptural times seemed to be bracketed with sin-
ners); and as such was not normally accorded the honor of
attendance by the gentry or the diplomats, although Prince
Hal and Sir John Falstaff used to meet and plot in pot-
houses; and Hitler and his accomplices met in bier-halles.
But since "bars" have moved into respectable lounges, cock-
tail-bars, and hotel establishments, they more often become
a rendezvous for statesmen and diplomats, where some information, gossip, or diplomatic business may be inconspic-
uously exchanged.   It is for this reason that the delegates'
bar-lounge in the United Nations Assembly building has acquired such importance, and is regularly crowded.

The bar has the connotation of a brass rail along the
counter in a tavern and, by extension, any counter where
drinks are served.   Indeed, drinking and the Law seemed
to have a certain affiliation.   Charles Dickens reminds us
in A Tale of Two Cities (Chapter V) that the days of the
1780's "were drinking days, and most men drank hard....
The learned profession of the law was certainly not behind
any other learned profession in its Bacchanalian propensi-
ties."   In the United States, Chief Justice John Marshall

had originated the custom of starting conferences of Supreme
Court Justices with a drink if it was raining--raining that
is, anywhere in the Courts' broad jurisdiction--but that custom has long ago died out and now such magisterial conferences, while in session, are not only dry, but in Court sessions also free from tobacco in any form.

Thus the plebeian term "bar"--deriving originally
from the tavern's brass-rail or counter--became more respectable in its affinity with the bar of Parliament and the
bar of the law courts.   To pass one's bar examinations has
a respectable connotation; to become a barrister rather than
a barman.   Temple Bar in London did not mean a corner
pub, but an ancient district barricade, and later the quarters
of the barristers-at-law; and many a diplomat has been a
member of the Bar.   Quite a number of Canadian ambassadors and ministers have the title K.C. or Q.C., a superior
legal recognition; and at the same time have had no small
familiarity with the beverage bar.

Attorney Clarence Darrow numbered among his colleagues a lawyer who was a heavy drinker.   One day when
he staggered into court, a friend commented, 'What a pity.
And he's such a brilliant lawyer, too." "Yes," agreed Darrow, "but he practices at the wrong bar."

Diplomacy is in some ways related to the law, and
many diplomats have to know or apply national or international law; in modern times a large proportion of diplomats,
like politicians, are lawyers.   One class of lawyers is barristers, who practice before the Bar of the Courts.   According to Martin G. Berch, in the New York Herald Trib-
une, "it is no secret that much of the world organization's
business is conducted near the lounge's long mahogany bar,
whose tenders are anxious to please.   They have now per-
fected the art of mixing a pasco pisco sour, a Peruvian
brandy concoction favored by Latins, and have laid in a supply of Moscovite vodka for new sputnik celebrations" [Cited
in Ottawa Citizen, Sept. 17, 1962, p. 7].   During my two
official assignments to the U.N. General Assembly, I soon
discovered that much of the "corridor diplomacy," the ac-
companiment to the more formal plenary sessions, was conducted in the Delegates' Lounge, at one end of which was a
very busy bar.   Many of the foreign delegates whom one
met were lawyers and were professionally acquainted with
the Bar; they found, nevertheless, that there was a certain
affinity represented by the capital letter "B" and the lower

case letter "b" and between the barrister and the barman.

MARINE ASSOCIATIONS

If the Bar of Parliament, the Bar of Courts, and the
bar of lawyers and barristers have terminological affinities
with the bar of the tavern and cocktail lounge, it is also interesting to notice the link in nomenclature between marine
or naval occupation, and drinks. Marine geography and top-
ography recognizes certain reefs, shoals and similar coastal
features and formations as "bars." It was a matter of skill
in crossing the bar; and, in the sense of a barrier or barricade, Tennyson had the half-line "And let there be no moan-
ing at the bar...." When old seamen speak of "crossing
the bar" they often have a double meaning. Was this double
entendre intended when small Alice watched the White King?
And after this effort is accomplished, the imbiber, perhaps
thinking of the overturning of a vessel in a squall or a
storm, proposes "Bottoms up!"--also signifying the tilted
and emptied glass. He also exclaims, in true nautical manner, "Down the hatch!" If he wishes to have a "straight"
or a "neat" drink, not weakened or allayed by water, but
with ice both to cool and to tinkle it, the expression "on
the rocks" is used. Finally, if he becomes tipsy from too
much imbibing, he thinks of the sailor-terms of shipwreck
--"three sheets in the wind" or "half seas over." As many
spirituous potables gained their first popularity among sailors, the marine tradition and terminology have persisted.
And while to a seaman there is both the bar ashore with
its brass foot-rail, and the bar which signifies an offshore
reef or mole, there is also the "reefer" which is slang for
a marijuana cigarette, named perhaps for the reef-sail to
a ship, or the action of "reefing sail." Even the name
"grog" was derived from the nickname of a certain Admiral
Vernon of the West Indies station. How much terminology
of the drink-bibber is based on maritime origins!

Nor, with these nautical analogies in mind, can we
overlook the similarity of the fore-and-aft-rigged, two-or-
more-masted sailing vessels known as schooners, which
word derives from the Dutch and Scandinavian, and the
North European term for a tall beer-glass or measure for
beer, said to be likewise derived from scun or scoon, to
skim or skip. Henry David Thoreau wrote in Cape Cod:
"Robinson having constructed a vessel which he masted and
rigged in a peculiar manner, on her going off the stocks a
bystander cried out "O, how she scoons!" whereat Robinson

replied: "A schooner let her be!"   From which time
(1721), says Tufts, "vessels thus masted and rigged have
gone by the name of schooners; before which, vessels of
this description were not known in Europe."   In drinking
from such a scooner or schooner of ale or beer, one im-
perceptibly thinks of the sea-foam of the crested wave, and
the "splendid ships, their white sails crowding."

COFFEE-DRINKING

It is not generally recognized that coffee was in early
Arab times considered an intoxicating liquor.   The earliest
origins of coffee are disputed between the claims of Abyssinia and India.   In the later assumption, it was said to
have been introduced into Persia by certain ambassadors.
From Persia it went into Arabia.   Its physiological action
in dissipating drowsiness and preventing sleep was taken advantage of in connection with the prolonged religious services of the Muslims, and its use as a devotional anti-sopo-
rific stirred up fierce opposition on the part of the strictly
orthodox and conservative section of the priests.   Coffee by
them was held to be an intoxicating beverage, and therefore
was prohibited by the Koran, and severe penalties were
threatened to those addicted to its use.   Notwithstanding
threats of divine retribution and other devices, the coffee-
drinking habit spread rapidly among the Arabian Muslims,
and the growth of coffee and its use as a national beverage
became as inseparably connected with Arabia as tea is with
China.   (See the Encyclopaedia Britannica (11th ed.), "Coffee.")

We are also told that "although coffee was not drunk
at Rome until long after it had been known to, and tasted
by, Italian travellers at Constantinople, the Church looked
with pleasure on a beverage, one effect of which was to
keep both Priests and people awake" [Doran, Table Traits].

Another angle on the inspirational and sensual effect
of coffee is given by the Frenchman Emile Souvestre, in A
Philosopher Under the Roofs";

Coffee is placed in a manner of speaking, midway
between nourishment for the body and nourishment of
the mind.   It acts in an agreeable way upon our
senses and thoughts at the same time.   Its mere
aroma has, for some reason or other, a pleasantly
stimulating effect upon the mental faculties; it is a

genie which provides wings for our imagination and
carries us into the land of the Arabian Nights.
When I am buried in my old armchair, with my feet
spread out before a blazing fire, my ears full of the
soothing burbling of my coffee-pot which seems to be
chattering to the andirons, my nostrils titillated by
the bouquet of the Arabian bean, and my eyes half-
closed beneath the cap that is pulled down over them,
then it often seems to me that every wreath of the
fragrant steam is assuming a distinct shape: I see
arising there before my eyes, like mirages in the
desert, various counterfeit images, one after another,
that my wishes would gladly have changed into reali-
ties.

Could the opium-eater Thomas De Quincey have expressed
better, from the benefits of his narcotic-elixir, the imaginative benefits which Souvestre found in coffee?

Edmond Taylor refers to this coffee-period in picturesque terms.   "In 1683 Vienna rendered a notable service
to Christendom by withstanding a Turkish siege,...   Vienna
recalls the victory with modest pride, but in the collective
memory of its citizens the really noteworthy event occurred
after the Turks had withdrawn, when a quick-witted Polish
mercenary picked up on the battlefield a sack of dark, aromatic beans, previously unknown in the West.   A bronze
plaque on the coffee-house that the Pole founded still com-
memorates the occasion; [since then] the Viennese have elaborated over the centuries...virtually a whole way of life"
[The Fall of the Dynasties, p. 27].

One writer, Dr. Doran, states that Yemen is the accepted birthplace, if we may so speak, of the coffee tree.
Pietro de la Vallé introduced it into Italy, La Royne into
Marseilles, and Thevenot brought it with him to Paris.   In
1643, a Levantine opened a coffee-house in Paris, in the
Place du Petit Chatelet; but it was Soleiman Aga, Turkish
Ambassador in Paris, in 1689, who was the medium
through which coffee found its way into the realm of fashion.   "His method of service was marked by all the minute
details of oriental fashion--small cups and foot-boys, gold-
fringed napkins and pages, coffee wreathing with smoke,
and Ganymedes wreathed with garlands, the first all aroma,
and the hand-bearers all otto of roses: the whole thing was
too dazzling and dramatic to escape adoption" [Table Traits].

Coffee was first drunk in London about the middle of
the 17th century. "The first coffee-house in London," says
Aubrey, "was in St. Michael's-alley, in Canhill, which was
set up by one Bowman (coachman to Mr. Hodges, a Turkey
merchant, who putt him upon it) in or about the year 1652."
Two thousand coffee-houses sprang up in a single generation, and they played an enormous role in the social, literary and political life of the 17th and 18th centuries. Coffee
was first mentioned in the English statutes in 1660, when a
duty of 4d was laid on every gallon of coffee made and sold.
A statute of 1663 directed that all coffee-houses should be
licensed at the Quarter Sessions. In 1675, Charles II issued a proclamation to shut up the coffee-houses, on the
ground that they were centers of political agitation and "the
resort of disaffected persons, who devised and spread
abroad divers false, malicious and scandalous reports to the
defamation of His Majesty's government and to the disturbance of the peace and quiet of nations"; but in a few days
he suspended this proclamation by a second. They continued
to be the centers of travellers' news, of literary discussions, the resorts of all the movements for temperance,
teetotalism and abolition of liquor houses, and of social relaxation.

When Cowper in about 1785, wrote The Winter Evening, he described a cottager's home, and said

> Let fall the curtains, wheel the sofa round,
> And, while the bubbling and loud-hissing urn
> Throws up a steamy column, and the cups
> That cheer but not inebriate, wait on each,
> So let us welcome peaceful ev'ning in.

Generally this has been assume to refer to tea-brewing;
but there are some who argue that it refers to coffee, "bubbling" in some sort of early form of percolator.

There was no restaurant in Paris before 1765; and
restaurants did not begin to flourish until the revolution
made the supply of servants at home scanty. The sidewalk
café, a result of the introduction of coffee into France in
the middle of the 17th century, was essentially a place where
one drank coffee. Until then France had only known the
auberge, the traveller's inn. Coffee appealed to the French
temperament, but Louis was distrustful of the café; he
feared it as a center of sedition, just as Charles II, across
the Channel, in spite of Catherine of Braganza's addiction

to tea, regarded the coffee house with suspicion. Both the
café and the coffee house survived their monarchs' stric-
tures and their separate fates are indicative of the difference between France and England. The sidewalk cafe has
retained its pristine character. The French go to cafés before and after meals; to drink coffee and eat a pastry in
the afternoon, to sip an apéritif before dinner, to take a
cordial with their coffee after dinner. Not only artists and
Bohemians and boulevardiers do so; but also, not infrequently, diplomats.

The English coffee-houses, on the other hand, became clubs. White's and Brook's and Boodle's, where far
less coffee was drunk than port or brandy, where cards
were played for extravagantly high stakes. (See Alec Waugh,
"Modus Bibendi," Playboy, 1961, p. 135.)

David Livingston, describing his experiences among
the Makololo tribe in Africa wrote: "They are eminently
gregarious in their eating; and as they despise any one who
eats alone, I always poured out two cups of coffee at my
own meals, so that the chief, or some of the principalmen,
might partake along with me. They all soon became fond
of coffee; and indeed, some of the tribes attribute greater
fecundity to the daily use of this beverage.... Sekeletu,
relishing the sweet coffee and biscuits, of which I then had
a store, said: 'he knew my heart loved him by finding his
own heart warming to my food!' He had been visited during my absence at the Cape by some traders and Griquas,
and 'their coffee did not taste so nice as mine, because
they loved his ivory and not himself.' This was certainly
an original mode of discerning character" [Travels and Researches in South Africa].

TEA-DRINKING

Then, a century or two later, among the upper
classes, came the vogue of tea-drinking, mostly in the salons of good society, where both politics and the arts were
discussed to good advantage.

Tea is said to have been first used in China as a
medicine, or a corrective for bad water. Sometime it
found its way into India. In the 17th century it was brought
to Holland, where "half the physicians of the country published treatises, in favor of tea," but mainly on medicinal
grounds. Nevertheless, it remained unpopular generally.

It is said that a Russian ambassador refused a pound or two
of it, offered him by the Mogul as a present to the Czar,
on the ground that the gift was neither useful nor agreeable.
Tea is supposed to have been first imported into England,
from Holland, in 1666, by Lords Arundel and Ossary. It is
said to have been in favor at the Court of Charles II, owing
to the example of Catherine, his Queen, who had been used
to drink it in Portugal.

Three hundred years ago tea was unknown in England;
250 years ago it was little known and extremely expensive,
besides being generally regarded as a sort of medicine. In
1660 the famous Samuel Pepys, records in his diary: "I did
send for a cup of tea, a China drink which I never had drunk
before." This, be it noted, was the very year of the Restoration, when the old stern restrictions had been recklessly
lifted, and novelty was an irresistible recommendation.
Catherine, the unhappy queen-consort of the so-called Merry
Monarch, had become fond of tea and had introduced it and
encouraged it among her friends at the court, in the vain
hope that it would bring about some improvement in the manners and morals of the fashionable wastrels who flocked
about Charles and brought his reign into disrepute. Vain the
hope proved. But later the popularity of tea increased, especially in the 19th century, when it became "the thing" to
ask for a cup of tea instead of something more potent. Tea
rooms sprang up in England, more sedate than the tea
houses in Japan and China: there were the "God Begot" in
Winchester, the "Old Bishop's House" in Chester; Anne Hath-
away's "Garden" in Stratford and hundreds more. Tea-
drinking also became the social form in the fine houses and
salons. There were fluctuations in the tea hour; at one time,
in Jane Austen's day, it was in the evening, after dinner; for
many years it was at five o'clock; more recently it became
four o'clock.

In 1618, Catherine de Vivonne, born in Rome (in
1588) to the French Ambassador to the Vatican, designed a
salon in the Rue St. Thomas-du-Louvre in Paris, that became the most famous in history. Congenial members of
the nobility, clergy, and military mingled with poets and
scholars there. Corneille came around. Manners and learn-
ing both were traded and taught; social graces were polished,
and music, and above all the arts of conversation. Since
the introduction of tea as a fashionable drink, the private
salons continued to be the center of literature, politics, and
diplomacy.

Social tea-drinking seems to have flourished particularly in the 19th century; and it may have been influenced by the attitude of such sedate sovereigns as Queen Wilhelmina of Netherlands, and Queen Victoria who set the fashion in England for nearly sixty years. Alice found herself caught up in such tea parties with the King and the Red Queen, the White Queen.

The Victorian Age in England was ostensibly a Puritan Age, at least in respect to domestic morals and conduct. In reality this was not so; but in outward aspect and tradition and theory it was a very proper era. Queen Victoria was sedate, and encouraged sobriety in her court. It is not likely that she was abstemious, but she was temperate. Perhaps she got a trace of this from her father, the Duke of Kent. In the British fortress of Gibraltar, military discipline had grown disgracefully out of hand. In 1802 a new governor was sent: King George III's fourth son, His Royal Highness the Duke of Kent, who was specifically charged with establishing a "due degree of discipline among the troops," and specifically warned that doing so would require "much exertion." The Duke held that "drunkenness was the bane of the soldiery," so he struck straight at its root: he closed all but three of the wine houses and allowed those three to sell only beer. The outrage of the troops, deprived of their sole relaxation, boiled over on Christmas Eve in murderous riots and an attempted mutiny. The Duke took prompt action. He arrested the ringleaders, shot three of them in the presence of the whole garrison, and gave two others a thousand lashes apiece. The civilians thanked him for his firmness, but the military were less enthusiastic. Their private reports on the affair reached London before his own, and presently the Cabinet recalled him. The Duke, safe at home, married and duly sired a child. When it was born, a girl, he remembered Gibraltar and the gypsy woman there who had predicted that a daughter of his would become a mighty queen. This daughter he christened Victoria. (See Holiday, March 1961, p. 183.)

I remember that the tea-call custom was still in vogue in some parts of Europe in 1920's. In The Hague, for example, court ladies and wives of ambassadors used to have regular "at home" days, when gentlemen and ladies of society were expected to make a formal call for tea; and junior diplomatic secretaries, if they wished to be comme il faut, were expected to pay their duties. Also it was customary for guests, following a dinner, to call on the hostess

the next day by way of thanks, and instead of leaving per-
functory cards at the door, to take tea with the hostess if
she were at home.   These tea-calls were purely formal,
and quite brief; and were not the so-called salon "routs"
where invited larger groups assembled for social intercourse
on politics or the arts.   The afternoon social tea-custom derived from earlier times when diplomacy was a leisurely and
largely social business; for the more modern professional,
it was a great nuisance, as it interfered with the afternoon
work in the chancery, which grew ever more pressing and
demanding.

    The "pink teas" of the Victorian salons, at which
young diplomats in striped trousers were lampooned as
cookie-pushers, are mostly gone.   With them has passed an
age--of stately dignity, culture and refinement, of magnificent salons and of intellectual hosts and hostesses and guests,
and distinguished literary or political talk.   The weekly "at
homes," the regulation calls and dropping of cards, the invitations that meant social recognition, are rarer today.
The diplomatic memoirs of that age were readable, but now
seem a little nostalgic.

CHOCOLATE

    Incidentally, alongside of coffee and tea-drinking in
Europe was chocolate-drinking, which had a great vogue in
England around the beginning of the 18th century among
people of fashion.   The large evergreen cacao tree, which
grows in the steamy tropics, had been grown in ancient
times in the lush valleys of the Amazon and Orinoco rivers.
The Indians of South and Central America had learned to
make chocolate from the cacao beans hundreds of years before Columbus discovered the New World.   At one time cacao beans were used as money.   It is said that chocolate
played a part in the Spanish conquest of America.   Hernan-
do Cortez, conqueror of the Aztecs of Mexico, received
many gifts from the Indians and was perhaps the first European to taste a drink of chocolate.   Charmed with its flavor,
he demanded more.   When Montezuma was defeated in battle,
Cortez demanded tribute, and among other things, demanded
that the Aztecs should pay 300 loads of chocolate.   To the
people of Europe it was unknown until Cortez shipped some
of it back home from America; and then, both as a sweetener (chocolate) and as a beverage (cocoa) it became extremely popular.   The cacao tree was taken to other countries.
It thrived in West Africa, and became one of the economic

mainstays of the Gold Coast, now known as Ghana; from
there most of the world's chocolate is supplied. It also
flourished in the West Indies.

The Aztec Indians claim that one of their prophets
brought the wonderful cacao tree down from heaven. When
Linnaeus named it Theobroma Cacao, he derived the name
from $\theta\varepsilon\acute{o}s$ (god) and $\beta\rho\omega\mu\alpha$ (-food), as an indication of the
high appreciation in which he held the beverage prepared
from the seeds, which he considered to be a food fit for the
gods. After it had been introduced into Spain, it passed to
other parts of Europe. The Public Advertiser (London) of
June 16, 1657, contained an announcement that "In Bishops-
gate St., in Queen's Head Alley, at a Frenchman's house,
is an excellent West India drink, called chocolate, to be
sold, where you may have it ready at any time, and also
unmade at reasonable rates." Chocolate became a very
fashionable beverage in the early part of the 18th century;
and has never ceased to be a popular drink and confection.
In the 1700's it may have had an appeal to diplomats, as
well as others, who moved in fashionable society; but today
it can scarcely be regarded as a diplomatic drink, even at
dinners where coffee or tea might be served.

THE SPIRITUOUS AGE

The American-innovated cocktail party has almost
eclipsed those old sedate customs of the past. Of this we
shall have something to say in a subsequent chapter. Society ladies no longer sit at home in the afternoons ready
to receive visitors and callers for a cup of tea and delicate
toast or sandwiches; they are more actively engaged outside
their homes, in charity works, and visiting art exhibitions
or attending afternoon concerts, or disporting themselves
riding or golfing or playing bridge, while most of the men
are occupied in their chanceries and ministerial bureaus.
Any personal visits more often result in the proffering of
drinks or cocktails than in cups of tea and sandwiches.

Thus from coffee and tea, we may pass on to wines
and spirits. The "cup" is no longer of delicate china, but
of crystal glass. Despite Fitzgerald's version of Omar
Khayyam, the "cup" of wine is, in reality, the flagon, the
beaker, the glass, the goblet, the "tulip," that holds in ap-
pealing visibility the wine or liquor, whether sparkling or
bubbling, or merely still and colorful. Most wines and
liquors that we drink are lovely when the light shines

through them; the red wine, the rosés, the white wines, the
bubbling champagnes, the colorful whiskeys, the cloudy per-
nods, the pink or golden vermouths, the dusky sherries, the
rich green menthes, the rainbow cocktails, and even the
amber ales crested with foam.   For this reason, the glass
is the proper vehicle for wines and spirits.

The poet Robert Herrick said as much in the mid-
1600's:

> Fill me my wine in christall; thus and thus,
> I see't in's puris naturalibus:
> Unmixt.   I love to have it smirke and shine,
> 'Tis sin I know 'tis sin to throtle wine.

And glass is akin to mirrors, and thus connected
with the Diplomat Through the Looking Glass.   In that mir-
rored reflection, we see the symbolic Envoy, glass in hand,
helping promote by this universal solvent, amity and con-
cord and good relations, and good will among men, with the
ultimate hope of Peace on Earth.   Richard Brinsley Sheridan,
at one time in his parliamentary career Undersecretary of
State for Foreign Affairs, penned in his play The Critic the
lines:

> A bumper of good liquor
> Will end a contest quicker
> Than justice, judge, or vicar.

We hear of an early member of the ancient noble
family of Ruthven, one Patrick Ruthven (1573-1651), who
distinguished himself in the service of Sweden, which he entered about 1606.   As a negotiator he was very useful to
Gustavus Adolphus because of his ability to "drink immeas-
urably and preserve his understanding to the last."   He also won fame as general-in-chief of the Royalist Army of
Charles I of Scotland.

The Hon. Dean Acheson tells of how once, drinking
on President Truman's yacht Williamsburg, the Rt. Hon.
Winston Churchill turned to his intimate friend Lord Cher-
well, and told him that he had been thinking that from the
age of sixteen to that evening, about sixty-two years, he
had consumed on the average about a quart of wines and
spirits a day, sometimes none, when none was available,
sometimes more, but on the average about a quart ["Sketch-
es from Life," Sat. Eve. Post, March 18, 1961, p. 74].

Sir John A. Macdonald, Canada's first Prime Minister, was
a notoriously heavy drinker; but his successor Alexander
Mackenzie, was a total abstainer, like several other of his
successors.

TOASTS

In formal social and official celebrations, spirits or
wines are inseparable from the ritual of drinking toasts.
This is an inescapable part of diplomatic protocol and practice and has existed from earliest times.   The custom of
drinking "health" to the living is apparently derived from
the ancient religious rite of drinking to the gods and to the
dead.   The Greeks and the Romans at meals poured out li-
bations to their gods; the Norsemen drank the minni of
Thor, Odin and Freya, and of their kings at their funeral
feasts.   But the Greeks and Romans drank to the health of
living men.   The English drinking phrase, "toast"--to
"toast someone"--was adopted in the 17th century.   The
origin is curious.   In Stuart days there appears to have
been a time-honored custom of putting a piece of toast in
the wine cup before drinking, from the fanciful notion that
it gave the liquor a better flavor.   If the verb "to toast"
is derived, through Old English and Old French, from the
Latin tostus, from torrere, meaning "to parch," it is a
curious inversion to signify "to unparch" or to drink.   But,
in diplomatic life, the libation or toast is a wellworn custom.

Kings were always toasted.   The toast to majesty is
first mentioned in the book of Samuel (I, x, 24): "And all
the people shouted and said: God Save the King."   Shakespeare, in Hamlet, has the murderer King Claudius an-
nounce his accession to the throne of Denmark by artillery
salutes and the drinking of the "King's rouse"; he also proposes a toast to Crown Prince Hamlet: 'The King shall
drink to Hamlet's better breath."   At the coronation of the
restored and popular Charles II--himself a more austere
and abstemious man than his father James I--we are told
that his health was drunk so often that the streets were full
of vomiting citizens, and even the diarist Secretary of the
Navy, Pepys, confesses that he was "never so foxed in my
life."   Such toasts were repeated throughout the country to
the Sailor-King William IV, in everything "from champagne
to water."

Health-drinking had by the beginning of the 17th cen-

tury become a very ceremonious business in England. At
Christmas 1623 the members of the Middle Temple drank to
the health of the Princess Elizabeth, who with her husband
the King of Bohemia, was then suffering great misfortune,
and stood up, one after the other, cup in one hand, sword
in the other, and pledged her, swearing to die in her service.   Toasts were often drunk solemnly on bended knee,
sometimes bare knees.   A Scotch custom still surviving,
was to drink a toast with one foot on the table and one on
the chair.   Pepys, in his diary for June 19, 1663, writes:
"To the Rhenish wine-house, where Mr. Moore showed us
the French manner when a health is drunk, to bow to him
that drunk to you, and then to the person that you drink to,
which I never knew before, but it seems it is now the fashion."

The Rev. Henry Teonge, chaplain on board His Majesty's Ships Assistance, Bristol, and Royal Oak in 1675-9,
records in his diary:

> November 1675.   I was invited to dinner with our
> Captaine, and our Doctor, our Pursor, Capt. Mauris,
> and Capt. North, to our Consulls on shoare; where
> wee had a princelike dinnar, and every health that
> wee dranke, every man broake the glasse he drank
> in; so that before night wee had destroyed a whole
> chest of pure Venice glasses; and when dinner was
> ended the Consull presented every one of us with a
> bunch of beads, and a handfull of crosse, for which
> he sent to Jerusalem on purpose, as he tolde us af-
> terwards [Henry Teonge, Adventures of a Naval Cap-
> tain].

This custom of the pledge to a table-companion has
extended to Scandinavian countries, Germany, and at one
time to the American West.   All this seems to be a survival of a very early and universal belief that drinking to another was a proof of fair play.   The modern "loving cup"
sometimes has a cover, and in this case each guest rises
and bows to his immediate neighbor on the right, who also
rising, removes and holds the cover with his right hand
while the other drinks; this little comedy is a survival of
the days when he who drank was glad to have the assurance
that the right or dagger hand of his neighbor was occupied
in holding the lid of the chalice.   At other times it was
customary for a toaster's adjoining companions to stand with
him: not only perhaps to support him if he were shaky on

his feet, but also possibly to be sure that he could not lay hand to arms or sword in a moment of excitation.

Perhaps one of the most unique healths was one proposed by Lord Dufferin. In 1877 the first telephone in Ottawa was installed in the Prime Minister's Office, and the next year the Governor General of Canada experimented with another invention, Thomas Alva Edison's phonograph. "Ladies and Gentlemen," said the Marquis of Dufferin, as he spoke into the machine, "I have never had occasion to bottle my speech until now. I propose calling on you to give three cheers for Her Most Gracious Majesty, Queen Victoria. Hip! Hip! Hurrah!"

It is said that the bibulous Roman Emperor Caligula, somewhat in his cups at a banquet, proposed a toast to his favorite racehorse Incitatus, which he thereupon proposed to appoint Consul. In modern times, many a toast had been drunk to distinguished or prize-winning racehorses.

The Knight, in Through the Looking Glass, sang in his song:

> 'An that's the way' (he gave a wink)
> 'By which I got my wealth--
> And very gladly will I drink
> Your Honour's noble health!
>
> I thanked him much for telling me
> The way he got his wealth,
> But chiefly for his wish that he
> Might drink my noble health!

But there are occasional lapses, when the host has been not only well dined but too well wined. One host entertaining a high Japanese ambassador, proposed the health of "Our distinguished guest--the Ambassador of - er - China!" As recently as 1960, at the United Nations, a certain diplomat proposed a toast to "the distinguished representative of Colombia," who happened not to be present; it turned out that the toast was intended for the distinguished representative of Peru.

Sir Toby Belch, upon hearing criticism that his crony Sir Andrew Aguecheek was drunk every night in his company, retorted "With drinking healths to my niece. I'll drink to her as long as there is a passage in my throat and drink in

Illyria; he's a coward and a coistrel that will not drink to
my niece till his brains turn o'th'toe like a parish-top"
[Twelfth Night, I, iii, 42].

　　　During the reign of another Sailor-King, George V,
there was some sort of Canadian-American convention held
in a border city, at which a banquet became very convivial.
The principal Canadian rose to propose a toast to the President of the United States. In reciprocation, the American
leader, somewhat shaky in his history and politics, rose
and proposed a toast to the health of "His Majesty King -
er - King - er - King George III!" The story is also well-
known of the overwined guest who, after other toasts, including one to the ladies, had been drunk, rose to propose
a flowery, jocular and somewhat tricky toast to mothers.
He said uncertainly, "Here's to the happiest hours of my
life, spent in the arms of another man's wife--... er - er
- ..."; he came to a halt. His nearest neighbor at the table
helpfully stage-whispered, 'my mother!" "Oh yes," continued the toaster, "this chap's mother!"

　　　I remember a semi-diplomatic dinner once held in
Tokyo, at which Lord Lovat, a tall braw Scot, was one of
the principal guests. A toast was proposed to his health;
and responding, he replied that he had responded to so many
toasts to his health that his health was by now all but
ruined! In this, he was only repeating what Jerome K. Jerome said in The Idle Thoughts of an Idle Fellow, "We drink
one another's healths and spoil our own"; and the same idea
was expressed in 1650 by John Taylor in A Navy for Land-
ships: "So the sailors in this ship [the Carouse] have taken
a use to drink other men's healths, to the amplifying of their
own diseases." But we might go even further back, for
when Timon of Athens gave a great banquet in one of his
rooms of state, and cried "Let the health go round!," the
churlish philosopher Apemantus muttered: "Those healths
will make thee and thy state look ill, Timon" [I, iii].

　　　"Even nowadays," says Jerome K. Jerome in Idle
Thoughts,

　　　　　the thirstiness of mankind is something supernatural.
　　　　　We are forever drinking on one excuse or another.
　　　　　A man never feels comfortable unless he has a glass
　　　　　before him. We drink before meals, and with meals,
　　　　　and after meals. We drink when we meet a friend,
　　　　　also when we part from a friend. We drink when we

are talking, when we are reading, and when we are
thinking. We drink one another's healths, and spoil
our own. We drink the Queen, and the Army, and
the Ladies, and everybody else that is drinkable; and,
I believe, if the supply ran short, we should drink
our mothers-in-law. By the way, we never eat anybody's health, always drink it. Why should we not
stand up now and then and eat a tart to somebody's
success?

It was customary in China in the early part of this
century to offer numerous toasts to health at diplomatic dinners, especially those with military officers in attendance.
Normally an abstemious people, when in a toasting mood the
Chinese offer formidable challenges to one's capacity. The
proposer drains his cup at one draught; the guest addressed
is expected to do likewise; both say "Gambei" (a challenge
to empty the cup). Paul Reinsch tells an anecdote about one
such gathering:

> General Yin, who seemed in high spirits, was on his
> legs half the time, 'gambeying' to the other guests,
> especially to myself and the other Americans, the
> military attaché, the Chinese secretary, the command-
> ant of the guard, and other officers. General Yin
> must have performed this courtesy at least forty
> times in the course of the evening [along with] the at-
> tentions paid us by the other members of the table
> round,... It must however, be confessed that I
> largely shirked this test, in company with the ami-
> able General Yin Chang, my Manchu neighbor, by ir-
> rigating a large plant in front of us with the liquid
> dedicated to friendship [An American Diplomat in Chi-
> na, p. 110].

One of the more triste of these toasts occurred when
I was High Commissioner in New Zealand. The Governor-
General, Lt.-General Sir Willoughby Norrie, was concluding
his terms of office there; he kept a few racing horses, of
which he was very proud and confident. He entered his favorite in the last major horserace which he would attend and
his heart was set on winning it and taking home, as his New
Zealand souvenir, the trophy cup of the National Race-Club.
Unfortunately for him, his horse came in second, beaten by
a horse owned by a great and rich New Zealand lady racing
stable owner. Instead of proudly receiving the cup himself,
it fell to Sir Willoughby Norrie, after the race, to bestow

the trophy and propose a toast to his successful competitor.
With his customary tact and graciousness he expressed his
own personal disappointment, which was deep, but added
that he had always heard that "it is more blessed to give
than to receive." And so he left New Zealand for home without his hoped-for souvenir, but with memory of his toast to
his rival. Not infrequently do toasts have to be proposed
to the proposer's rival.

An Irish poet, William McGinn, in "A Thirst-imony
in Favour of Gin-Twist," compared other drinks with his
favorite gin-and-water, or gin-and-brandy, called gin-twist,
and then chose the latter for royal toasts.

> The people of Nantz, in the Kingdom of France,
> Bright brandy they brew, liquor not to be kissed;
> It may do as a dram, but 'tis not worth a damn,
> When watered, compared with a jug of gin-twist.

> Antigua, Jamaica, they certainly make a
> Grand species of wine, which should ne'er be dismissed;
> It is splendid as grog, but never, you dog,
> Esteem it as punch, like a jug of gin-twist.

> As for porter and ale--fore Gad, I turn pale,
> When people on such things as these can insist;
> They may do for dull clods, but, by all the gods,
> They are hog-wash when matched with a jug of gin-twist.

> Yet since I've made out, without any doubt,
> Of its merits and glories of flourishing list,
> Let us end with a toast, which we cherish the most,
> Here's God Save the King in a glass of gin-twist.

And so in these ubiquitous toasts we get a miscellan-
eous vocabulary of "healths"; in China "gambei," in Japan
"kampai," in Germany "hoch" and "Sieg heil," in Poland
"na zdrowie," in Scandinavia "skoll," in North America
"bottoms up," and in France "à votre santé."

NATIONAL DRINKS

"The Grape," observes Lawrence Durrell, "is a Rum
Thing. I should say it was the Diplomat's Cross.... Just
think of the varieties of alcoholic experience which are presented to one in the Foreign Service. To take one single
example--National Days.... To drink vodka with Russians,

champagne with the French, slivovitz with Serbs, sake with
Japs, whiskey and Coca Cola with the Yanks--the list seems
endless. I've seen many an Iron Constitution founder under
the strain..." ["Esprit de Corps," White Man's Milk].

Diplomats are representatives of their nations and it
is not uncommon for them to face the question of national
drinks as well as national anthems. It is a common observation that national entities have their own distinctive potables, even though international commerce has disturbed this
distinctiveness by introducing alien beverages, and in a new
form of Babel, contributing to a confusion of drinks. In
most cases the national beverages reflect the national climate and productive capacity. Sake in Japan results from
the rice-growing character of domestic agrarian production;
wine and champagne result from the French vineyard soil;
the date wine of the East, which Mohammed prohibited, was
the product of the indigenous date-palm; whiskeys flourish
where barley or corn is grown; rum is most popular in the
lands where the sugarcane grows. The national taste follows the national plant product, unless the taste becomes
corrupted by alien importations. Tequila is the popular national drink of Mexico, and is named after the town of Tequila; pisco is the principal potable of Chile.

It is difficult to say what is the national drink of
Canada. This is partly because there are so many ethnic
components of the Canadian population, who prefer their traditional beverages. The French Canadians still like their
wines, even the vin ordinaire produced in the Canadian vineyards, especially of the Niagara district, the most southerly
of Canada. The Canadians of English stock still like their
beer and Canadian beer is probably stronger than the English product; the Scottish and Irish like their whiskey; and
the East Europeans their vodka or slivovitz, etc. Nationally, the working classes generally consume home-produced
beers and ales, because of their relative cheapness, as the
taverns, "beverage rooms" and tap-rooms of most licensed
hotels indicate. The better-off classes prefer whiskey or
gin or their derivatives and for them, "cocktail lounges"
exist in the licensed hotels in such provinces which do not
have restrictions. Apart from the teetotalers and temperance addicts, who have made Coca Cola, ginger ale and
mineral waters their predilection, along with fruit juices,
the national taste in alcoholic beverages is heterogeneous,
as a short poem of the 1940's indicated:

> The Frenchman loves his native wine;
> The German loves his beer;
> The Englishman loves his 'alf and 'alf,
> Because it brings good cheer.
> The Irishman loves his 'whiskey straight, '
> Because it gives him dizziness.
> The Canadian has no choice at all,
> So he drinks the whole damned business.

But in upper-class circles in Canada, which include the diplomatic circles, whiskey--either "rye" or imported Scotch--
is probably the most popular drink; at cocktail parties,
whiskey or gin martinis seem to have taken the place of
fancy mixed cocktails in recent years; while at the table,
imported wines, topped in the list by champagne, are still
the customary beverages.

It may be noted that in certain countries, like Afghan-
istan and Saudi Arabia, prohibition of the use of any alcoholic or intoxicating liquors is not a historic episode, based on
war-time public consideration, as in the U.S.A., but is a
religious custom faithfully observed for centuries. Even the
foreign diplomats, with their 'privileges," lost caste by exercising their own practices and flouting local custom, thus
earning the epithets "foreign devils" or "barbarians." Modern Pakistan, being Islamic, was also prohibitionary, but
some of the Westernized Pakistanis who had acquired a European taste for alcoholic liquor, explained that the Prophet
Mohammed's interdiction referred only to the use of "date-
wine," a detrimental intoxicant among the desert people, but
did not specify either the wine of the grape, or whiskey, not
yet invented! Although the Persians and their offshoot the
Parsees are generally abstemious concerning fermented
drinks, Omar Khayyam the astronomer-poet and hedonist
was a backslider who eulogized the cup of wine.

> Indeed the Idols I have loved so long
> Have done my credit in this World much wrong:
>   Have drowned my Glory in a shallow Cup.
> And sold my reputation for a Song.
>
> And much as Wine has play'd the Infidel,
> And robb'd me of my Robe of Honour - Well
>   I wonder often what the Vintners buy
> One half so precious as the stuff they sell.

If it was Sir Walter Raleigh who brought back from

America and introduced into England tobacco, the Indian
weed which is now the addiction of the world, it is also
claimed that in modern times tobacco changed the wine
tastes of England. Lord Frederic Hamilton remarks on the
decline of the heavier wines in a heavy drinking age. "I
am certain of one thing," he wrote in his retrospective
memoirs The Days Before Yesterday; "it is to the cigarette
that the temperate habits of the twentieth century are due.
Nicotine knocked port and claret out in the second round.
The acclimatization of the cigarette in England only dates
from the 'seventies.' As a child I remember that the only
form of tobacco indulged in by the people that I knew was
the cigar. A cigarette was considered an effeminate foreign
importation; a pipe was unspeakably vulgar."

But if the relatively recent adoption of cigarette
smoking caused the decline of drinking of port and claret,
as Lord Frederic Hamilton suggests, there was, long before, a recurring effort of social reformers to discourage
the consumption of alcoholic beverages, or the grave abuse
of over-indulgence.

There has almost always existed opposition movements against drinking, apart from Mohammed's prohibition
of intoxicating liquor. During the gin age in England, pro-
hibitory laws were passed but were constantly broken, and
where import restrictions were applied, home-brewing and
distilling expanded. There have continued apace the efforts
of abolitionists, prohibitionists, and temperance societies,
many of whom base their actions on moral and religious
instead of medical grounds. The religious grounds seem
particularly shaky; wine was frequently referred to with tol-
eration in both the Old and the New Testament. Jesus himself participated in the conviviality of wedding, where the
wedding feast invariably included some form of fermented
beverage, and at the wedding-party at Cana, He came to the
rescue of a depleted supply by performing His first "miracle"--converting water into wine for the party celebration.
Wine is again mentioned in the Acts of the Apostles. Because it is supposed that it was wine that Jesus drank out
of the "silver chalice" or Holy Grail at the Last Supper,
many Church sects allow real wine to be drunk at Holy Communion or at Mass, while other sects substitute grape juice.
The legend of the Holy Grail has its own vast literature,
associated with the Arthurian Cycle and the foundation of
Glastonbury Abbey; Thomas Costain, in The Silver Chalice,
has written a fictional novel about it.

An official "finding" tabled in Parliament in April
1960 by the Canadian Department of National Health and
Welfare claimed that alcoholism had become a "serious
problem" in the civil service; but a special four-man team,
undertaking to investigate this finding, reported back to the
Executive Committee of the Headquarters Staff of the Public
Works Department, in October 1960, that in all the Canadian Civil Service in Ottawa, numbering some 40,000, there
were only 11 alcoholics--all "old" cases with psychological
and psychiatric backgrounds.   What was called moderate
"social drinking" was admittedly prevalent, as in other employment fields, but was not excessive.   It was specifically
mentioned that "social drinking" was often a part of the
working routine of certain groups, such as the Foreign Service and the Department of External Affairs, due to the pressures of the cocktail and reception obligations in diplomatic
life.

WINE

Wine, from most ancient times, has ever had a ceremonial importance.   Wine was the drink at wedding-feasts,
as we know from the story of the wedding at Cana; and it
was doubtless the usual beverage at small reunions and suppers among Judeans.   At the Last Supper, the Gospels relate that Christ partook of wine and gave it a symbolic
meaning; ever since the Christian Church became institution-
alized, the Eucharist has been an essential ritual.   The
Church soon became schismatic and broke into the Eastern
Orthodox, the Roman Catholic, the Alexandrine Monophys-
ites, and the Coptic churches; and after the Reformation,
the Protestant Church branched out, like a great delta, into
hundreds of sects and denominations; but in most, the Eucha-
ristic rites of Communion are retained, and the libation of
symbolic wine, either by the priests or by the congregation,
is an essential ritual.   Only in a few sects, influenced by
temperance ideas, is the liturgical wine replaced by symbolic unfermented grape juice for Communion purposes.

Benjamin Franklin quotes the reply of an Indian ora-
tor, after hearing a missionary account of the Fall of Man;
"What you have told us is all very good.   It is indeed bad
to eat apples.   It is better to make them all into cider."

WINES IN RELIGIOUS USE

It may be noted that the most celebrated Neapolitan

wine is Lacrima Christi, produced on the slopes of Mt.
Vesuvius.   The name means "Tears of Christ" and there
are many stories to explain its origin.   The lovely Bay of
Naples country has been called "a fragment of Paradise"
and according to one story the Lord, returning to earth,
found this heavenly region "inhabited by demons"; touched
and distressed, He wept, and where His tears fell, green
vines sprang up--the vines of the Lacrima Christi vineyards.

If Italy can offer for export the "Tears of Christ,"
Germany, not to be outdone, can furnish, and does furnish,
Liebfräumilch, or "Milk of the Blessed Virgin."   No disre-
spect, let alone impiety, is intended.   Both wines are made
by some of the most devout farmers in Western Europe,
and are supplied, under these names, as altar wines to the
Church.   Wine has an old and close bond with the Christian
(as well as the Hebrew) religion, as our own West Coast
Missions can attest, and wines with Biblical or ecclesiastical names are fairly common.   One called "Blood of Judas"
is produced in Lombardy, and "Tears of the Magdalene" is
popular in the Tyrol.   (See Holiday, Jan. 1961, p. 127.)

Although for the West the Greeks secularized and
democratised wine, and recognized the popular god Bacchus,
in the Far East wine long remained a drink restricted to
religious observances or for the use of the privileged.   In
ancient times, Indra, the warrior-god and the most popular
deity of the Hindu pantheon, was in some mystic sense
identified with or symbolized by soma, an intoxicating drink.
Soma was poured as a libation and drunk at religious ceremonies.   Soma may have been fermented honey, or perhaps
a beer-like drink, but it was at least as likely that it was
fermented grape juice.   But in general, the cultivation of
the vine was rare in Asia, and date and palm wine in the
Middle East and rice wine in the Far East were much more
popular.   Palm wine is at least as old as the pyramids, as
shown in wall paintings of the beginning of the second millenium B.C.   Both in the valley of the Nile and in Mesopotamia, grape wine was being made well before 2000 B.C.
In Egypt, the pharaohs and the hierarchy of priests seem
to have kept viticulture as a monopoly of church and state
(which were one); vines were trained on pergolas, much as
they are in some parts of the world today.   In the days of
the kings of Assyria, including Sennacherib and Nebuchadnezzar, the royal palaces had extensive wine cellars and
lists of the best wines were compiled; one list is still in

existence, although the names are of course meaningless.
Thus, wine has always had sacerdotal and aristocratic character.

The first European contacts with America, around
A. D. 988, seem to be associated in an uncertain form with
the vine. The Vikings Leif Ericcson and Thorwaldson on
several occasions touched the Atlantic coast at some inde-
termined point, possibly in what is now Labrador, or Nova
Scotia, which, because of the vegetation they encountered,
they called Vineland. As far as I know, there is no proof
that these plants were wild grapevines; there are many other species of climbing vine-like wild plants in that area.
I do not recall any record in the Icelandic sagas stating that
the "vines" they found provided grapes suitable for wine making, or that the indigenous Indian or Eskimo inhabitants
made beverages from them. For the next thousand years,
it does not appear that the natives made or drank wine, nor
that the bleak East Coast climate of the New World was
conducive to the growth of the grapevine, which had to be
introduced into warmer areas, like the Niagara peninsula,
the southernmost and warmest sector of Canada, and the
more hospitable regions of the United States, particularly
California, and the lands of South America. Nevertheless,
the unknown northern landing spot received the name of
Vineland (or, Vinland) and thus has left the impression that
a fruit like the grape existed in North America during the
first millenium A. D.

GRAPEVINES

There is in all fields of human activity what is called
the "grapevine" telegraph, that is, the filamentary channel of
gossip, rumor and authentic news by underground or invisible
means. Although not always reliable, it is uncannily quick;
and although it is not scientifically controllable, it often
serves as an expeditious means of news transmission, like
African drums and the so-called "whispering galleries" of
certain capital cities.

We may note also one of the world's most renowned
fruit-producing grapevines. Many a time, as boy, as young
man, and as oldster, have I visited Hampton Court Palace,
which was presented by Cardinal Wolsey to King Henry VIII
in 1525. Situated on the River Thames about ten miles from
the center of London, it is one of the most beautiful, as
well as historic, estates in the district. As a boy I lived

for several years at Kingston and Teddington and Richmond
and, being so close, used to have many picnic excursions
to their fine park and palace.   There is so much to see and
love there; the flowers and lawns and fountains; the long
water vistas in the park; the Tudor tennis court, built by
Henry VIII; the Orangery with the Mantegna cartoons, the
lovely little Pond Garden, and the celebrated Maze to get
lost in.   And there is also the Great Vine.   It lives in a
specially constructed glasshouse close to the Orangery.   It
was planted in 1768 by "Capability" Brown, the great landscape designer, at the command of George III, the original
cutting being taken from Valentine's Park at Ilford, Essex.
Now, after nearly two centuries of growth, it is of immense
size.   The girth of the main bole is 81 inches, and the
main branch is 114 feet long.   At one time the vine bore
well over 2000 bunches of grapes a year, but nowadays, in
order to preserve the strength of the tree, the number of
branches is limited to about 650, weighing on the average
between one and two pounds each.   They are of the excellent eating variety known as Black Hambo.   The grapes are
at the disposition of members of the Royal Family, but often
find their way as gifts to friends or to hospitals; but a proportion of them are sold to visitors at six shillings for a
one-pound bunch.

The Hampton Court Vine, however, for all its im-
pressiveness, is not the largest in Britain.   That honor
must go to the vine at the village of Kippen in Stirlingshire,
which, indeed, claims to be the largest in the world, producing about 2000 bunches every year.   It is unfortunate that
these famous grape-vines can make no contribution to wine
or champagne production, which has never succeeded in England because of the climate.   Viniculture on a commercial
scale could never flourish under glass.   The occasional
grapevines are there, in hothouses; but in insufficient quantity for an English wine industry.

Thomas Jefferson devoted pages of his diary to French
wines and sketched with his own hand detailed maps of
French vineyards.   Benjamin Franklin wrote of them with
eloquence.   A roster of those who have praised French wines
in the last thousand years would constitute a "Who's Who" of
the Western World.

Nearly a third of all the wine in the world is produced in France--seven billion bottles a year--ten times as
much as the United States makes.   Frenchmen drink it with

their meals, not because water in France is bad (it isn't),
but because it is cheap, goes well with food, is cheering
and pleasant and hardly more intoxicating than beer. They
like it so much that France imports more wine than she exports, consuming even more wine than her over three million acres of vineyard can provide.

In modern society circles, vintage wines are of
course the formal beverage at meals. They have a vast literature and history; they form an art and a cult and a hobby
among many educated men. Connoisseurship is almost an
esoteric art. In diplomatic circles, an ambassador is
judged by the wines he serves and by his reputation as a
connoisseur of wines; but in this latter respect there is often great rivalry and pretension of expert knowledge.

Connoisseurship among wine experts is fraught with
as much rivalry and discordant opinion as can be found in
other of the pursuits. Petrarch smiled at the discord of
philosophers, among whom he found "no more agreement
than among clocks"; it is almost an adage that doctors of
medicine often disagree, and even with royalty several physicians and consultants are called in, rather than one, to obtain if possible an agreed joint opinion. In economic questions, of course, controversy invariably rages, leading to
rivalry of parties and policies in economic-political fields.
Likewise gastronomically, what is one man's meat is another
man's poison; there is no accounting for taste; chaque
homme à son gout; and thus restaurants gain their rival cli-
entéles. The judgment of the qualities of wines is equally
exposed to the idiosyncracies of taste; and he would be a
vain, conceited and presumptuous man who would be arbitrary or dogmatic in such a refined art. Nevertheless,
many a diplomat has assumed this arbitrary authority as a
judge of wines.

Montaigne, who was generally an abstemious gentleman and water drinker, has been criticized for his lack of
fastidiousness in regard to wine, when he followed his con-
fession by as foolish a boast as a wise man can ever have
uttered, to the effect that he who is fastidious can be made
happy only by good wine, whereas the unfastidious can always find pleasure in wine whatever its quality. Although
"Blessed is he that expects little, for he shall not be disappointed," it is rather Philistine to be undiscriminating or
devoid of epicurean taste.

Of the erroneous pretensions among connoisseurs of
wines, the diplomat Castiglione, writing in 1514, remarked,
of a discussion, "Do you not remember that, when drinking
a certain wine, you would at one time pronounce it to be
most perfect and at another to be most insipid? And this
because you were convinced they were different wines, one
from the Riviera of Genoa, and the other from this region;
and even when the mistake was discovered, you refused to
believe it--so firmly was that wrong opinion fixed in your
mind, which opinion came however from the report of others"
[The Book of the Courtier].

Of course, the profession of diplomacy is often an
expensive one. Ambassadors and ministers have often found
it difficult to "keep up with the Joneses"--their more wealthy
colleagues--in the business of official representation of their
country and in the entertainment involved. Since professional diplomats are no longer necessarily richly-endowed aristocratic gentlemen of the court, but may be required to be-
have as such while receiving inadequate official emoluments,
they have either to rely on their own financial wealth, or
act more humbly than their status warrants or than their
country merits. The United States, and other countries,
have found that the diplomatic or court traditions surviving
in capitals of certain old Great Powers, require a lavish
expenditure which none but the extremely wealthy can meet.
Those appointees who, on grounds of other merit, find themselves in posts where social life is grand and expensive, but
who are themselves limited in personal wealth, are forced
to run their embassies on an economical basis; and sometimes their limitations or seeming parsimony are noticeable.

Charles M. Thayer refers to William Dodd, a professor of history whom Roosevelt had recruited as ambassador to Germany. Dodd was a great scholar of German history and culture, but had little knowledge of, or flair for,
diplomacy or the diplomatic social life. Moreover, he was
frugal partly because of his lack of private means. At one
of his earliest official receptions in Berlin, Ambassador
Dodd, taking his youngest vice-consul aside and with an air
of admonition not unmixed with pride, confided that one
could give a reception for two hundred people with only one
bottle of gin if one was careful. The punch he served bore
unmistakable evidence of the ambassador's carefulness.
Thayer goes on to say:

Parsimony can take many forms. One American

ambassador used to serve cheap local wines from
bottles bearing the labels of famous Rhine or Bur-
gundy vineyards. Once when entertaining a visiting
foreigner known to most of the guests as a great
authority on Rhine wines, the ambassador served a
particularly ordinary native product in a Rhine wine
bottle. As the distinguished guest took a sip and
carefully rolled the liquid around his tongue, the other guests watched in awkward silence. Then the
guest put down the glass and bowed to the Ambassador. 'Most unusual,' he commented and ostentatious-
ly reached for his water-glass [Diplomat, p. 232-3].

One catches a little glimpse of the Mad Tea Party.
"Have some wine," the March Hare said in an encouraging
tone. Alice looked all round the table, but there was nothing on it but tea. "I don't see any wine," she remarked.
"There isn't any," said the March Hare. "Then it wasn't
very civil of you to offer it," said Alice angrily. In very
similar terms Lord Frederic Hamilton describes a certain
cher collègue at Tokyo who was determined to avoid bank-
ruptcy, if it were at all possible. "He had in some mad
fit of extravagance bought two dozen of really fine claret
some years before. The wine had long since been drunk;
the bottles he still retained with their labels. It was his
custom to buy the cheapest and roughest red wine he could
find, and then enshrine it in these old bottles with their
mendacious labels. ... The palate...pronounced [it] sour,
immature vin ordinaire. The label on the bottle claimed
it Chateau Margaux of 1874,... Politeness dictated that
we should compliment our host on this exquisite vintage,
which had, perhaps, begun to feel (as we all do) the effects
of extreme old age" [The Vanished Pomps of Yesterday, p.
338].

Many diplomats consider that it is part of their social grace to be expert connoisseurs of wines; it is not only Frenchmen who are experts. Among my own Canadian
diplomatic colleagues I have known a number who were real
or imaginary connoisseurs. The only trouble is that each
one is inclined to be jealous or distrustful of his colleague's
"expertise."

There was one ambassador who, having spent twenty
years in France and further years in other European posts,
regarded himself as a master. He once entertained at an
embassy dinner, a visiting fellow Canadian Ambassador,

who, though of shorter residence in Europe, and though an
Ontario English-Canadian, instead of a Quebec-born French-
Canadian, was by chance an equal authority of the cult of
French wines.   During the dinner, the guest-ambassador
congratulated his host on his most excellent specifically
identified and named wine.   The host replied that his guest
was mistaken: the wine served was a different, named
kind.   The guest's judgment being thus impugned, he argued
the point.   The host, much irritated, said that after all, he
should know best what wine he was serving.   If his word
was not accepted, he would ask his butler to confirm it.
He called in his butler, and asked him to reassure the guest
as to the wine served.   The butler was most embarrassed,
and then whispered in his master's ear: "You instructed
me to serve the XXX wine, but I found it was out of stock,
so I substituted the YYY wine."   The very brand that the
unknowing guest had identified!   After that unfortunate ex-
posure and betrayal of the "expert" host, the two ambassadorial colleagues were barely on speaking terms for a very
long time.

Another French-Canadian ambassador who had also
spent over twenty years in France and considered himself
a perfect connoisseur of French wines, persuaded me, as
his counsellor, to stock my cellar with his choice of fine
wines.   I did so, on his recommendation.   The war inter-
vened, all our properties were safely put in local storage;
and seven years after the war, I paid a return visit to the
post and examined my stored possessions.   I discovered,
to my surprise, a small stock of my pre-war wines.   As I
no longer had any need of them, I offered to sell them to
the new Canadian Ambassador at my former post.   He invited me to dinner, bringing some sample bottles to taste.
After tasting them, he declined to buy--mainly, I think, because they had been the selections of his rival colleague
and therefore could not be as well chosen as those he chose
from his own "expertise."   Fortunately I was quickly able
to dispose of my remainder stock, with greatest appreciation, to senior members of his staff, who were not influenced by jealousy or rivalry, but who held the wine-judg-
ment of my former chief in high esteem.

When I was head of mission in Warsaw I once wished
to give a farewell dinner to a departing American colleague.
The diplomatic restaurant in those days was in the basement
of the ruined and half-demolished Europejski Hotel, owned
before the war by the princely Czetwertynski family.   Prince

Stefan Czetwertynski could not rebuild the immense, formerly de luxe, hotel, but he did reconstruct the restaurant.
He himself was an experienced restaurateur.   I told him of
my proposed dinner and asked him to help me with the
menu.   He then asked me about the wines to be served.   He
said that he had three categories: cheap wines, middle-
quality wines and a few treasured (and expensive) pre-war
wines which he had preserved in his "cave."   I said that the
party was mainly American and Canadian; cocktails would be
served first, and after that, their taste would not be too
critical or fastidious; and suggested a medium-quality wine.
He asked me who my principal guest was.   I named the
American chargé d'affaires.   He said: "In that case, I
candidly advise you to serve only the best wine that I have
in my cave.   It will be expensive.   But Mr. Crocker happens to be one of the first wine-connoisseurs I have known
and nothing but the best can be served to him."   And so,
to satisfy my expert connoisseur guest, I ordered a valuable
and expensive wine which Prince Czetwertynski extracted
from the cobwebs of his hidden cave.   It cost me a pretty
penny, being black-market wine-stocks; but it won the admiration and compliments of my guest-of-honor, a very
long-time American friend and colleague.

This taught me the lesson that one cannot fool the
true expert, and that you must meet his taste with nothing
less than the best.   He will know; he will recognize his
wines; and he will judge his host accordingly.   It matters
not whether he is French, Norwegian, American, Italian or
Canadian.   The palate and the passport have no relationship.   With luck, the maître d'hotel of any well-known restaurant will know all his clients' tastes; and if on good
terms, can best advise a prospective host concerning his
prospective guests' tastes and knowledge.

During my period in Washington, the beloved doyen
of the diplomatic corps, Sir Esmé Howard (later Lord Howard of Penrith after his retirement) was about to terminate
his mission as British Ambassador to the United States,
and was reported to have announced the following views.
The United States was then under Prohibition, by the Eigh-
teenth Amendment and the Volstead Act.   American citizens
were not allowed to sell or purchase, or transport, or consume, spirituous liquor.   Diplomatic missions were, of
course, exempt from this law, and naturally were most popular among thirsty American guests.   But the diplomats'
disregard for the national law was as much a defiance (how-

ever popular) of the law as disregard for red lights and
traffic regulations might be. Diplomatic immunity and privilege certainly existed; but it should not be flagrantly abused
in the face of local law and custom. It was the duty of foreign diplomats to respect and reasonably to observe the local practice. The British Ambassador announced therefore
that for the next few months prior to his departure, he
would conform to American law and ask permission no more
to import, under diplomatic privilege, any further liquor
supplies, generally illicit in the United States. This announcement apparently won widespread appreciation among
the Americans jealous of the diplomats. Sir Esmé Howard,
however, made it clear that this personal act would in no
way commit his successor, or any other foreign diplomat.

The joker in this well-received announcement was,
first, that the ambassador did not reveal that previously he
and his embassy associates had stocked up on liquor supplies sufficient to last at least for the next six months, so,
with cellars full, there was no need to ask for further import permits; and secondly, that he did not discontinue serving wines and liquors at his diplomatic parties, which remained as popular and welcome as before in circles of
Washington society.

The Italian Chianti is one of the best known and most
popular wines in the world. With spaghetti, it has invaded
and conquered many countries and has doubtless done more,
in its humble and charming way, to make friends for Italy
than a hundred ambassadors. It is the one non-French
table-wine that Parisians gladly drink, and its gay, round-
bellied, straw-covered bottles are as familiar in Copenhagen
and Chicago as they are in their home province of Tuscany.
"The Chianti bottle is a primitive idea, an old form, and is
surprisingly cheap to produce. It is nevertheless one of the
most successful commercial packages ever devised. It is
round-bottomed and extremely thin, and is therefore given
a straw base so that it will stand upright on a table, a
straw jacket to protect it, and straw strings to hang it up.
Its picturesqueness is accidental, and in Italy it costs no
more, hand labor and all, than an ordinary wine bottle"
[Frank Schoonmaker, Holiday, Jan. 1961, p. 126].

John Keats was not a diplomat, only a pharmaceuti-
cal student and a humble poet--and one not averse to wine,
the nectar of the gods, as an ambrosia of mundane poets.
In one of his letters, written on February 18, 1819, he
wrote:

Now I like claret--whenever I can have claret, I must
drink it. 'Tis the only palate affair that I am at all
sensual in. Would it not be a good speck to send you
some vine-roots? Could it be done? I'll enquire.
If you could make some wine like claret, to drink on
summer evenings in an arbour! For 'tis so fine. It
fills one's mouth with a gushing freshness, then goes
down, cool and feverless; then you do not feel it
quarrelling with your liver. No; 'tis rather a peace-
maker, and lies as quiet as it did in the grape.
Then it is fragrant as the Queen Bee, and the more
ethereal part of it mounts into the brain, not assault-
ing the cerebral apartments, like a bully in a bad
house looking for his trull, and hurrying from door
to door, bouncing against the wainscot, but rather
walks like Aladdin about his enchanted palace, so
gently that you do not feel his step.

James Russell Lowell, in Leaves from My Journal in
Italy (1854), meditated: "Suppose that a man in pouring down
a glass of claret could drink the South of France, that he
could so disintegrate the wine by the force of imagination as
to taste in it all the clustered beauty and bloom of the grape,
all the dance and song and jollity of the vintage." Sir Vincent Corbett, in his diplomatic Reminiscences Autobiographical and Diplomatic (1927), looking back to the 1870's, remarks rather plaintively:

It is true that, to the trained palate, smoking in no
wise interferes with the appreciation of the flavour
of champagne, nor does it very much affect the taste
of that strange artificial product that we call vintage
port, but it has totally killed the consumption of claret, which used to form the finale of any well-organ-
ized dinner. I wonder if there are any country
houses left where, after a seven o'clock dinner, a
decanter of claret, fine vintage claret properly decanted and just properly warmed, is placed on the
mahogany, or perhaps a specially devised crescent
table before the hearth, to be slowly and apprecia-
tively sipped and discretely renewed until, at ten or
half past, it is time to rejoin the ladies for half an
hour in the dining room? Such was the custom in
very many houses in my youth, especially in Ireland
[p. 338].

It is perhaps of some interest to note that, instead

of "bathtub" gin and home-brew and "moonshine," some
private individuals in Canada, particularly Italian immigrants
from wine-producing areas at home, make their own wines.
It is said that four million gallons--about half of the production of the nine Canadian vineries in Ontario, are thus home-
manufactured. Italians make their wine in October; the Portuguese wait until November. Most drink their fermented
wine around Christmas time. There are few legal restrictions on home wine-making. In Ontario, a maker may ferment up to 100 gallons a year at home without a permit.
To make more than that he must obtain a permit from the
Liquor Control Board, a government monopoly agency, which
is issued free. In the last 20 years, fewer than 1600 permits have been issued; only about two were issued in 1961.
The home-maker may not legally sell his product, or let it
be taken off the premises; this is to prevent large-scale
bootlegging of wine and its sale to juveniles. The commercial product is heavily taxed by both federal and provincial
governments. But the home maker can make wine cheaper
than pop at about $1.70 for a gallon of juice, or $1.50 if
one crushes and presses the grapes oneself, it is said that
wine can be made at home as good as the Chianti bought in
the licensed liquor stores.

CHAMPAGNE

Of all varieties of wine, champagne of course takes
the lead. It is sipped at Christening parties and is quaffed
at weddings; it is the beverage of toasts; and it is used
ceremonially for the launching of ships or laying of corner-
stones or the opening of buildings; it is drunk to celebrate
birthdays, and the publication of first novels, and the var-
nishings of art exhibitions. It is, par excellence, the ceremonial wine, and the most virtuous wine. Champagne
shares the glory, which Marlowe's Faustus saw in Helen's
eyes, of launching a thousand ships. Moreover when the
Union Pacific Railway finally joined its western and its
eastern links by the closing of the last gap and driving of
the last spike, locomotives from both sections of the line
drew together "until their noses touched," while their gala
decorations received a christening from the contents of
champagne bottles broken over their cabs. That May 10th,
1869, marked the first rail link between the Atlantic Ocean
and the Pacific Ocean, and history was honorably commem-
orated with the traditional ceremony.

Around 1920, G. K. Chesterton read in a newspaper

paragraph that influence was being brought to bear on the American Government to induce them to break a bottle of water instead of a bottle of champagne when they launch a battleship. He exploded in an article, "Four Stupidities." First, he argued, it was inconsistent.

Note the notion: that there is something so intrinsically and supernaturally evil about an intoxicant that the pure temperance man will not touch it even when it cannot intoxicate anybody. It is as if a man were to insist on having a teetotal boot-polish or a teetotal printing-ink. A cup of tea, or even a hot milk, becomes diabolic if you have boiled the kettle with methylated spirit...." [Second stupidity:] The extraordinary confusion by which it becomes not only wicked to possess wine (though you never drink it), but becomes wicked even to destroy it.... If a champagne bottle is smashed to smithereens over the prow of a ship, I should have thought the most logical teetotaller would merely have been glad that there was one champagne bottle less in the world.... [Third stupidity:] The confusion in men's minds over maintaining ancient forms and customs, but 'watered down' to be without meaning or symbolism.

The fourth stupidity is in the abandonment of the human sentiment, expressed in a special sort of ceremony, of sacrifice. "The thing sacrificed may be anything: wine, as on the battleship; gold, as when the Doge threw the ring into the sea; an ox or a sheep, as among the ancient pagans; and very occasionally, when tribes savage or civilized are seized with Satanic panic, a man. But it must be something valuable, or the particular thrill, wholesome or unwholesome, is not obtained. ...[A]nd these men evidently understand none of [this] when they fill the bottle with water" [in The Uses of Adversity].

Though the cultivation of the vine in the Champagne area in and around the Marne district, dates back at least from the days of the Roman emperor Propus in the third century A.D., sparkling or effervescent wine appeared only in the 18th century. Its discovery is attributed to Dom Pérignon, a monk who managed the cellars of the Benedictine Abbey of Haut-Villers near Rheims from 1670 to 1715. It seems that he also first used cork as a material for closing wine bottles. Up to that time such primitive means as pads of tow, hemp or cloth steeped in oil had been em-

ployed. It is very likely that the discovery of the utility of
cork for stoppering led to the invention of effervescent wine,
the most plausible explanation being that Dom Pérignon
closed some bottles filled with partially fermented wine with
the new material, and on opening them later observed the
effects produced by the confined carbonic acid gas.

The art of making this type of wine was kept secret
for some time, and many mysterious fables were circulated
concerning it. For example, it was believed that the Evil
One had a hand in its manufacture. It was not until 1718
that the sparkling wine of Haut-Villers was called "champagne" and it became popular or consumed on large scale
only around the end of the 18th century. Since then it has
always been a favorite.

Diplomats, as wine tasters, are not necessarily poets or poetasters; although many of them are by training
and taste classical scholars or orientalists. When they
drink wine, rarely does it bring to them poetical allusions.
They do not think of the flagons in the Odyssey, or the
drinking horns of Bacchus, or the nectar of the Grecian
gods. Therefore they do not stop to question John Keats'
anachronism in "To a Nightingale":

> O for a beaker of the warm South
> Full of the true, the blushful Hippocrene,
> With beaded bubbles winking at the brim
> And purple-stained mouth ...

Even the later lyricist Alfred Noyes could be misled by this
Keatsian metaphor, as when he says, in "The Haunted Palace":

> At last, one royal rose-hung night in June
> When the warm air like purple Hippocrene
> Brimmed the dim valley and sparkled into stars
> I saw them swim out from that summer shore ...

Keats, though himself trained as an apothecary, seemed to
have confused Hippocras—an ancient medical drink or cordial made of wine mixed with spices and strained through
a woolen cloth called "Hippocrates' sleeve"--and Hippocrene,
"fountain of the horse," the cold water spring on Mount
Helicon in Bocotia, sacred to the Muses and Apollo and
hence taken as the source of poetic inspiration. The hippocrene to which Keats mistakenly referred was not an

aerated or sparkling wine, and produced no "beaded bubbles,"
but was only water; he doubtless intended Hippocras.

But he was mistaken further. That the cordial called
Hippocras was purple might well be; but that it had "beaded
bubbles winking at the brim" (i.e., was fermented or aerated) is extremely doubtful. Sparkling wines were not known
in the Hellenic age of the fifth century B.C. Bubbling or
sparkling wine was apparently not known in Europe until
around 1700. Keats was certainly adopting poetic license in
applying the modern type of sparkling red wine to the Greek
"Hippocras." As for the "blushful" or dark wine, he perhaps was influenced by reading Chapman's Homer, in speaking of the purple-stained wine; for one of the most mysterious of Homer's cliché-epithets is the description of the col-
or of the Mediterranean Sea as "wine-dark"--which, apparently, it is only at sunset when Athens is violet-crowned.
To Homer, and thus to Keats and Noyes, the Aegean was
ever twilight colored; and not the sapphire-blue which it is
by day. But a poet is always permitted to take imaginative
liberties, and since he was confessedly fond of claret, and
was no doubt familiar with champagne, he conjured up a
Grecian wine, purple and sparkling, which he misnamed
Hippocrene.

Of the superior merits and social prestige of champagne, reference is scarcely necessary. Lord Kinross has
summed up the general view: "Champagne is, by tradition,
hospitality incarnate, the quintessence of all that is bounti-
ful and beneficient and bubbly. This is an age of hospitality, when all the best mantelpieces are stocked with invitation cards from strangers, regardless of whether they
chance to be enemies or friends. Hence it is an age of
champagne, of champagne for the general" [Punch, April
6, 1960].

Even in the wildernesses of the mighty East, this
precious beverage was not overlooked. The Marquess Curzon wrote:

> If a man is marching with a caravan, where his im-
> pediments are carried either on the backs of animals
> or, as in Africa, on the heads of native porters, or,
> as in many parts of the East, slung on poles from
> the shoulders of men, we may be sure that the cases
> of wine or spirit will be there in sufficient quantity;
> that these will be broached at the end of the day, and

that, after an exceptional spell of exertion, the corks
will fly and the day's toil will be rehearsed to this
merry tune.   If I may relate my own humble [sic!]
experience, when I was galloping for nine long days
from Meshed to Teheran, getting up in the darkness
of the night long before sunrise, and riding through
the heat of the day, with no more liquid than the contents of a flask in one of my holsters, I used to think
fondly of the prospective amenities of the British
Legation, and to murmur to myself the magic incan-
tation: 'Wolff's Champagne' [Sir H. Drummond
Wolff, British Minister at Teheran].   When at length
I rode exhausted into the Legation Compound, and a
friendly secretary asked me what I would like, I answered without the slightest hesitation, 'Wolff's
Champagne.' And I got it! [Leaves From a Viceroy's Notebook, p. 346].

Even the Soviet Russians, anti-monarchist, anti-
aristocratic, proletarian and plebeian dressed, have not escaped or eschewed the allure of the courtly champagne that
was the elixir of the rich. Indeed, they produce champagne
in their Caspian and Black Sea vineyards, in rivalry to the
authentic French, even as in Czarist days; and at every
Communist party, at least where foreigners are present,
champagne is as popular as their native vodka. When in
1960, Nikita Khrushchev made an official visit to France,
one of his excursions was to the famous Champagne region,
and his hosts showed him through their best cellarages.
As Lord Kinross noted, it was appropriate that Mr. Khrushchev should be entertained at Epernay with a hospitality ex-
ceeding, in the concern for the guest, all that was lavished,
in a more casual century, on his predecessor the Czar Alexander I.

Champagne is the appurtenance of diplomacy; indeed,
its sine qua non. How many a brilliant toast has been proclaimed, how many a diplomatic banquet has been enlivened
and brightened and made convivial, how many a treaty has
been celebrated, with the aid of this incomparable and be-
nevolent wine! Dom Pérignon should better be recognized
as the deus ex machina who has contributed as much to diplomacy, treaty-making and world history, as he has to the
launching of the world's marine, commerce, and naval ar-
gosies--a thousand times more than Helen of Troy's beautiful face.

In August 1963, the foreign ministers of the United
States, Britain and the Soviet Union put their signatures to
the nuclear test-ban treaty, in the Kremlin in Moscow. The
world press published photographs of the important diplomatic occasion, and showed that immediately after the sign-
ing, champagne was served all around, before the diplomats
resumed the discussions of further East-West problems.
Even the U. N. Secretary General U Thant was pictured hap-
pily clinking his champagne glass with the pleased and ami-
able Premier Khrushchev.

SHERRY AND SAKE

"If I had a thousand sons," said the old toper Captain John Falstaff, "the first human principle I would teach
them, should be to forswear thin potations and to addict
themselves to sack." It was indeed a false and conditional
pledge of Falstaff's that if he gained a reward "I'll purge
and leave sack, and live clearly as a nobleman should do."
Whether called sherry or sack, this notable potable has been
associated with Britons so long that many believe that the
Spanish wine was produced in England. In Shakespeare's
time playgoers at the Mermaid Tavern drank sherry without
regard to time of day. Ben Jonson applied the name "sack"
to the Canary wine which, as Court Poet, he received from
King's cellars annually. A dubious attribution of the word
"sack" is that the English called it so after Sir Francis
Drake "sacked" 3000 casks of sherry from Spanish ships in
1587. But it is more generally, though by no means entirely, accepted that the name came from the French vin
sec, because the Spanish wine was of a strong dry kind usually sweetened and mixed with spice and mulled "burnt."
It became a common name for all the stronger white wines
of the South, and was in common use in the Elizabethan
period and thereafter. The name is preserved in the sherry
known as Humbert's "Dry Sack," one of the most popular of
sherries.

I like the farewell stirrup-cup proposed by Venator
to Piscator on the Fifth Day of the Compleat Angler's conversations, as Izaak Walton describes it. "Pray let's now
rest ourselves in this sweet shady arbour, which nature
herself has woven with her own fine fingers; 'tis such a
contexture of woodbines, sweetbriar, jasmine and myrtle;
and so interwoven, as will secure us both from the sun's
heat and the approaching shower. And being set down, I
will requite a part of your courtesies with a bottle of sack,

milk, oranges and sugar, which, all put together, make a
drink like nectar; indeed, too good for any but us Anglers.
And so, Master, here is a full glass to you of that liquor."

In the 19th century, the English essayist and art
critic, John Ruskin advised: "I consider just and tolerable
the drinking of sherry from dawn to dusk." * Spain's 11
o'clock sherry break, las once, soon became a British institution known as "elevenses."

Whether or not the older name "sack" comes from
Jerez seco, the name "sherry" itself is said to come from
the 3000 year-ago Phoenician region in Spain called by them
"shera," and by the later Moors, "scheris," until the old
Spanish conquerors rendered it "xeres," and finally "Jerez."
This is the region from which almost all of the true sherries have come.

In modern production, there are three main sherries,
imitated in many countries but originally Spanish. These
are fino, amontillado, and oloroso. Walter Starkie, in Don
Gypsy, mentions that there are four distinct types. "In
Spain, what is called Fino is popular in clubs, instead of
our cocktails. It is pale in color, and has a light bouquet.
One of the authorities told me that if the Fino is allowed to
get old it will become an amontillado wine, which is peer-
less for fragrance and subtlety. The name amontillado is
derived from Montilla in the province of Cordoba."

Some official descriptions indicate that "fino should
smell like green apples, taste of almonds, and look like
topaz; amontillado should smell like vine blossoms, taste of
filberts, and look like liquid gold; oloroso should have a
raisin taste (due to the sweet Pedro Ximines which has been
added to it), it should taste of walnuts, and glow like ru-
bies." At Jerez there are several famed establishments,
or "bodegas," and they have their distinguishing badges.
"Sandeman has tame storks walking soberly about. Garvey,
founded by an emigrant Irishman, has an image of St. Patrick and a grand wine named after him. Williams and
Humbert have mice which drink the sherry before your eyes,
stagger back to their holes, and then come back for more.

---

*But it has been elsewhere mentioned that John Ruskin depended for his
wealth on the fortune made by his father, an English agent of the Spanish
sherry firm of Domecq; no wonder he would say a good word for this popular wine.

Misa has the best stunt of all--three huge alligators roaring and whistling at their incredulous visitors" [John D. Stewart, "Drunk as a Vineyard Snail," The Compleat Imbiber, p. 163, 165]. Amontillado has become a familiar type in America--the more so, perhaps, because of Edgar Allan Poe's famed horror tale "The Casque of Amontillado"; it is a dry sherry which takes on a deep golden hue and nutty flavor as it ages. The other popular form, specially favored in the United States, is oloroso, a fragrant sweet sherry. It serves as an apértif, afternoon refresher, pre-theater treat, or wee-hour nightcap. These sweeter Spanish sherries are considered particularly suitable with dessert or cheeses, while the drier type is usually served at dinner with soups.

In diplomatic circles, I have noticed that while a Scotch-and-soda is more commonly taken by men, as a "man's drink," the ladies exercising more delicacy, frequently choose a glass of sherry as their apertif; it seems to be considered more genteel for the fair sex.

In Japan the national drink is sake, a mild form of rice-wine, imbibed warm. Its nearest taste is sherry, but it seems thin and mild. Japanese may readily feel its effects, since they seem to have weak stomachs as regards alcoholic beverages, but foreigners find it relatively innocuous, with food, especially as it is served warm in tiny sake cups, a little at a time, and very ceremoniously, sipped delicately rather than swallowed at a gulp like vodka. It may be that the Portuguese or Spaniards introduced their vin sec into Japan in the 16th century, and from "sec" the Japanese learned to call their rice-wine "sake." The Encyclopaedia Britannica [11th ed., 'Wine"] however, disputes this, and says: "It seems possible that sherry was the first wine known as sack in England, but it is at least doubtful whether this word is, as some contend, derived from seck or sec, i.e. dry. According to Morewood it is more likely to have come from the Japanese sake or Sacki, derived in its turn from the name of the city of Osaka."

I myself tasted saké for the first time when, before I left Ottawa to take up my diplomatic appointment to the first Canadian legation opened in Japan in 1928, the Japanese Minister to Canada gave me a farewell party, at which his national beverage was served to me. Incidentally, this first Japanese Minister to Canada had installed himself in a residence on Elgin Street next door to a distinguished

Protestant Church. Once he received a telephone call from
the church, asking if he was expecting a consignment of
wine. Such was the ignorance in those early days of the title of diplomatic "minister" that, seeing the title, the delivery had been made to the church's minister!

The former diplomat Lawrence Durrell in "White
Man's Milk" [Esprit de Corps] tells the fictional story of
Kawaguchi, a Japanese minister in Prague who with his wife
drank nothing but sake which they imported in little white
stone bottles. "When they had to go out to a banquet or
rout he always sent his butler over in the afternoon with a
few small bottles of the stuff which were always placed before him at table." On one fatal New Year's Eve party
given by the French, the Kawaguchis as usual had a table
near a corner, with their own special beverage. Suddenly
they rose, and to the waltz music of the band, began to go
into a beautiful and impeccable Vienna waltz. They went
faster and faster, and the band played for them faster and
faster, until all the other dancing diplomats were dizzy and
exhausted, and until finally the Kawaguchis, in a sort of
frenzy whirled their way "like a meteor" right out of the
ballroom on to the terrace and right into the shallow lake,
just three minutes before midnight was to strike. This
calamitous end to the Minister's burst of energy resulted in
the failure of his mission and his immediate departure from
Prague. "It was purely inadvertent," says Durrell. "The
butler gave the whole thing away some weeks later. Apparently the normal case of saki had not come that month.
They were out of drink. There was nothing a responsible
butler of any nationality could do. He took some of the
saki bottles and filled them with ... guess what?" "Bad
Scotch whiskey." "Dead right! 'White Man's Milk,' he
called it."

At any party given in Japanese style, ordinary or
formal or diplomatic, sake is served as an essential beverage, prior to the native and formal serving of tea. As with
post-prandial cognac in Europe, or even champagne during
the meal, sake with meals is the means among Japanese for
"warming the cockles of one's heart" and of relaxation and
amity. It may repeatedly be poured and served by the host;
but more often the cups are refilled by the kneeling attendant neisan or geisha who officiates at such Japanese dinners
--or by the wife if one is a guest in a private home.

Among the Japanese, in the lovely spring season,

"cherry-viewing" parties are customary and as in Izaak
Walton's moment of rest with his friends, sake flasks are
always brought along for refreshment.   One wonders whether this traditional custom is not a relic of ancient ceremonies connected with fertility rites and vernal celebrations
of spring and nature's rebirth.   The sake bottles themselves
were in all shapes and forms and since early times, like
modern perfume bottles, generally artistically designed and
handmade with all the aesthetic taste and care that characterizes Japanese handicraft.

Diplomats and others who enjoy the honor of attending a dinner given at the Imperial Palace, in the presence
of the Emperor, are served their sake in small porcelain
or silver cups engraved with the Imperial crest.   These
they are allowed to keep, afterwards, as souvenirs.   My
own minister, Sir Herbert Marler, collected these precious
souvenirs and had them displayed in a glass-fronted china
cabinet as evidence of the number of times during his six
years he had enjoyed an Imperial audience and State dinner
invitation.   The Belgian Ambassador to Japan, Baron de
Bassompierre, who was in Japan for 20 years, had a much
greater collection, followed by that of the Netherlands Minister, General Pabst, who had been in Tokyo for 15 years.

This was of course quite opposite to the old Russian
custom of shattering the vodka glass against the wall at the
end of every toast--on the principle that a glass of honored
occasion should never be put later to mundane use.   But
those were in the more extravagant Czarist days.   I have
seen it done in more modern times, but only as a relic of
an antiquated tradition.   It is a wasteful practice in modern
times when hosts are not so affluent, and when deliberately-
smashed glassware is an egregious exhibition of wealth.
Japanese prefer to regard their sake cups ever since early
times, as precious works of art, and preserve them, or
make gifts of them to their guests as mementos of each
happy occasion of hospitality.   Foreign visitors, statesmen
and diplomats are usually proud to preserve these mementos
coming from the Imperial Palace, or from Japanese nobles.

GIN

The origin of gin is fairly well established.   Some
sort of wine flavored with juniper had been drunk in France
in the 16th century.   It was invented by the son of Henry IV,
and was known as "the wine of the poor."   But a new form

was invented in Holland; it was a distillate or spirit of juniper berries.

> Professor Franciscus Sylvius of Leyden, in the course of important experiments, produced a distillate from rye and juniper berries. The professor's beverage was important because it was such a high proof as to be almost pure alcohol. And perhaps because juniper berries (junever in Dutch and genièvre in French--in English it was once called "geneva," although it has no connection whatever with the Swiss city) have a therapeutic value to the kidneys--or maybe because of the aromatic bouquet and flavor they imparted to the drink--these berries became an important ingredient in the new drink. ... The Dutch predilection for this dry, fruity, potent potable--which they drink neat, uncluttered by mixers or ice--remains to this day. Perhaps it is because they are convinced of its healthful qualities, for, when Dutch traders settled in far-off places, such as the East Indies, or Sumatra, they took with them this unique drink to ward off many of the ills of the tropics [Joseph Scholnick, "Gin by Juniper!" Argosy, Aug. 1960, p. 57].

The first uses of gin were purely medicinal. The apothecaries sold it as an infallible remedy for all diuretic ills, besides benefitting sufferers from gout, rheumatism, kidney trouble, and various such infirmities. It continued to be sold in chemists' and apothecaries' shops until the 19th century. Of gin, it has been said that "medical science created it; war and its political aftermath brought it to England."

Gin was among those potables whose history is mixed up with wider issues of foreign policy and war. For example, the Dutch had long been drinkers of spirits, while the English were rather drinkers of ale and to a lesser extent of wine. But English troops, as far back as the reign of Edward III, had discovered the encouraging effects before a battle of aquavit, the "burning wine," and had developed the continental habit of drinking each other's health in it afterwards. Later, on the long damp campaigns in the Low Countries, they derived a new "Dutch courage" from the new and more palatable spirit "geneva," or gin. In the 16th century, medical authorities with a British army in Holland reported that on an ill-fated expedition to Walcheren, only those officers who drank gin and smoked escaped from fever.

In due course, with the returning British troops to
England, the medical value as well as the taste were
brought with them, and became popular.   In a short time
the enterprising English started to make it for themselves.
Both Charles II and James II gave charters to brewers con-
ferring on them the right to distill.   But since their foreign
policy was favorable to France, the importation of French
brandy still thrived, and the English gin industry, thus un-
protected, made only gradual headway.   This situation
changed when James II fled to France and the Dutch prince,
William, acceded to the throne with his Queen, Mary.   This
was a "Glorious Revolution" in among other things, the
drinking habits of the English.   Brandy and foreign spirits
became prohibited from importation, along with nearly all
trade with France, and from about 1690 King William's
Parliament promoted English corn and the distillation of
spirits from it.   Thus prospered both farmer and distiller.
Geneva (gin) was drunk for King and Country and was given
out to workers as a part of their wages.   (Wine still is in
a few cases in France.)   No longer was ale the premier
potable of England.

King William III was given the credit for introducing
gin into England by his support of a certain distiller Alexander Blunt, who in 1729 wrote a poem in praise of his
product (see Lord Kinross, The Kindred Spirit), in part as
follows:

> ... Martial William drank
> Geneva, yet no age could ever boast
> A braver prince than he.   Within his breast
> Glowed every virtue!   Little sign,
> O genius of malt liquor!   That Geneva
> Debilitates the limbs and health impairs
> And mind enervates.   Men of learning famed
> And skill in medicine prescribed it then
> Frequent in recipe, nor did it want
> Success to recommend its virtues vast
> To late posterity.

In consequence, gin drinking became cheap, popular
and common in England.   It was gin on which customers of
a Southwark liquor shop could get drunk for a penny or dead
drunk for tuppence.   The addiction of Englishmen and wom-
en to this cheap beverage led to appalling drunkenness and
to many deaths.   Dram shops of the time and their horrors
were immortalized by Hogarth.   The sale of gin after a

time became rigidly controlled by Parliament but consumption was not reduced. *

The great gin-drinking period in England was between
1720 and 1750. The dire consequences of that change in the
habits of the poor have been immortalized in Hogarth's famous delineation of the horrors of "Gin Lane" contrasted with
the prosperous "Beer Street." In the third decade of the
century, the epoch of the Beggar's Opera, statesmen and
legislators had deliberately encouraged the consumption of
gin by throwing open the distilling trade and by placing on
spirits too light a tax. But as the appalling social consequences were gradually brought to their notice by the bur-
geoning philanthropy of the age, a series of hesitating steps
were taken to mitigate the evil. But it was not really
checked until 1751, when spirits were highly taxed and their
retail by distillers and shopkeepers was stopped. "The Act
of 1751," says an historian of 18th-century London, "really
did reduce the excesses of spirit-drinking. It was a turn-
ing-point in the social history of London." Even after that
date medical men still attributed an eighth of the deaths of
London adults to alcoholic excesses. In the country at large
its ravages had been severe, but ale had held its own better in the village than in the town. After 1750 the worst
was over, and after the middle years of the century tea became a formidable rival to alcohol with all classes, both
in the capital and in the country at large.

It is thought that the restrictive legislation had a salutary effect on the nation's health and morals. To some
extent this was of course true. But in the London Magazine
of 1736 there is this account:

> When the Bill against the spirituous liquors was past,
> the people at Norwich, Bristol and other places, as
> well as at London, made themselves merry on the
> death of madam gin, and some of both sexes got
> soundly drunk at her funeral, for which the mob made
> a formal procession, but committed no outrages.
> Riots were apprehended in the metropolis, so that 'a
> double guard for some days mounted at Kensington;

---

*An enterprising British Army officer got around the law by nailing the
sign of a cat to his ground floor window and installing a lead pipe under
it.   Passers-by were invited to put their money in the cat's mouth and to
murmur "Puss! give me 2d worth of gin." In a month, the gallant officer
cleared 220 pounds sterling.

the guard at St. James's and the Horse Guards at
Whitehall were reinforced, and a detachment of the
Life Guards and Horse Grenadiers paraded Covent
Garden, etc.' But there was no disturbance. To
evade the Act the brandy shops in High Holborn, St.
Giles, Tothill Street, Rosemary Lane, Shore Ditch,
the Mint, Kent Street, etc., sold drams under the
names of Sangree, Tow-row, Cuckold's Comfort,
Parliament Gin, Bob, Make Shift, the 1st Shift, the
Ladies Delight, the Balk, King Theodore of Corsica,
Cholic, and Grape Waters, etc..

In the 19th century, the squalid dram shops were replaced by resplendent "gin-palaces" which became neighborhood social centers. Temperance societies characterized
gin as the "skeleton spirit and demon of depravity" and urged
total abstinence. (Earlier a German temperance society
agreed that its members would not drink more than seven
glasses of alcoholic liquor at any one time, and that not of-
tener than twice a day.) The architectural heyday of the
pub came in the middle of the 19th century. As Alec Waugh
has remarked "The Victorian gin palace with its efflorescence
of applied ornament, its elaborate brass rails with their
triple gas burners, the decorated plate glass softening the
glare, the embossed wallpaper, the Corinthian capitals, the
rich mahogany, was for the slum-dwellers of the day what
the movie palaces were to be to a later generation."

Much of the credit for making gin respectable, it is
said, is given by gin distillers to officers of the Royal Navy.
While rum was ordinarily the drink of the ratings, gin has
reigned in the wardroom for 150 years. The prophecy of
Alexander Blunt that this colorless beverage would eventually become acceptable for "lady delicate and courtier grand"
seems to have come true.

When the modern era of the "cocktail" was ushered
in, gin became even more respectable, as a major ingredient of those drawing room convivial beverages. Endorsed
in former centuries by the British Army, elevated as an officers' drink by the Royal Navy, perhaps popularized by the
era of Prohibition in the United States, which made bootleg
or easily made "bathtub gin" an illegal adventure and a social sport, it finally came into high vogue in official and
diplomatic social life. Beverages of mixed components became more and more potent as the gin content strengthened.
And more and more, diplomats had to adjust themselves to

martinis or other cocktails before sitting down to an array
of selected wines. If rarely adding to the serious "hazards" of the diplomatic profession, the custom at least corrupted the palate and the connoisseur's taste for vintages
and champagnes.

Writes Robin McDouall:

> Wars make people drink, and those who survived the
> 1914-18 one emerged drinking not only more but new
> things and at new times. Though it was still not the
> custom to have drinks before luncheon at home, it
> was not exceptional to have a gin-and-bitters or a
> sherry and bitters in a club before luncheon--but
> probably before your guest arrived. Gin and sherry
> were gaining respectability. Gin, "mothers' ruin,"
> the charwoman's drink--"Don't 'ave any more, Mrs.
> Moore"--had, thanks to the Navy, become respect-
> able ["Convivial in Clubs," The Compleat Imbiber,
> Chapter iii, p. 33].

Speaking personally, I was first introduced to the
liquor of the juniper when I was a diplomat in Holland, especially after the head of the De Kuyper dynasty called on
me to induce in me an interest in his firm's famed products.
I tackled my Dutch gin, but never with thrilling relish. It
always seemed to me to have a "rotten-pear" flavor--prob-
ably the taste of the juniper. Then I encountered akvavit
(or aquavit) in Scandinavian countries--not dissimilar but
seemingly more potent and flavored with caraway seed. It
was a ritualistic business at table to down an akvavit, usually followed by a chaser of Danish or Swedish beer, with
pickings of salt fish, anchovies or herring. In company
one was not supposed to drink by himself: one had to catch
the eye of a neighbor and after saluting each other by a
look across the glass brim, to drink together. If it was a
lady one drank opposite, so much the better: "Drink to me
only with thine eyes ... "--she was probably thirsting to have
another sip, which she could not take alone. I did not mind
the aquavit appetizer so much; its caraway flavor was a
great improvement on the Dutch gin.

When I was suddenly dispatched, at 24 hours' notice,
from London to Greenland, I ordered to have shipped to me
by the next available ship from Canada, a supply of whiskey
and gin sufficient to serve my entertainment needs for the
whole forthcoming winter of closed navigation. The con-

signment, in due course, arrived; but the soda water and
ginger ale which were to accompany it failed to come, before the ice-barrier of late autumn closed off navigation and
supplies. I was thus left in the dilemma of having to accustom myself, and the local Danes whom I entertained in
return for their aquavit and beer parties throughout the
winter, to whiskey and water or gin and water--which sometimes took on the character of an anti-freeze mixture in the
long dark Arctic days and nights. The joke of it was that
this deprivation was all a misunderstanding. The soda had
been shipped: in the form of a syphon and a vast stock of
cartridges or sparklets. I had not been told of this substitution and never looked for them. They were packed in a
case containing stovepipes and plumbing fixtures for our
next spring's consular house that we were to construct. Because those building supplies arrived, by shipping error,
after the ground was frozen and snow was already on the
ground, they were left to lie under the snow, unopened, until the following spring, when we built our house. I little
guessed, all winter, that my soda supplies were lying there,
unlisted in the packing cases, almost outside my very door
throughout the whole long winter, while I was blaming my
government for a supposed omission of my supplies.

The geography of the Canadian Arctic owes some in-
debtedness to gin. One of the most famous distilleries of
England was Booth's; the greatest of the family was a certain Felix Booth, who after becoming enormously rich (at
his death at the age of 70 in 1850 he left £2 million),
turned philanthropist, and among other contributions, backed
the Ross Expedition in search of the North West Passage,
sponsored by William IV. The long-sought passage was not
discovered until Amundson's days, but Captain Ross mapped
an area of some half a million square miles, including a
vast peninsula 1300 square miles in size which, in honor of
his patron he called Boothia; he named Felix Harbour, on
Cape Felix, and paid a delicate compliment to Felix's sisters in Brown Island and Elizabeth Harbour. He also added
to the map Brentford Bay and North Hendon, commemorat-
ing the village of Hendon in Middlesex near which Sir Felix
Booth lived. In addition Ross named another vast Arctic island after his sovereign--King William's Land. But the
outstanding achievement of the Ross expedition, in terms of
scientific discovery, was that his nephew and second-in-
command, James Clark Ross, established the true position
of the North Magnetic Pole. Here, on the west shore of
the Boothia Peninsula, he planted the Union Jack, drinking

the healths first of King William and then of the gin tycoon
Felix Booth. When I was sipping my gin and water in my
outpost in Greenland, I little realized then that a large part
of the neighboring Canadian Arctic carried names commem-
orating the leading gin establishment of England! But, except for that period of Arctic sojourn, I never developed a
taste for gin, even when, in other posts, it was served
more graciously, well-disguised with fruits and vermouths
and other condiments to become strange "cocktails" of a
multitudinous variety.

VODKA

During the First World War, Russia, until the Bolshevik Revolution of 1917, was one of the Allied nations opposed
to the Kaiser's Germany. Naturally there was an exchange
of diplomatic intercourse, of which we have many interesting
memoirs. Vodka was the traditional lubricant. During the
second World War, Stalinist Russia was once more one of
the Allied nations, opposed to Hitler's Germany, and again
there was diplomatic intercourse. Vodka, as usual, was the
liquorous medium. For Westerners this powerful drink, although normal to Russians, was hazardous. Even brandy-
loving Winston Churchill in his encounters with Joseph Stalin,
had to prepare himself for the drinking bouts by a prior
dose of olive oil.

Vodka, the Russian form of gin, is made usually either from rye-malt or from potato starch. In A Dictionary
of Thoughts, Dagobert D. Runes made the caustic remark
that "Royalty used to carry a sceptre, now it sports a vodka bottle." But it is not apparent to what royalty he was
referring. Although it has become an ingredient, in place
of gin, in certain varieties of cocktails, its major use is
found in Russia, Poland and Finland as the national beverage. And it is in those countries that foreign diplomats,
on the principle that "while in Rome, do as the Romans,"
have to accustom themselves to the vodka habit. I myself,
during nearly four years' official residence in Poland, ac-
commodated myself to this national custom; and learned
partially to enjoy the quick downing of thimble size cups of
vodka together with canapés of herring, eel, or other salted
delicacies. A swift swallow of vodka--or aquavit or slivo-
vitz--leaves no time for the tastebuds to experience the
taste; the enjoyment, after the quick burning descent down
the throat, is in the "delayed reaction," the reflex response
of the taste and aroma as it recoils to the sensitive palate.

Because vodka is a clear, colorless liquid, it is easily mistaken for water; and thereby hangs many an anecdote of experience. Leigh Hunt, writing on "Coaches" in The Indicator (August 23 and 30, 1820) comments:

> We remember in our boyhood an edifying comment on the proverb of 'all is not gold that glistens'.... It was a severe winter; and we were out on a holiday, thinking perhaps of the gallant hardships to which the ancient soldiers used to accompany themselves, when we suddenly beheld a group of hackney-coachmen, not, as Spenser says of his witch, 'Busy, as seemed, about some wicked gin,' but pledging each other in what appeared to us to be little glasses of cold water. That temperance! thought we. What extraordinary and noble content! ... There are a set of poor Englishmen, of the homeliest order, in the very depth of winter, quenching their patient and honorable thirst with modicums of cold water! ... We know not how long we remained in this error, but the first time we recognized the white devil for what it was--the first time we saw through the crystal purity of its appearance--was a great blow to us....

The Duke of Edinburgh, then in command of the Mediterranean squadron, came to Rome to pay his respects to the King in 1888. Vincent (later Sir Vincent) Corbett was at that time a secretary in the British Embassy. He records in his memoirs that one day at luncheon the conversation turned on the extravagant hospitality one met with on Russian ships. He said that he tried to avoid it as much as possible as he could never get off them sober. The Duke of Edinburgh replied: "I can give you a recipe for that. Whenever I am invited to dine on a Russian ship, I always take the precaution of drinking half a liqueur glass of salad oil just before I start; I can then drink brandy to their claret and drink them all under the table; the oil prevents any fumes rising to the brain so that I remain perfectly sober; of course I take a strong purge directly I get home" [Reminiscences Autobiographical and Diplomatic, p. 133].

Of course this is a time-honored practice among Western diplomats confronted with the need to down vodka with their Russian colleagues. It was perhaps this sort of entertainment that led the Italian Minister Daniele Vare to declare that diplomacy consists of "protocol and purgatives." These preventatives were anticipated nearly four hundred

years ago by Sir Hugh Plat, who wrote: "Drinke first a
good large draught of Sallet Oil, for that will floate upon the
wine which you shall drinke, and suppresse the spirites
from ascending into the braine. Also what quantitie soeuer
of newe milke you drinke first you may well drinke thrise
as much wine after, without daunger of being drunke. But
howe sicke you shall bee with this preuention, I will not
heere determine, neither woulde I haue set downe this experiment, but openly for the helpe of such modest drinkers
as sometimes [find themselves with] quaffing companions
they would be loth to offend..." [The Jewell House of Art
and Nature (1954)].

        Mr. Eric Cleugh, later British Ambassador to Pana-
ma, was consul-general in Poland in 1945. In his memoirs
he refers to the Russian, and incidentally, the Polish addiction to vodka. Although he decried its over-use at receptions, he added that in reasonable quantities,

> vodka has great merit. At one official review which
> necessitated standing still for some time in the open
> I was pressed to drink an alarming quantity of vodka
> beforehand, but it did indeed prevent me from feel-
> ing the penetrating cold, besides mitigating boredom.
> If the Scots hadn't invented whiskey they would cer-
> tainly have done well with vodka. I don't think either
> race capable of inventing Coca-Cola. Vodka, how-
> ever, like Swedish aquavit and Mexican tequila, is
> an acquired taste and we generally preferred Scotch
> whiskey to dissipate gloom and warm our bodies
> [Without Let or Hindrance, p. 158].

        C. W. Thayer relates in Bears in the Caviar (p. 23)
how at the end of the war, he accompanied General Clark
and American staff to visit Marshal Konev at his headquarters at Baden, Austria. After the serious prupoaes of the
meeting were over, Clark and Thayer and the others sat
down to a full banquet. All the soldiers were still celebrating the German surrender with great quantities of liquor and
General Clark, although not willing to drink so much himself, nevertheless wished to appear to be so as not to dis-
turb the mood of the banquet. Thayer says it was given to
him to insure that the General's vodka glass was filled with
water at all times, and since he felt he was "not particularly light with [his] fingers," the only way he could do this
was to drink his glass of vodka the moment it was poured,
refill it with water, substitute this for Clark's glass (and

drink that down too), all the while evading some Soviet general's sharp eyes.   Thayer says "We can skip the details of what went on that night at Baden."

On one occasion, I recall while I was in Japan, the Soviet Ambassador, Mr. Trojanovski, gave a National Day Reception in his new embassy in Tokyo, on November 7th. As I entered, after due introduction, I was offered a glass of champagne, with which to toast the "glorious Bolshevik Revolution" of October 17 (by the new Russian calendar, November Seventh).   Then I was ushered into the salon having a resplendent buffet, with caviar ad libitum and other delicacies.   One after another, the Soviet secretaries greeted me, and invited me to join with them in a vodka "toast." After some five of these, I began to refrain, saying that I had to drive my car soberly back home.   They only laughed and said: "Never mind your car; we will see that it is delivered to your house.   Meanwhile, 'na zdrovie'!"   And so, after a couple of more hazardous ceremonial gulps of vodka, in respect to their National day, I went home on foot, and found my automobile stationed at my door.

I also remember once, at a Rumanian reception in Warsaw, standing beside the British Ambassador to Poland, Sir Donald Gainer, who mentioned to me his thirst.   He saw what seemed to be a normal water decanter in the center of the buffet-table and reached out and poured himself a tumbler full.   I quickly remarked that while the odds were that it was water, he had better make sure, before drinking, and suggested that he sniff, and carefully sip the beverage.   Sure enough, it proved to be a transparent but powerful vodka.   I thus saved him from a dangerous imbibation, for which he was duly grateful.

But then, at another such party, I myself had an impulse to taste some vodka.   With two English companions I explored the buffet bar, and seeing a vodka bottle and an array of small vodka glasses, we each poured out a shot. With great solemnity, we toasted one another and gulped it down.   It tasted funny, and a little gaseous.   I thought to myself perhaps this is a new and unfamiliar type of Slavic "sparkling vodka."   I was intrigued.   But finally I said: "Boys, I think we have made a mistake.   This is only soda-water," in which we proudly had been toasting one another! Soon we found identical bottles containing real vodka, and made amends.   But it is all a tricky business.   One does not always know what one is about to swallow.

Vodka has lately become a popular drink in the United States and Canada. But when I once asked if the government-controlled Liquor Commission of Ontario sold imported vodkas, I was informed that all vodka on their sales-list were Canadian-produced. 'What's the difference?" the salesman asked, "it's simply raw alcohol from potatoes; and foreign vodka is no different or better than that which we produce ourselves. We sell only homemade vodka. It's all the same."

Stalin's Russia followed the old habits; it was vodka-drinking. But Khrushchev's Russia has lately been trying to try "deterrent tactics." According to the English authority on modern Russia, Edward Crankshaw, Mr. Khrushchev, who used to be a fairly boisterous drinker himself, has become virtually teetotal and is doing his best to discourage heavy drinking generally. He is up against the powerful vested interests of the state drink monopoly. Further, he has to destroy the old Russian tradition that the main reason for drinking is to get drunk--a tradition until lately fortified, and in the provinces still fortified, by the drabness and emptiness of life under Soviet rule. He is said to have made some headway.

Oddly enough, while vodka is allegedly losing its respectability and becoming non-U in the better-class circles of Russia's "classless" society, it has recently been insidiously penetrating, against all former prejudice and contempt, into the cocktail-drinking circles of England and America. It is becoming fashionable in the West, as a martini ingredient substituting for gin, just as it is beginning to go out among the Soviet élite. (See Edward Crankshaw, "Drinking in Russia," The Compleat Imbiber (3) p. 130.) But whether this latter trend is true or not, it is almost certain that in all diplomatic receptions in Russia, the national drink, vodka, will be served with the hors d'oeuvres.

WHISKEY

Unlike so many other alcoholic drinks common in Elizabethan times, such as ale, port, sack, and other wines, it is odd that whiskey is given little notice. For example one searches far to find a reference to whiskey in Shakespeare's works. And yet Holinshed's Chronicles published in 1577, which was a source book for Shakespeare, gave this comprehensive depiction of the usquebaugh or whiskey of that day:

He distinguisheth three sorts thereof--Simplex, Composita, Perfectissima.... Beying moderatelie taken, saith he, it sloweth age, it strengtheneth youth, it quickeneth the spirites, it cureth the hysdropsie, it healeth the strangury, it pounceth the stone, it repelleth gravel, it puffeth away ventositie, it kepyth and preserveth the head from whirling--the guts from rumbling--the hands from shivering--the sinoews from shrinking--the veynes from crumpling--the bones from aking--the marrow from soaking-- ... and trulie it is a sovereign liquor if it be orderlie taken.

Joseph Scholnick ascribes the invention of whiskey to a certain simple physical phenomenon. This is the fact that the boiling point of water is 42 degrees higher than the $170°$ boiling point of alcohol. This difference is of great importance to civilization--often playing a part, says Scholnick, in maintaining mankind's sanity--for it means alcohol can be separated from water through distillation. And thus any number of alcoholic beverages can be concocted. "Just who discovered this great truth we will never know. The discovering of the elixir, however, is fittingly traced to the early Irish. Recognizing the value of the liquid, they named it, in Gaelic, Uisge Beathe (water of life). It is from the original Gaelic name that our word whiskey is derived" ["Gin by Juniper!" Argosy, Aug. 1960, p. 55]. But then it became the favorite drink of the Scots; and after a time became popularized abroad, was a major export, and soon found its imitations overseas in the rye whiskey drunk in Canada and the bourbon (corn) whiskey popular in the United States.

Although "whisky" and "whiskey" are used almost interchangeably in the ordinary way, trade usage in Britain favors "whisky" for Scotch and "whiskey" for Irish. In the U.S.A. "whiskey" is the commonest spelling for both; in Canada, on the other hand, it is generally known as "whisky."

Before we bring attention to whiskey as a diplomat's drink, we may cite some examples in which whiskey has played a role in general history. When the Act of Union brought Scotland within the jurisdictional orbit of England, the close commercial relations between Scotland and France were abridged, for the British protection of national interests, including distilleries, interfered with the trade of Scotch whiskey and French wines which had formerly been

carried on between the two independent countries.   The
Scottish Government was required to tax its exports of whiskey to Frence, while French wines were also under British
customs restrictions.   In this situation, following the Union,
Robert Burns, a former French supporter and Scottish patri-
ot, found himself paradoxically a government excise man,
whose business was to check the trade to Scottish whiskey
to France.   Although he hated the job, "hungry ruin had him
in the wind" and drove him to this employment under the
new English laws.   This was paradoxical for a man of his
taste for whiskey.   The lesser alternative was to be employed on a sugar and rum plantation in the West Indies.
He was glad to have escaped this, but he was not happy
with its substitute.   After all, he had formerly attached himself to one of the smuggler bands which had defied the customs laws.

        Whiskey played a minor role in the constitutional de-
velopment of the United States.   The common prejudice in
America against excise in any form was felt with especial
strength in Western Pennsylvania, Virginia and North Caro-
lina, where many small whiskey stills existed and protests
were made.   Among the many Scots-Irish settlers, they had
brought with them the habit of making whiskey out of grain,
and by 1791 their stills on every farm furnished so much of
the liquor that it superseded the New England rum, which in
colonial times was the chief tipple throughout the colonies.
An attempt to enforce the law led to stormy scenes and ri-
otous violence, the Federal revenue officers in some cases
being tarred and feathered.   In September 1794, President
Washington, using the new powers bestowed by Congress in
May 1792, despatched a considerable force, an unnecessary
15,000, of militia against rebellious Pennsylvanians, who
thereupon submitted without bloodshed.   In America the so-
called "rebellion" or "whiskey-war" is important chiefly because of the emphasis it gave to the employment by the federal executive of the new powers bestowed by Congress for
interfering to enforce federal laws within the states.

        On November 18, 1921, in an address to the Canadi-
an Club of Toronto, Admiral Earl Beatty jocularly told that
he had heard that the Canadian-United States boundary had
been determined, in part at least, by means of a case of
whiskey.   "... [They had arrived at deciding the frontier
line between the two countries, and after much talking and
a great deal of consideration they went away without deciding anything at all.   Those who were responsible sent other

commissioners back to meet, and they met, armed with a
brass-band and a case of whiskey.   The brass band could
play only two tunes.   One was 'God Save the King.'   The
other was 'Pop Goes the Weasel.'   The relationships between them were so good, and such an understanding created, that when the case of whiskey was finished they did
not know whether the band was playing 'God Save the Weasel' or 'Pop Goes the King'." *   As a result of this convivial
confraternity of boundary commissioners, diplomatic negotiations apparently were easily resolved!   Whiskey proved a
most excellent solvent.

Prohibition in the United States resulted in enormous
smuggling operations, largely from Canada, which brought
many problems to foreign ministries, diplomats and international lawyers.   Whiskey was no less a contraband and
smuggled commodity than rum in olden days, or gin.   The
Department of Internal Revenue, aided by its auxiliary agency the U.S. Coast Guard, was kept busy in preventive operations, and in a constant and militant battle with the power-
fully organized "bootleggers."   Numerous unfortunate "incidents" occurred.   In one, a bootlegger had his house constructed bridging the Canada-U.S. border, so that in one
room he was in U.S. territory and in another room he was
in Canadian territory; the borderline bisected his garden.
In an excess of zeal, two American revenue officers chased
him; he fled through his Canadian room into his garden, followed hot-at-heel by the officers.   In a final scuffle in his
garden, he was shot and killed.   His widow took steps for
a claim, based on violation of Canadian territory.   As she
was the only witness, the investigating authorities had to
reconstruct the case; and with surveyors, delineate the invisible international boundary running through the garden.
Finding that the scuffle and fatal attack had taken place on
the Canadian side of the line by excited American officers,
the Canadian government, while reprehending the Canadian
bootlegger, had to lay a claim against the U.S. government
for violation of territory by its agents; and the claim was,
with due apology, ultimately met.

---

*This would seem to be an elaboration or duplication of an old anonymous
limerick: There was an old person of Tring/ Who, when somebody asked
her to sing, / Replied "Ain't it odd?/ I can never tell 'God/ Save the
Weasel' from 'Pop goes the King'."

The I'm Alone case was another diplomatic problem, as well as a problem in international law. A master of a liquor-running ship, the I'm Alone, had been intercepted by a U.S. Coast Guard cutter. As it fled, another faster U.S. cutter pursued it, allegedly just inside the U.S. 12-mile limit, overtook it, and after firing warning signals to stop it, fired on the vessel, killing the captain and all but sinking the ship. In law, this involved the principle of "continuous hot pursuit," where one vessel of the chase passed on its pursuit to a faster vessel, and also the question of the "freedom of the seas" outside territorial waters. The news of this incident broke on the day I was leaving my post in Washington. I was paying my farewell call on the British Ambassador, Sir Esmé Howard, and showed him the morning's newspaper. After glancing at it, he said he hoped that the ship, or its captain, was Canadian; and then the British Embassy would not be involved and the case would be entirely Canadian. So it turned out. The Canadian government appointed a legal commission; it made a formal protest against the infraction of maritime international law; and made a claim for the killing, on the high seas, of a French-Canadian captain of a Canadian registered ship. After long legal process, the U.S. government admitted its responsibility and finally paid compensation to the Canadian Government.

The social historian must take note of a new trend in France, a revolution in French drinking habits. Not so many years ago, the standard beverage in a Parisian nightclub was champagne. The patron, as I so well remember, was expected to buy at least a half-bottle of it for himself, and a half-bottle for every member of his party. Now it is reported that in many nightclubs there is not a champagne bottle in sight. Some years ago, also, it was a rare host who in preparing for a cocktail party, laid in a supply of Scotch. Now it is usually the most asked-for beverage at such a party and a host would be very imprudent not to have it on hand. For example, at the fashionable parties that introduced the new French liner The France, Scotch was the drink most in demand. After wine, whiskey is becoming the most popular drink even in the Parisian home. The importation of Scotch whiskey into France increased, in sales, almost six-fold from the late Fifties to the early Sixties. No whiskey manufacturer can advertise his wares in France; and even the placing of a sign in a bar is illegal. Yet the popularity and consumption increase. How has this revolution occurred? Some contend that the basis of the change is rooted in the drinking of Scotch in French motion pictures and popular French romantic novels, not to speak of the American films and novels which more and more frequently include whiskey drinking.

Of course, at every celebration of "Burns Nicht"--commemorating the birthday of the great and beloved Scottish poet--two elements are always presented: the traditional haggis and plenty of "Scotch." Burns had a taste for the latter, though his weak stomach betrayed him and in the end caused his death by a drunken fall in the snow; but he panegyricized John Barleycorn. On at least two occasions, in places as far apart as Tokyo and Buenos Aires, as a Scottish descendant I have delivered addresses on this subject, and other diplomats of Scottish blood have done likewise, in fair sobriety, in eulogizing the attractions of this usquebaugh which was the life and death of the great poet, and the commemorative drink at every Burns Nicht celebration.

Both the English and the Scots are good canny businessmen. It was recently reported (May 1963) that a Chelsea liquor store, handling Scotch whiskey, posted a sign offering "Scottish Water" at one shilling a bottle "to go with your Scotch whiskey!"

In the 38-acre Ballantine distillery plant at Dumbarton, in 1959, two human watchmen needed help in patrolling the plant. A crusty autocratic gander and five female companions were enlisted, and proved so reliable that the staff was enlarged to its present size. Goose-stepping through the warehouses full of whiskey, a gaggle of fifty geese stand sentinel duty over 30 million gallons of spirits. Keener of ear and sharper of eye than any dog, and twice as quicktempered, geese have a long and distinguished history as guards. They once saved ancient Rome from the Gauls by awakening the capital's garrison with their cackles, and only a few years ago they were used as sentinels on lonely British outposts in Malaya. Because of these characteristics of alertness, they have been adopted in the Ballantine plant.

Tales referring to the personal use of whiskey are relatively few in the more personal annals and memoirs of diplomacy--possibly because as it is in recent times such a common beverage, it arouses no special comment. Nevertheless it has been the symbol of a form of diplomatic

entertaining which has its critics.   Diplomats in foreign
countries are expected to serve good whiskey, as they are
expected to serve good wine.   And as whiskey in any quantity costs money, even at distillery and duty-free prices,
senior diplomats usually enjoy a special entertainment allowance, over and above their salary, to cover such representational and entertainment expenses.   These allowances
provided by governments to their envoys ultimately are
paid for out of taxes; and in the United States at least, there
is a public jealousy of this diplomatic prerogative or per-
quisite.   Americans abroad in fact have long felt it their
right to stop by and be entertained by "their" embassy.
Says C. W. Thayer, "Not a few career diplomats, eyeing
their precious supply of whiskey, have listened tight-lipped
as American visitors demanded a double Scotch from the
butler, explaining loudly, 'What the hell, we taxpayers pay
for it!' "   [Diplomat, p. 222].

I recall that some of my Muslim Pakistani official
friends, who were Westernized to appreciate whiskey, used
to justify their apostasy by explaining that when the Prophet
forbade the drinking of liquor in the Koran, it was date-
wine to which he referred, and not whiskey, which at that
period was still unknown; and that consequently there was
no religious interdiction against Scotch whiskey.   One Pakistani diplomat whom I used to know had formerly been may-
or of Karachi and had signed various municipal regulations
controlling the serving of liquor in public bars and hotels.
Occasionally he would himself seek a drink in such a place
and would be refused by the bartender.   On protesting, the
bartender would show him the regulations and then point to
the authority, "under your official signature, Your Honor."
The disappointed mayor could make no reply and would
leave, his thirst unquenched.

On another occasion, a high Pakistani diplomat gave
a garden-party reception on his premises, the lawn of which
was exposed to the street.   When his diplomatic guests arrived, he would whisper in their ear: "You know I musn't
serve alcoholic drinks publicly; I have lemonade out here.
But if you want a whiskey, walk through the house to the
kitchen, where there is a full bar, and help yourself.
What you have in your glass as you emerge into the garden
will be indistinguishable from lemonade to any prying public
eyes."   The diplomatic guests' trail into the house and out
again, glass in hand, reminded me a little of a procession
of soldier-ants.

In Egypt too, another Muslim country, where I served as ambassador during the early Nasser regime, whiskey-drinking was not always eschewed by the military officers who formed the government.   Many of them, while observing other Muslim rituals, had acquired Western tastes, even as regards alcoholic beverages.   The ancient Arab taste for date-wine, proscribed by the Prophet among his Arabian herdsmen because of excess, dies hard, despite religious decree, and is transformed into a taste for the whiskey of the West.   President Nasser himself, however, was believed to be an abstemious ruler.   Among the Egyptian diplomats, when abroad, habits vary; but the old rule of "When in Rome do as the Romans" is not without observance.   As regards the less restricted foreign diplomats, Western tastes generally prevail.

Malaysia's "father," Prime Minister Abdul Rahman, the "Tunku" (prince), belongs to an abstemious nation; but he himself, educated at Cambridge, is not averse to brandy and soda or to wining and dining important political guests with whom he is negotiating.

I remember a diplomatic colleague in Cairo whom I sometimes called on in a morning hour, the papal nuncio. In offering me the usual hospitality of a beverage, he would suggest various items, but always included the option of a whiskey-and-soda, which I generally accepted.   I gained the impression that this, instead of port or sherry or vermouth, was what he himself liked most around the noon hour, when, as the old British saying was, "the sun is over the yard-arm" and it was permissible to broach the bottle or pour the decanter with the silver pendant, "whiskey."

No doubt many a diplomatic relationship has been smoothed by mutual conversations over a congenial glass of whiskey; and it is now becoming a popular alternative beverage served at diplomatic cocktail parties everywhere.

In former days it was the practice of a certain Canadian distillery company to send a complimentary case of its brand of whiskey to all Canadian Government Trade Commissioners abroad.   It was of course a common form of advertising, before the recent reaction against "payola" forms of commercial gifts.   When legations and embassies were created, not only the trade commissioners, but the ministers and ambassadors, were honored by this attention as a mark of goodwill.   Every Christmas a complimentary case of whiskey was shipped to them. When I was head of mission in Poland, such a gift was dispatched to me, there being no commercial secretary or trade commissioner on my staff. The Canadian vessel arrived at Gdynia, where the British vice-consul was also the local shipping agent, who had to check and certify the manifests. The captain of the vessel told him that, in his own custody and off the manifest, had been a case of Canadian whiskey addressed to the Canadian Head of Mission in Warsaw, but in passage this had been destroyed "owing to boisterous weather." In conveying this captain's report to me, the vice-consul inserted after "boisterous weather" a few exclamation points and question marks. The captain, however, had a conscience. He averred that having lost the consignment addressed to the Canadian acting minister, he was substituting, out of his own ship's stores, a case of a rival Canadian distillery company's whiskey, which I duly received. Reporting this episode as requested to the original sender, together with my appreciation and thanks for their intentions, I said that in any case I was none the worse off, as I had a case of the rival whiskey to help me through Christmas in the right spirit. This of course did not satisfy my original benefactors, who promptly shipped me another case of their own product, which duly arrived safely and I was consequently the beneficiary of two complimentary cases of Canadian whiskey instead of one.

I was somewhat astonished to learn, on my recent return to Canada, that the good old custom of presenting one or more bottles of wines or spirits to friends at Christmas time or on another special anniversaries is strictly for bidden under Ontario's Liquor Laws! During the period of Ontario's restrictive blue laws--almost similar to the Prohibition days in the United States--residents of Ottawa could drive across any one of the three interprovincial bridges to the town of Hull, in Quebec Province, and unrestrictedly purchase liquor, or have drinks late at night or on Sundays. Theoretically, if they brought back in their car some "Quebec" bottles of liquor they were violating Ontario liquor laws, and if discovered could be arrested, charged and fined. But this legal rule was more honored in the breach than in the observance. Even in the Province of Ontario, there was permitted a "local option," by which one town might permit spirituous beverage licenses and another town, more Puritan, might forbid them. This differentiation was perhaps a compromise arrangement by which the provincial Government of Ontario left decisions to municipalities,

which were influenced by the rival pressures and lobbies of
the Temperance League and churches, and the brewer and
distillers and tavern- and hotel-owners' self-interests.

According to Mr. Watson Sellers, lately Auditor-
General of Canada, the introduction of prohibition in Ontario
in the 1920's was a factor in the increased use of unpopular
interdepartmental telephones in Ottawa. Mr. Sellers, who
was at that time private secretary to the finance minister,
recalls that

> one day in 1925 I wandered into Deputy Minister
> Saunders' room while he was on the phone. As usu-
> al, he was ruffled because he was somewhat hesitant
> in conversation, slow in decision making and disliked
> phone calls. As he hung up he ejaculated, 'damn
> Prohibition!' This puzzled me because his side of
> the conversation had given no indication of that being
> involved. Mr. Saunders led me to the window and
> pointed to the Bodega Hotel--since razed to make way
> for the War Memorial. 'In the old days every civil
> servant worth a damn, and some who weren't, made
> it a point to drop in at least once a day. Things
> could then be settled leisurely and face to face.
> Since Ontario has gone dry we have to use this
> thing!' ["Intimate Memories in the Government Serv-
> ice," Ottawa Journal, Sept. 10, 1960].

Ottawa and Hull are separated by a river and joined
by an Interprovincial Bridge and several other bridges. In
Ottawa, the Ontario Liquor Control Board sells domestic
wines and a few expensive imported wines, and nothing in
between. On the Quebec side, one can very cheaply buy,
through the Liquor Control Board stores, imported French
table wines which, although not luxury items, are very good.
Therefore there is a considerable "smuggling" trade going
on over the Ottawa-Hull bridges all the time. Fortunately
no one seems very interested in trying to stop it.

Another peculiarity of local law is that it is strictly
forbidden to carry liquor around in anything except the unopened bottle in which it is sold by the Liquor Control
Board of Ontario. If a travelling man likes to have a bottle handy--for protection against snake-bite for example--
the law says that he either has to finish protecting himself
in his hotel room before moving on to his next destination
--which is a fast way of becoming an alcoholic if you move

often enough--or else leave what's left behind. This is non-
sensical. Under Ontario's laws it is also illegal, except
under a hotel or club license, to sell or give a bottle of
liquor to any other person as a gift.

And what are we to say about old topers who, like
brandy-loving Sir Winston Churchill, have built a political
preëminence in spite of a heavy consumption of alcohol?
Canada's first and renowned Prime Mininster, Sir John A.
MacDonald, was a heavy whiskey drinker and yet he dominated Canadian politics for 18 years and died at the respectable age of 76. Sir William Muloch, another famous
Canadian cabinet minister, in his later years consumed a
quart of whiskey a day, and yet he lived in good health and
active mind until the age of 101.

There are other times when whiskey may be an official restorative. Sir Esmé Howard (Lord Howard of Penrith) describes the ordeal of the Coronation of King Edward
VII, in 1901, when he was in charge of arrangements for
the placing of the foreign diplomatic corps in Westminster
Abbey. The ceremony lasted all morning, from about 8
a. m. when the guests began arriving until noon.

> I had provided myself with some chocolate and bis-
> cuits, and a flask of brandy for any diplomatic lady
> who felt faint, but had fortunately no use for the lat-
> ter. At the end of the ceremony after midday, the
> old butler from Norfolk House, who had had a simi-
> lar kindly thought for his fellow-men, came up to me
> and in a conspirational whisper asked me if I would
> like a whiskey and soda. As I had been on my legs
> in my tight and heavy diplomatic uniform since six
> in the morning, I replied in a similar whisper that
> I would. So it came about that in the privacy of the
> empty space under the diplomatic stand in the north
> transept of an Abbey I refreshed myself with a whis-
> key and soda from Norfolk House, again thanking
> Providence that there were no Cecil minions about,
> for it might have been difficult for a papist to es-
> cape hanging, drawing and quartering for such an of-
> fence as that. [Theatre of Life, vol. I, p. 321].

RUM

Apart from use in punches, rum is mainly a drink
of the equatorial regions, and of the Caribbean. Any in-

viting travel literature offers illustrations of romantic
scenes of rum-drinking parties in the delectable semi-tropi-
cal islands and resorts.   And to many of such parties, tour-
ing statesmen, politicians and diplomats come, in their elegant white tuxedos, to sip the mint juleps and other so-
called "native" drinks made primarily from rum.   Even in
the temperate zones, the modern pseudo-Polynesian and
"South Pacific" and "Hawaiian" restaurants and nightclubs
(generally owned by Chinese) promote rum drinks as their
stock-in-trade.   But rum, while it has its important history,
is not generally a diplomats' drink except in the West Indies.

During the earlier part of the 19th century, rum,
alone or with hot water, sometimes flavored with pineapple,
was drunk by almost everybody in England.   Rum seems to
have been the favorite drink of Cuilp, that mighty drinker,
and of Mr. Stiggins, described in the Pickwick Papers.
"Shrub," a mixture of rum, fruit juice and sugar, had been
popular from the middle of the 18th century.

A curious story is told by Jermann about the imperial kitchen at St. Petersburg in the days of Czar Paul.   The
empress was given to inspect the "domestic accounts" and
she was puzzled by finding among them "a bottle of rum"
daily charged to the Naslednik, or heir apparent!   Her imperial Majesty turned over the old "expenses" of the household, to discover at what period her son had commenced
this reprobate course of daily rum-drinking, and found, if
not to her horror, at least to the increase of her perplexity,
that it dated from the very day of his birth.   The "bottle of
rum" began with the baby, accompanied the boy, and continued to be charged to the man.   He was charged of drinking upwards of thirty dozen of fine old Jamaica yearly!   The
imperial mother was anxious to discover if any other of the
Czarevitch babies had exhibited the same alcoholic precocity;
and it appears that they were all alike; daily, for upwards
of a century back, they stood credited in the household
books for that terrible "bottle of rum."   The empress continued her researches with the zeal of an antiquary, and her
labors were not unrewarded.   She at last reached the original entry.   Like all succeeding ones, it was to the effect
of "a bottle of rum for the Naslednik"; but a sort of editorial note on the margin of the same page intimated the where-
fore: "On account of violent toothache, a teaspoonful with
sugar to be given, by order of the physician of the Imperial
Court."   The teaspoonful for one day had been charged as
a bottle, and the entry once made, it was kept on the books

to the profit of the unrighteous steward, until discovery
checked the fraud.   (See Doran, "Their Majesties at Meat,"
Table Traits.)

Until about a generation ago, rum was considered to
be a rather "low" drink (from the social point of view) and
its consumption was chiefly confined to sailors.   When cocktails became popular, however, in the 1920's, it became a
popular ingredient of mixed drinks, and nowadays, encouraged by the efforts of West Indian shippers, it is drunk
with soda water, lemon or other fruit juice, milk, Coca
Cola, or bitters, as well as in cocktails.   It has always
been one of the ingredients of punch.

Rum is said to be a corruption of the Malay "brum"
or "bram."   (The other connotation of the adjective "rum,"
i.e., "odd" ("he's a rum 'un")--is from a Gypsy word
"rom," meaning a Gypsy man.)   How the Malay noun came
to the West Indies or into English is not clear.   Rum, being made from fermented sugarcane, is mainly a product of
such cane-growing countries as the West Indian islands, and
the southern United States.   In Alice's Wonderland, the Dor-
mouse told of three little sisters who lived in the bottom of
a well--a "treacle-well," to which Alice angrily replied
"There's no such thing!"   Nevertheless, although no one has
known a treacle-well, treacle is very largely the basis of
rum.

The most popular rum today is Jamaican; but actually it is said that if you want rum as delicate and light as
whiskey, not the dark Demerara from British Guiana, you
ask for Trinidad rum.   But the one for connoisseurs, it is
said, is from Barbados.   Although I have visited Trinidad
and Barbados, I had no opportunity of seeing the processes
of rum manufacture, which evidently is an odoriferous one
--so much so that the Jamaican Negroes could not tolerate
it and so East Indians were imported.   Perhaps it was they
who brought the word "rum."

Whether as a legitimate article of trade, or an illicit
article of smuggling, rum was inevitably associated with the
West Indies, and the slave-operated sugar plantations there.
Lord Frederic Hamilton mentions that there is a curious un-
inhabited rock lying amongst the Virgin Islands.   It is quite
square and box-like in shape, and is known as "The Dead
Man's Chest."   "Before seeing it," he writes, "I had always thought that the eternal chant of the old pirate at the

Admiral Benbow, in Treasure Island:--'Fifteen men on the
Dead Man's Chest, / Yo-ho-ho, and a bottle of rum!'--re-
ferred literally to a seaman's chest though reflection might
have shown that one chest would afford rather scanty seat-
ing-ground for fifteen men" [Here, There, and Everywhere].
But it turns out that this was a reference to a spot at one
of the rum-producing West Indian islands.   The old buccaneer Sir Henry Morgan came hither, and his shipmates took
to the native drink, as John Masefield has commented
("Captain Stratton's Fancy"):

> Oh some are fond of red wine, and some are fond
>   of white.
> And some are all for dancing by the pale moonlight;
> But rum alone's the tipple, and the heart's delight
> Of the old bold mate of Henry Morgan.

Captain Henry Morgan (1635?-1688), it may be mentioned, was a reprobate and scoundrel, a British buccaneer,
who led the Barbados pirates about 1666, but strangely
enough was later given British authority for his exploits.
He was knighted as a hero in 1674, and was made Lieutenant Governor of Jamaica.

In olden times, rum shipments were frequently exposed to piracy.   Moreover, because of customs duties levied on imported rum in the British Isles, smuggling developed its own lurid history.   It was smuggled ashore in kegs
from small boats by bearded rascals, at dead of night, as
in the smugglers' scene in Carmen.   Robbie Burns, the
later excise man, in his youth lived among such smugglers.
In one of his letters the poet wrote: "I spent my nineteenth
summer on a smuggling coast....   The contraband trade
was at that time very successful, and it sometimes happened to me to fall in with those who carried it on.   Scenes
of swaggering riot and roaring dissipation were till this
time new to me; but I was no enemy to social life.   Here,
I learnt to fill my glass, and to mix without fear in a
drunken squabble."

Burns' great "flight that failed" to the West Indies,
around 1786, gave us instead the wonderful poems and immortal memory of the greatest Scottish poet.   In those days
the West Indies were Britain's most intriguing colony.   It
was a colony of black slaves who worked to produce wealth
and fortune for the sugar traders and the rum makers.   The
managers of the plantations were in a great majority of

cases Scotsmen of Burns' own rank and condition. He had
heard of their life, their success, their independence, from
letters coming home. At various times in his earlier years,
long before his poetry was known, through the mediation of
his acquaintances in the seaport of Irvine he had applied for
and nearly obtained appointments to the West Indies. When
the father of Jean Armour, his primary love, whom he had
made pregnant, rejected the document of his irregular marriage to Jean, Burns proposed to go immediately to Jamaica
to seek better fortunes. He made various efforts to buy his
passage but, being short of a payment of the small sum of
nine pounds, he decided to indent himself as a seaman before the mast. But then, when "hungry ruin had him in the
wind" he decided to capitalize on the only asset he had.
This was the loose collection of his locally popular rhymes.
From the six hundred copies which he "threw off," he
gained nearly twenty pounds. He "woke to find himself famous," like Byron; and he was invited to Edinburgh. His
ship sailed without him; Jamaica never saw him; his was a
narrow escape from an obscure life in exile and death "from
fever and exhaustion" in the West Indian rum-islands.

Rum has some macabre associations. Nelson's flag-
ship, the Victory, after the battle of Trafalgar, was towed
into Gibraltar for a refit, with the admiral's body still
aboard, in a cask of rum. The Royal Navy's nickname for
rum, "Nelson's Blood," traces back to the sentry found
drunk while guarding the depleted cask.

After the defeat of the Spanish Armada, the West Indies became England's treasure house of rum. Pepys, in
his diary from 1660 to 1669, names 300 establishments in
London where it was possible to get a noggin.

The "red authority of rum" flourished in America for
two centuries. George Washington, himself a port and Madeira man, kept "one Barrel of Best Rum; one ditto of Lymes
if good" behind the stairs at Mount Vernon. In the New
England states rum was the popular drink.

Indeed, rum used to be made in some parts of the
United States, either from local sugarcane grown in the
South, or from imported molasses. The New England rum
industry dates back to the early 18th century. In those
days, New England made rum from molasses shipped from
the West Indies, which were supplied with slaves brought
from Africa. The ships of Boston that carried the slaves

took the rum east-bound to European and African customers, thus completing the "New England Triangle." When, later in the century, the British Crown imposed taxes on molasses shipped north, the indignation of the colonies was extreme, and economists are inclined to rank it among the principal causes of the unrest which led to the "Boston Tea Party" of 1773 and consequently to the secession of the colonies from the British Crown. Production of New England rum has declined however, since the repeal of Prohibition in 1933, although its popularity as an imported drink is on the rise.

The late John P. Marquand, in his last book, retells the story of Timothy Dexter, who lived in Newburyport, Massachusetts, in the 18th century. Starting as a tanner, he made a fortune by sending, as legend has it, a cargo of warming pans to the West Indies, where by dumb luck they brought high prices as sugar ladles. Thus New England gave to the Caribbean islands some products in exchange for the molasses imported; each contributed to the manufacture of rum.

According to one recent commentator, "the most intemperate period in American history began in the decade before the Revolution and lasted for some 80 or 90 years. In most communities "the good creature of God," as liquor was called in some colonial laws, not only was considered as salutary as vitamins are today but rated every bit as much of a necessity as bread. Rum was the popular drink, and men, women, and growing children took a dram every few hours if they could afford it. Even babies were quieted with doses of rum, often laced with opium, and the occasional teetotaler was considered a crackpot. Workmen usually received part of their wages in rum or some other potent liquor, and work agreements with their employers stipulated that they would be given a certain number of days off "to get drunk." No farmer could expect to keep hired hands unless he dispensed liberal tots of rum at regular intervals. Offices and business establishments set the precedent for today's coffee-break by closing down each morning at 11 o'clock so employers could relax over a drink, commonly called " 'leven o'clock bitters." Nobody seems to have drunk more during this period than clergymen. The ministry was regarded as a hard-drinking calling, about like the newspaper or advertising business today. Few Americans seem to be aware that their ancestors were such rumpots." (See Joe David Brown, "A Kind Word for Drink," Sat. Eve. Post, May 25, 1963, p. 64.)

After slave trading in Africa came to a halt in 1808, the rum industry in America began to decline. Rum of course was not a native drink, since its raw material had to be imported; and whiskey, made from rye or corn, both abundant homegrown crops, gradually became the national drink. By 1850 rum was literally scorned. On temperance platforms, it was Demon Rum, the Devil's Lubricant. It was not until the early 1940's that the demonic imputation in its name was no longer heeded. It began to climb back into favor, with "Rum and Coca-Cola" belted out in a calypso beat by the Andrews sisters. The lyrics alluded to the rum of Trinidad first; then the islands of the Antilles got into the act with the Cuba Libre, and rum was well on its way. Also, rum has become detached from strict identification with the Caribbean; vast amounts of it are consumed in "Polynesian" drinks served in the rapidly proliferating South Seas-type restaurants in atmospheres of bamboo and palm fronds.

Rum became a standard drink in the Royal Navy. In 1740 Admiral Edward Vernon was West Indies naval commander-in-chief.

> He was known as 'Old Grog' from his habit of always having his breeches and linings of his boat-cloaks made of grogram, a species of coarse white poplin (from the French gros grain). It occurred to 'Old Grog' that, in view of the ravages of yellow fever amongst the men of the Fleet, it would be advisable, in the burning climate of the West Indies, to dilute the bluejackets' rations of rum with water before serving them out. This was accordingly done, to the immense dissatisfaction of the men. They at once christened the mixture 'grog'... [The Days Before Yesterday].

"Splicing the mainbrace" was a naval term for issuing an extra ration of rum on some special occasion.

Although still more or less a standard Navy issue in British ships, I do not recall ever having rum when I was young Royal Navy officer on H.M.S. Riviera in the Mediterranean during the First World War. But when we were on Army active service in Italy, the officers and men received a daily ration of a mug of rum. At first I usually by-passed this rum issue parade, but finally learned to take my issue and pass it on to one of my mates. I was an-

noyed when on one occasion the service mess decided to
dump the whole unit's rum issue into the cauldron of the
regular tea-issue. For rum drinkers, the tea spoiled the
rum; for me the rum spoiled my enjoyment of tea.

My own most-remembered contact with rum was when
I was consul in Greenland. My colleague and vice-consul,
Danish-born but an old Arctic hand, was as familiar with
rum as with his native aquavit. When he joined me in that
Arctic outpost, he brought with him a private keg of Jamaican Navy Rum, pure and undiluted and of highest "ester."
He intended to, and later succeeded in rebottling it, diluted
to a normal 80 proof, for ordinary consumption. But before this had been achieved, we took a boat cruise of several days down the coast through the chilling ice floes. The
hard-bitten, hard-drinking skipper would come down from
the deck every once in a while to warm himself in the
cramped cabin and would pour out for himself and his two
passengers a drink of aquavit or brandy. As Robert Service somewhere remarked, the men of the Northland and
Arctic are of heroic mold, and can drink with the best; and
this was true of my Danish Arctic-trained friend and of the
hardy skipper of our motor launch. He regarded himself
as a well-seasoned drinker. But then my very quiet and
reserved colleague, by way of reciprocity, asked him if he
had ever tasted Jamaica navy rum; he had a little supply
with him. He produced it, and refilled the glasses, but
with a warning wink toward me. It was still undiluted, 140
proof--pure and potent spirits--the kind that one could ig-
nite and watch burning with a pretty blue flame. Our skipper tossed it off in a single gulp; but then began gasping for
air, as though a firebrand had seared and burned his throat,
esophagus, and all his inner tubes. He wondered what had
hit him. Well forewarned, I had cautiously sipped my
share: it was like a flame.

My Danish colleague told me of a well-known incident
of a new superintendent or inspector of the Arctic, an Ottawa civil servant, who was dispatched to a very rough frontier outpost. Although unused to such pioneer conditions,
he determined to show himself as a real "he-man" who
could "take it." On his arrival at the camp, he found that
a welcome had been arranged, which of course included a
rather heavy drinking reception. After his arrival, the lo-
cals gave him a very large brandy-glass, with which he was
completely unfamiliar. As the guest of honor, he was the
first to be served. His rough hosts set out to offer him

the first fill; and he had no precedent to observe.   It was
a large glass.   His host poured a small portion, and asked
him to say "when."   In misplaced bravado, he said "go on:
fill it up!"   So, they filled his huge glass--thinking to themselves: "My God, what a man!   He can drink all that!"
Then they poured their own flasks, somewhat more moder-
ately.   The toast was proclaimed in his welcome: everybody drank.   The inspector, trying to live up to expecta-
tions of the frontiersmen, bravely drank down his oversized
share.   But in his complete ignorance, he had misunder-
stood and mis-estimated.   Five minutes passed, with great
éclat and the admiration of his rough pioneer hosts.   Suddenly he turned a sickly green, and passed out completely
with a great thud to the floor.

It cannot be said that rum is generally a diplomats'
drink, except perhaps among those who are stationed in the
West Indies where it is the national beverage.   But as an
ingredient of punches and cocktails, it has gained some social respectability and is frequently used also in high cuisine in various dishes.

BEER

Since beer is not of the grape it is not, generally
speaking, a diplomatic drink.   Hops or barley malt have less
prestige than the time-honored Dionysian and Bacchic grape;
and ales and beers do not enjoy the vintage or the devotion
of connoisseurs, that wines enjoy.   Nevertheless, the making and drinking of beer or ale has the prestige of a much
older history and even in modern times the froth-topped
tankard and ale glass have sometimes been an accessory to
diplomacy.

Brewing seems to have started in ancient Mesopotamia, some 6000 years ago.   Probing in the ruins of Nine-
vah, an archaeologist discovered a tablet alleged to be from
Noah's Ark which listed beer among the provisions.   But
since it is also claimed that when Noah left the Ark, he
promptly planted a vineyard for the production of wine, both
stories may be legendary.   It is documented that beer in
some form was known to the Sumerian, Chaldean and Phar-
aonic Egyptian peoples.   Some archaeologists have claimed
that beer may have been invented before bread.   It is probably the closest thing to a truly universal beverage, historically speaking.   The Chinese loved beer.   So did the Babylonians, Egyptians, Greeks, Romans, and Anglo-Saxons.   It

was considered an improvement on water in olden times and
was consumed like water.   Moreover, beer had a solid religious background.   In Egypt for example, beer had its own
goddesses, temples, and use for sacrifices.   Rameses III
once parted with 25,000 gallons of his choicest brew to placate some angry gods.   The god Osiris was credited with
the introduction of beer into Egypt; Diodorus says that if
Osiris "found any territory unsuitable for the vine, he
caused the people to make beer, a drink composed of barley and water, not much inferior in taste, savor and
strength to wine."   In the middle ages, too, every monastery had its own brew-house; monks were selected as brewers.   Once, when I was visiting a Canadian Catholic monastery in the heart of Japan, I was well, though frugally
entertained to a meal.   One of the Fathers was introduced
to me as the teacher of chemistry in the Church school.
He proudly produced for the guests some home brew, which
even the visiting Bishop partook of.   In many monasteries,
ale is a favored beverage, even today.

It was King Wenceslaus (1361-1419) who first granted
the people of Pilsen, in Bohemia or present Czechoslovakia,
the right to brew beer; the remark has been made that it
was after this that he was known as "good King Wenceslaus."   Ever since then, Pilsner beer (the true variety)
has been renowned.

When Columbus arrived in the Americas, he found
that the Indians knew how to ferment grain and make beer.
(It was only after the civilized white men settled in America, conquered and confined the surviving Indians to reser-
vations, that, while the whites might drink all the spirits
and beers they wished, the Indians were restricted.   Recently this discrimination between white citizens' privileges,
and Eskimo and Indian citizens' privileges, has been very
earnestly debated in Canada.)   Back in the 15th century the
Journal of Elizabeth Woodville, afterwards the Queen of Edward IV, contained the following entry: '10 May, 1451.
Six o'clock (a.m.) breakfasted.   The buttock of beef rather
too much boiled and the ale a little the stalest.   Memoran-
dum: to tell the cook about the first fault, and to mend
the second myself, by tapping a fresh barrel directly."   If
a queen quaffed beer or ale in those times, and even decided to tap the barrels herself, it was evidently a royal
drink.   No doubt the Norsemen drank it regularly, as the
Danes do today, and the Danish King Canute may have encouraged its use in his court during his reign in England.

I found in an old book in my father's library the story
of bottled ale. Beer and ale had of course been drunk from
time immemorial.   Here it is said that Nowell, Dean of St.
Paul's, London, for 42 years--who lived from 1507 to 1602--
grew strong by drinking ale; and that he was the accidental
inventor of bottled ale.   He was out fishing with a bottle of
the freshly-drawn beverage at his side when intelligence
reached him of peril to himself under Queen Mary.   After
flinging away his rod and thrusting his bottle of ale under
the grass, he fled.   When he could again safely resort to
the same spot, he looked for his bottle, which on being disturbed, drove out the cork like a pellet from a gun, and
contained so creamy a fluid that Nowell took care to be well
provided with the same thereafter.   Dean Nowell was the
first church dignitary who laid the foundation of the red
noses by bringing bottled ale to the notice of the clergy.
(See Doran, Table Traits, p. 12.)

From before the beginning of the 18th century, the
age of Queen Anne, ale had been the countryman's drink all
over Britain.   Except in the cider counties of the West, ale
had been almost unchallenged in former centuries, until it
began to feel the rivalry of strong spirits, gin especially,
on the one hand, and of tea and coffee on the other.   It was
still the drink of ladies.   Children still drank very small
beer and it was in many cases better for them than the impure water which was too often the only alternative.   Beer
and ale were at that time still considered a drink of the
gentry as well, especially as served in tankards; and in
some countries and seasons it is still respectable.   In Holland and the Scandinavian countries, and in Germany, beer
with formal meals is acceptable.   In Germany the Bier-
halles and Bierstubes and in England the taverns and pubs
were popular social institutions; and to some extent remain
so today.

In the days of the Venetian Republic, Iago, while
calling for rousing ale--"And let me the canakin clink,
clink.   And let the canakin clink!"--said of his song: "I
learned it in England, where, indeed, they are most potent
in potting; your Dane, your German, and your swag-bellied
Hollander--drink, ho!--are nothing to your English" [Othello
II, ii, 65].   The abstemious Samuel Johnson wrote a ditty:

> Hermit hoar, in solemn call
> Wearing out life's evening grey;
> Strike thy bosom, Sage, and tell
> What is bliss, and which the way

Thus I spoke, and speaking, sigh'd,
    Scarce repress'd the starting tear,
When the hoary sage reply'd,
    'Come, my lord, and drink some beer!'

And earlier, Shakespeare, in The Winter's Tale, sang:

The white sheet bleaching on the edge--
With heigh, the sweet birds, O, how they sing!--
Doth set my pugging tooth on edge,
For a quart of ale is a dish for a king.

Beer has undergone only two major refinements in brewing since ancient times, both German discoveries. In the 14th century, they first added hops to help in fermentation. Then in the 19th century they mass-produced lager beer; it came into use because German monks found, long before refrigeration, that beer stored in cool mountain caves would keep during the hot months when brewing had to be suspended.

For people whose interest in beer goes deeper than the bottom of a glass, Munich has established a special beer museum. Bavarians, known for their love of the golden barley, malt and hops mixture, claim it is the only beer museum in the world. The museum traces the history of beer from its origin in ancient Babylon 3000 years ago to the industrially produced beverage of today. Among the oldest exhibits are clay jugs used by Babylonians and Egyptians to ferment bread with water in order to make beer. They drank this brew, not out of steins, but right from the jug through clay tubes. A sieve was inserted to keep one from sucking up the mash. Romans, as documents show, referred to their beer as barley wine. Exhibits from the early Germanic days illustrate how housewives used to make beer for their bearskin-clad husbands--sieving it from the suds of a grain-honey-water fermentation. Metal containers for cooking beer were first used in the ninth century. One such boiler, from an ancient monastery in St. Gallen, Switzerland, is among the museum's treasured possessions. Beer brewing became a fine art in the middle ages. The first beer brewers' guilds sprang up around 1200. Local town administrations, always eager to rake in extra revenues, introduced a beer tax in Munich around 1280. This, too, is documented in the museum. A beer-cooling device invented by Germany's Earl von Linde enabled brewers to make beer all year round from the middle of the 18th century. Before

then, beer brewing was restricted to the cooler months of
the year. (From the article "Munich Sets Up Beer Museum," Ottawa Journal, Aug. 17, 1962.)

The popularity of ale and beer in England among the
common people, mainly because it was cheap, finally led to
the conversion of posting-houses and inns into taverns,
which have in the past two or three centuries been an important feature in English social history. Indeed, as the
French Ambassador J. J. Jusserand indicated in his English
Wayfaring Life in the Middle Ages, many roadside inns at
that period were very largely ale-houses, where travellers
stopped in an atmosphere of conviviality and warmth. Chaucer's Pilgrims gathered in the famous Tabard Inn in Southwark in a convivial spirit. The old English inn was essentially an ale-house; and that it has remained, in spite of the
changes that have been forced upon English habits by the
caprices of their rulers' foreign policies. During the 14th
and 15th centuries England owned Aquitaine, and the noble
wines of Bordeaux flowed on English tables. Then there
was a change toward the sweet heavy fortified wines of
Spain and of Madeira, which proved an effective antidote to
the chill, damp climate. The age of port began when William of Orange's hatred of Louis XIV of France encouraged
him to place exorbitant taxes on French wines and spirits
and lower the tariff on wines from Portugal. But beer has
always been the national drink in England.

Down through the centuries the British inn or tavern
has had a great tradition of warmth and hospitality. Its
heyday was in the Coaching Era. All along the post roads,
picturesque taverns flourished. The custom of hanging out
a sign to call attention to an inn or tavern actually goes
back to the early Middle Ages when people could not read.
A hosier had a sign with a stocking; a tailor, a pair of
scissors; a pawnbroker or money lender, three balls. Inns
and taverns provided the same pictorial guidance. Sometimes their welcoming signs were in corrupt spelling: one,
intended to read "May God encompass thee" became known
as "Goat and Compass." Excitement rose to fever pitch at
the arrival of a coach, known as a "diligence" or "true
blue." At its arrival, courtyards rang with the stamp of
horses' hooves and the shouts "Tally-ho!" of the post-boys.
Dickens' works glow with the joy of tavern companionship.
His characters arrive, weary and miserable; put on slippers
provided by the management; and almost automatically the
tankard is before them. Drowsy from their travel, from

the fireside and their drink, they are soon snug, all woes
forgotten. English historical novels are replete with such
descriptions. In modern times, the old inns and taverns
still exist, but in place of coaches are the tourist buses and
the private cars. And yet the warmth and hospitality con-
tinue. I have made many tours through England, with stop-
overs at the local inns, and have found them essentially still
the old-style friendly ale-houses.

When we come later to describe the variety of nomenclature of cocktail concoctions, we may look back to the
similar situation in respect to beers and ales in mediaeval
times. Jusserand, in his English Wayfaring Life ... (p.
138), quotes a 1577 authority in these terms:

> ... [P]eople were kept merry with ales and beers of
> various flavour and strength known by as significant
> names as those of present day dances, fox-trot,
> mothers' rest, and others, which tomorrow will they,
> too, need interpretation:... 'Such headie ale and beere
> in most of them, as for the mightinesse thereof ...
> is commonlie called huffa cap, the mad dog, father
> whoresonne, angel's food, dragon's milke, go by the
> well, stride wide, and lift leg.... Neither did Rom-
> ulus and Remus sucke their shee wolfe (or sheep-
> heards wife) Lupa, with such eger and sharpe devo-
> tion, as these men hale at huf cap, till they be red
> as cockes and little wiser than thair combs.

The Stars and Stripes, the American Army journal,
although perhaps not the best medium for praising the English public houses, remarked:

> If the anthropologists ever get round to chalking up
> England's major contribution to Western civilization,
> the pub should be high on the list. The pub is the
> heartbeat of the people and although there are but
> three basic styles, the variations make it possible for
> every toper to find just the atmosphere he wants for
> happy guzzling. The three types are the city tavern,
> which features spirits and wines above draught beers,
> the gin palace, typically Victorian if authentic, and
> the no-nonsense alehouse, plain, ancient and histori-
> cally traditional. If you decide to brave the English
> beer, there are three types, mild ale, bitter beer,
> and Burton ("old").... Most Englishmen prefer a
> mixture, but Burton is available only from September

to June. If you insist on chilled beer instead of
room-temperature types, most pubs now offer a pass-
able lager that has at least occupied a cool spot in
the cellar [quoted in Ottawa Journal, March 8, 1960].

Beer and ale cannot be omitted from a commentary
on diplomatic potables; because they were at least favorite
German drinks, and it was in the Bierhalles that the Nazi
movement was generated and where Adolf Hitler made his
name and fame. Even before that, the Prussian elite,
brought up in the universities of Germany, were united and
inspired by their Stein songs and the patriotic gaiety characterized in The Student Prince; and from those Studenten-
korps came the leaders of Germany, for better or for
worse, as well as some of the poets and philosophers and
musicians. Who can deny that beer has a distinguished
role in history?

Regarding such beer halls, two episodes will forever
stand out in the history of Europe of this century. Both
events centered in the Bürgerbräukeller in Munich. The
first was in the year 1923 when the almost unknown upstart
and Brownshirt organizer, Adolf Hitler, appeared on the political scene. Some three thousand thirsty burghers, seated
at rough-hewn tables, quaffing their beer out of stone mugs
in the Bavarian fashion, were suddenly raided by S. A.
troops. Hitler pushed forward into the hall, and after
threats of violence and fury, and much excitement, made
the attempt to pull off a coup d'état by setting up a new Bavarian government under his direction. His famous "beer
hall putsch" did not succeed; he was slightly wounded in the
street fighting that ensued, was captured, and tried on February 26, 1924, sentenced to five years and imprisoned.
In that imprisonment in the fortress at Landsberg, he dictated Mein Kampf.

The second occasion was on November 8, 1939. It
was a reunion of the "Old Guard" party cronies at the Bürgerbräukeller in Munich in commemoration of the 1923
Putsch. Hitler had just finished making his annual speech,
a shorter one than usual, and he and all the important Nazi
leaders had hurriedly left the premises. Several minutes
afterwards, a bomb which had been planted in a pillar directly behind the speaker's platform, exploded, killing seven
persons and wounding 63 others. Had this plot succeeded,
or had Hitler not shortened his speech and departed when
he did, the strange Sitzkrieg or phony war might have col-

lapsed, and no invasion and occupation of the Netherlands, Belgium and France, or attempted invasion of Britain might have ensued.

At least in Germany, beer had an official prestige. The American Ambassador to Germany from 1933 to 1937, William E. Dodd, tells in his published diary of the many diplomatic and political receptions he attended, which had the name of Bierabends. At one, given by von Papen, hundreds of guests were present, a number of reels of film were shown, and a lot of Saar wine was given away, to stress the German claims to the Saar territory. But beer was never lacking at such Bierabends. At one of the huge receptions given by the German Foreign Minister von Ribbentrop and his wife, at which at least 700 people attended, "supper was served on a huge table literally loaded down with food, beer, wine and liquors of all kinds."

One of the oldest and most notable beer festivals is the Oktoberfest at Theresienwiese, near Munich, which has been held for over 150 years. The tradition began when King Ludwig I of Bavaria married Princess Therese of Saxe-Hildburghausen in October of 1810. Democratic couple that they were, Ludwig and Therese allowed the commoners to celebrate the occasion by a great frolic in a nearby Munich meadow; and this has now become traditional. Great decorated horses haul beer carts through the city of Munich to the festival grounds where there are many tents and many barrels of beer. The mayor taps the first--then all festivities begin. "About four million quarts of beer are consumed. Costumed paraders from Germany, Austria, Switzerland and France form pageants up to three miles in length. Brass bands rev up the merry-makers to dancing, marching and singing throughout the fairgrounds. Acrobats, magicians and stuntmen enliven the sideshows, and after a day of beer and carnival, the night is a ferriswheel of lights whether you're on one or not" [Holiday, Sept. 1962, p. 111]. All this is due to the marriage of King Ludwig I a century and a half ago.

Marquess Curzon, Viceroy of India, tells in Leaves from a Viceroy's Notebook (p. 347) this memory of his travels in the Pamirs in 1894:

> I had run out of liquor altogether, and sometimes felt the want of some stimulant in face of the cruel cold at night and in the early dawn, and of the

scorching sun at noontide.... As I rode down the
grassy slope, I saw coming towards me in the dis-
tance the figure of a solitary horseman. It was [my
friend's] native servant. At that moment I would
have given a kingdom, not for champagne or hock
and soda, or hot coffee, but for a glass of beer! He
approached and salaamed. I uttered but one word,
'Beer.' Without a moment's hesitation, he put his
hand in the fold of his tunic and drew therefrom a
bottle of Bass. Happy forethought! O Prince of
hosts! Most glorious moment! ... [I]n this belated
tribute have I not done something to remove the stig-
ma of another British poet, Calverley?

'O Beer, O Hodgson, Guinnes, Allsop, Bess!
Names that should be on every infant's tongue,
Shall days and months and years and centuries pass,
And still your merits be unrecked, unsung?'

It is difficult to accept the reports that the late leader
of the Congo, Mr. Lumumba, had formerly been a beer
salesman; for one does not normally credit the black Congo-
lese as being beer drinkers, or if they have acquired that
taste privately in their homes, of being brewers on a commercial scale. Yet, if the ancient Egyptians and other
North African had this historic usage, there is no reason
why the once primitive custom should not have reached West
Africa.

There are two "Royal and Ancients": the Royal and
Ancient game of golf, for which Aberdeen claims first credit; and the Royal and Ancient Order of Froth-Blowers.
Froth overflowing a tankard was apparently a measure of
the quality of the beer, although in inverse ratio; it usually
marked the incomplete liquid-content of the tankard or glass.
When the froth was blown off, the glass might then further
be filled to the brim. In some Bierhalles and taverns in
Germany, Bavaria, Austria and Switzerland, I found that it
is the custom to stick a strip of paper onto the side of the
glass, and for the waiter to mark on it each refill, until
the account is ready to be settled, and the marks are up
for the number of drinks. This is a practical and convenient sort of scoreboard.

The humorist and Member of Parliament, Sir A. P.
Herbert, gave a sardonic vindication of beer-drinking in his
lines:

As I was saying only yesterday, Mrs. Thomas,
It isn't any use to fight our fates.
Well, if it isn't gin
Was meant to do us in
The chances are its lemonade or dates.
You never saw such saints as my two brothers,
Yet both of them are dead and gone, my dear;
Teetot'lers seem to die the same as others,
So what's the use of knocking off the beer.

This was perhaps an echo of Thomas Cogan, in 1588, 'Drink wine and have the gout; drink none, and have the gout."

Le Soir, a Belgian newspaper, recently published these per capita, per annum figures of beer consumption (given in litres--a little more than a quart): Belgium 130, Luxembourg 115, Australia and New Zealand 103, West Germany 85, United Kingdom 79, Austria 70, Denmark 64, Canada 58, and the U.S.A. 57. Americans drink on the average of 85 million barrels of beer a year, a per capita figure of about 13.2 gallons (Belgium consumes 31 gallons for every man, woman and child); but it is said that 8 per cent of the adult population in the U.S. drink 60 per cent of all the beer consumed in the country. It has been argued that among American beer-drinkers there is a certain snobbery or "status-seeking," as shown in the habits of some for drinking imported instead of domestic beer. This group like to have Augustinerbrau, or Heineken's of Holland, Carlsberg of Denmark, San Miguel of the Philippines, Fix of Greece, or Asahi of Japan, Pilsner Urquell of Czechoslovakia, Personi of Italy, Molson's of Canada, Barboa of Panama, Zywiec of Poland, Kronenbourger of France, Ballarat of Australia, and Carta Blanca of Mexico. Some 150 breweries in about two dozen countries of Europe, Latin America and Asia are exporting barrelled beer to the United States.

It was while he was working on beers and malts that Louis Pasteur discovered the process of pasteurizing milk.

The Dominion Brewers Association in Canada, in a small booklet, has proposed that beer is a temperate beverage. Canada's first brewery was started by Jean Talon in 1668 to get the settlers in New France off the hard liquor, which they were consuming in embarrassing quantities. Beer is less strong, is easier to make, and is much cheaper to buy. But it seems that beer brewers in England and Canada pile up just as large fortunes as whiskey distillers.

But nowadays, outside Germany and the Scandinavian countries, beer is rarely a haut monde society beverage (except after a round of tennis or golf, or on hot days around a swimming pool) and does not often appear in diplomatic parties--perhaps because it is regarded, for its cheapness, as a poor man's drink, a commoners' or laborers' thirst-quencher.

My drinking beer with a Russian in a Korean seaport before breakfast on a Christmas morning was the result of a poorly-guessed identification. I had been travelling down the length of Korea from Moscow, through Siberia, Manchuria, Harbin and Mukden, to the southern port then known as Fusan. (During the Korean War its name was transformed to Pusan.) The train arrived at this terminal at 8 o'clock on Christmas morning. On the train, the day before, I had observed another passenger, dressed like a squire in tweeds and plus-fours and looking rather English, but I had not made acquaintance. As we both descended side by side to the station platform in the early dawn, I said to him "Good morning--and Happy Christmas." He looked at me, smiled and in a foreign English, returned the salutation. I then remarked that the ferry steamer to Japan did not sail until 9 a.m. and we had over an hour to wait; so I suggested a bite of breakfast. We found that the station and port café were not yet open, but that at an adjoining bar we could get a beer. So I suggested that we might break our fast with a drink; and in this way become acquainted. He was a retired Cossack general, a hero of the White war against the Bolshevists, and for the past ten years had been living in exile in Peking, where he had a camera business. The beers made him friendly and communicative, in a comprehensible half English; and I learned, then and later on the steamer in which we sailed together to Moji, much of his interesting career. He told me that as a Cossack cavalry officer, it was the custom to lead in front of his troops, not to remain in the rear; and that for every wound received in battle, there was a promotion in rank. Thus, as a valiant leader in every Cossack charge, in which he received many wounds, he rose quickly to the rank of general; but on the victory of the Bolshevists, his army career came to an end, and he left Siberia forever. He told me of his Chinese camera business, making imitation Kodaks at low prices; of his production of cinema films by a machine which he had invented that would slice 35 mm commercial film into 16 mm small-camera film, with adapted perforated margins; of his optical experiments with

camera lenses, which he had specially made for him in
Switzerland and Germany. He wished to get some patents
in the United States and to make a fortune. Unfortunately,
after Moji, I never heard of him again or his dreams of
success. But it proved a profitable and entertaining encounter which the Christmas beer at dawn brought me; and
there was something of the "Christmas Spirit" that one finds
in Pickwick.

I think I was first inducted into beer drinking by association with Danish friends. Later I visited Denmark and
there discovered that it was a national beverage. As someone wrote, "There is beer for children, beer to be drunk
with breakfast, beer for snacks and beer for after dinner.
The principal fountains for this food are the great breweries
of Tuborg and Carlsberg, which supply beer not only for
Denmark but for much of the rest of the world. The profits
of Carlsberg, by deed or gift from its late owners, I.C. and
Carl Jacobsen, go for the furtherance of science and art.
Carlsberg Brewery sends expeditions to the Antarctic, does
research in cancer and the atom, and has built up the largest display of French art outside France" [J. S. Gordon,
"Denmark," Reader's Digest, Oct. 1962, p. 133]. Whenever I was invited to be a guest on one of the Danish or
Swedish ships visiting Buenos Aires, I encountered their traditional festive meal including aquavit and salt fish, chased
down by rounds of their famous beer. While posted in Danish Greenland for a year during the Second World War, I
naturally became habituated to their drink; but much of it
then had to come from the United States instead of Denmark.

Although the consumption of beer is enormous, I admit that I was astonished the first time I saw draft beer being pumped from a beer-truck through a hose into a pub's
cellars. I was used to beer served in bottles; I was familiar with its delivery and storage in heavy barrels, usually
surrounded by a characteristic damp, beery smell. But to
see a potable beverage, served at the counter by the glass,
being supplied by pipe, like fresh water pumped into a
docked ship, or like petrol pumped into the underground
storage tanks of automobile service stations, was a surprise
and almost an affront, until I became more accustomed to
the sight. After all, a tavern is only another form of filling station.

When I was an undergraduate science student at Toronto University, I was eager to utilize my free time by

some practical experience in a chemical laboratory--even
as bottle-washer. My old science high school teacher, Dr.
Charles G. Fraser of Harbord Collegiate, was working for
his doctorate in science, and had a laboratory in the University Chemistry Building. He invited me to come and
assist him in my free time and weekends. He was working
on malt fermentation, which had an application to beer making. I learned much about laboratory techniques, and also
a little about some scientific aspects of beer making.

This proved to be of some help when, much later,
I held a diplomatic position in Tokyo. On one occasion I
was invited by the management of the Asahi Brewery to inspect their factory. Japanese Asahi beer is an excellent
beer and, being more cheaply made than continental beers,
had a vast export market throughout India and other Asian
countries. The tour of the very up-to-date plant was most
interesting to me. I remember being shown a storage room
full of hops, which I was told were imported from Czechoslovakia; but as the total supply seemed small for the factory's total output, I concluded that this was only a supple-
mentary adjunct, and that much of the Japanese beer was
made without hops. The summer day was extremely hot,
and after the tour of inspection I was invited to the mana-
gerical boardroom to taste the product. I think we each
thirstily downed about six glasses during our conversation
with some of the managers.

Being all my life a thin type of person, I sometimes
tried to see if I could put on more weight by drinking ale
or stout, traditionally said to be fattening. But, after several experiments, I found that it had no effect. On the other hand, in Tokyo, I had a young English businessman as
neighbor; and he responded to beer like a concertina. After a month of beer diet, he grew so fat that his clothes
hardly fit him. He would then "go on the wagon" for a
month or two, and promptly deflate. Then he would com-
mence again, and again expand. His friends could often
tell by his figure whether he was on or off the wagon.

WATER

While Timon of Athens was banqueting his pseudo-
friends, and proposing "Let the health go round," the cynic
Apemantus mocked such healths, and said: "Here's that
which is too weak to be a sinner, / Honest water, which
ne'er left man i' th' mire." Even water, one of the basic

and purest beverages, is not beyond the story of diplomacy.
It too has its military and diplomatic associations.   For instance, old-time caravan routes, involving the trade and
commerce of nations, were dependent for the survival of
man and beast on the control of security of the life-giving
oases and desert springs yielding potable water.   In the
possession or protection of important oases in the desert,
both in North Africa and Central Asia, there have been not
a few clashes between desert tribes and Sheikhdoms.   Strife
over sources of water was a general feature of the desert.

Modern desert warfare has also sometimes been influenced by lack of water.   The ill-fated Gallipoli campaign
in the First World War was a failure for many reasons--
discord among war leaders at home, difficulties in conjoin-
ing naval operations with army forces; impossible landings
on open beachheads with enemy guns ranged above them--
but one of the accompanying factors was the lack of drinking water for the parched troops.   Shortly after that war a
Canadian veteran wrote for the Saturday Evening Post a
handsomely paid article entitled "The Most Precious Thing
in the World."   This most precious thing, according to the
survivors of the Gallipoli Campaign and the tortures of
Suvla Bay, was water.

Oddly enough, Rudyard Kipling spoke up for water as
a soldier's drink at least in Indian campaigning.   In Gunga
Din he wrote:

> You may talk o' gin and beer,
> When you're quartered safe out 'ere,
> An' you're sent to penny shots and Aldershot it;
> But when it comes to slaughter
> You will do your work on water,
> An' you'll lick the bloomin' boots of 'em that's got it.

In Mutiny on the Bounty and other books of shipwreck there
are powerful descriptions of the desperation and tragedy that
affected the castaway seamen when their water supply ran
out; and every narrative of shipwrecked sailors in similar
plight tells the same terrible story.

The muddy water of the Euphrates, which I once
watched in destructive flood, is a reminder of the Hebrews
under Nebuchadnezzar's captivity, for it was on those now
half-dessicated banks, lined with a few small "weeping wil-
lows," that the exiles nostalgically sat and pondered their

past and lamented their plight: "By the waters of Babylon
we sat down and wept." The water of the River Jordan,
which I have tasted in Palestine, is no better than most village streams; but it has traditional and religious significance.   It is as sacred as the filthy and contaminated water
of the Ganges is to the Bengalis; but it has a better reputation for purity.   The English traveller William Lithgow,
writing in 1614, recorded that "The water of Jordan hath
been transported to Venice in barrels, for that purity it
hath; which will reserve unspoiled bosth moneths and yeares,
and the longer it is kept, it is the more fresher; and to
drink it, is an excellent remedy for the fever quartan or
quotidian, being neare in vertue to the Wine of Lebanon"
[Rare Adventures and Painful Peregrinations, chapter xi].
Like the sacerdotal use of wine, from earliest Christian
times till the present, genuine Jordan water has been regarded as holy water, and precious.   It is still used in
coronation ceremonies and christenings of royal babies, and
was used even at the wedding of Princess Margaret to Anthony Armstrong-Jones at Westminster Abbey.   The symbolism is obvious and symbolism is the basis of the Christian
Church.   Fortunately, only a drop or two is sufficient to
hallow a font, or the contents of a priestly cup.   After all,
it comes from the ancient Jordan River, the stream in
which the wilderness prophet John baptized Jesus.   But I
have often wondered if the water of Jordan is as pure and
undefiled as the crystal water Hippocrene or the waters of
Castally that flowed out of the mountain springs under
Mount Parnassus and were revered by the pagans as sacred
waters of life and health.

Water was the symbolic drink of all those in England and Scotland, the anti-Jacobins, who sought the return
of Bonnie Prince Charlie, the ultimate Charles II, after the
Restoration, then in exile over the sea.   "Will ye no come
back again?"   There was some custom of which I have
heard of passing the hand over a glass of water, to signify
a wish for a return of the monarchy, separated by the
Channel from England.

A glass of water was used as a diplomatic symbol
in about 1820 prior to the union or condominium of Egypt
and Sudan.   One day about that year, Emil Ludwig tells us
in The Nile, a French explorer named Cailliard, came down
from the Sudan to Cairo, and met the Khedive Mehemet
Ali.   He brought special gifts and information.   The Frenchman recounted tales: of gold in the Sudan, which the ancient

pharaohs had worked; ivory to be had from countless ele-
phants; incense in Kordofan, and rumors of diamonds, tidings of which had come along the Nile from olden times.
Cailliard brought a glass or jar of water from the confluence
of the two Niles, for he was both an expert and an enthusiast.   These tales and this scientist's symbolic display of
worshipped Nile water impressed Mehemet Ali; and shortly
after, following an atrocious war, Khartoum was founded
and the Khedive paid a personal visit.   More wars followed,
and a struggle over the Nile headwaters went on for over a
century.   (See Emil Ludwig, The Nile, p. 192-4.)

This reminds me of an occasion in 1954 when I was
Canadian delegate to the United Nations General Assembly
in New York.   The late Mr. Andrej Vyshinsky, representative of the Soviet Union, * entered upon one of his customary
two-hour harangues, bitter, witty, and humorous in turn.
In the course of his long speech, he paused to pick up from
his desk a glass of water, but, "carried away with the ex-
uberance of his own verbosity," forgot, minute by minute,
to take the relieving sip.   Instead he waved the full glass
precariously in his hand as he gesticulated; dramatically
pausing an instant from time to time to prepare to moisten
his tongue, but at that very instant a new idea or sentence
would crowd upon him and the glass remained unsipped and
still upheld in his hand.   This dramatic performance continued for half an hour or more, and like a comedian on a
music-hall stage, he kept his audience spellbound, eyes on
his glass, ears attentive to his outpouring words, ever ex-
pectant and waiting for him to take that delayed sip.   It was
difficult to say whether this was unconscious, or whether it
was an act by a great forensic showman to hold his audience's attention.   But it was a memorable and dramatic performance or speaker's trick.   As far as I can recall, he
never did take the intended sip, but finished his oration with
the full glass replaced on his desk as he took his seat.
Soon afterwards this great actor, with his horrible background as prosecutor of the great Soviet purge murders in
the 1930's, sagged to his death from a heart attack while
still serving at the United Nations.

---

*Holofernes' words in Loves Labour Lost (V, i, 18) might apply to Mr.
Vyshinsky: "He draweth out the thread of his verbosity finer than the
staple of his argument. "

A modern poet Merrill Moore wrote these lines in "Hymn for Water":

> Water has sunk more grievances than wine
> And will continue to. Turn the water on,
> Stick your hand in the stream; water will run
> And kiss it like a dog, or it will shake
> It like a friend, or it will tremble there
> Like a woman sobbing with her hair
> Falling in her face.

Of course a considerable history could be written on the diplomatic consequences of "taking the waters" at the spas and Bads of Europe, or at Bath in England. The Romans were famous not only for their ablutionary baths, but also for their arrangements for drinking the mineral waters with so many medicinal attributes. Many votive offerings and coins have been found in such fountains and pipe courses; and of course they were always centers of political gossip and negotiation. Bath, in England, was built as a large city by the Romans, who called the place Aquae Sulis, after a local god Sul, whom they identified with Minerva. After being restored as a watering place about 1650, it became a century later the most fashionable in England, thanks to the indefatigable efforts of Beau Nash. Among the innumerable visitors of eminence in the 18th and early 19th centuries were Chatham, Pitt, Burke, Nelson, Wolfe, Clive and Sir Sydney Smith, English and foreign ambassadors, Gainsborough and Lawrence, and most of the great literary luminaries of the time. It became familiar to readers in Humphrey Clinker and The Rivals, and numerous other works down to the Virginians and the Papers of the Pickwick Club. But the competition of the Continental spas afterwards diverted a great part of the stream of guests.

Most of the famous spas in Europe, so fashionable in the 19th and early 20th centuries, were not only medicinal baths, but hostelries and social gathering places for drinking the mineral waters of the district. They became more fashionable than beer taverns and wine resorts. King Edward VII was a keen frequenter, and by attracting other statesmen to such resorts, probably accomplished much of his personal diplomacy in them.

One of the most renowned of these spas in Europe was of course Vichy, in central France. Although its waters were known to the Romans, Vichy came into favor

only in the late 17th century, when Madame de Sévigny made
it known to the court of Louis XIV, but it did not become
truly fashionable until the Second Empire.   Vichy was visited
several times by Napoleon III, who founded the Nouveau Parc
and had a villa nearby.   As it became more popular and
fashionable, as the chief watering-place in France, a casino
and concert stages were built and it became a mecca for the
aristocracy of Europe.   We have elsewhere mentioned the
reference by Genêt to what he called "spa diplomacy," such
as that adopted by M. Briand in the resort at Thoiry; Vichy
likewise was a center of diplomatic activity.   During the
Second World War it became the seat of government of occupied France, under Maréchal Pétain.

There is another similar Vichy mineral water source
in Catalonia, Spain, frequented by Spanish royalty: King
Alfonso XII, about 1883, used to drink the waters there, to
calm his liver, and by royal decree confirmed the name of
Vichy Catalan.   This gift of nature was "Declared of Utility to the Public" by the Royal Order of the 5th of March
1883; and later adopted the official description "Under the
Protection of the State."   The bottled product indicated on
the label: "Taken straight or mixed with milk, wine or
beer, it gives excellent results in acid dyspepsia, in debil-
ity of the stomach, flatulence or gas pains, for defects in
secretion.   Gastritis from overeating, chronic blockages of
the liver, spleen or prostate.   Small kidneys or liver
stones.   Chronic inflammation of the uterus and the consequent sterility.   King's Evil; rheumatic dermatitis.   A spe-
cific for Glycosuria; Diabetes."   Being under Royal warrant,
it is anomalous that it should be mentioned as a remedy for
the King's Evil!   And, of course, no one in Spain would
touch milk, or think of watering down beer, or corrupting
good wine.   "A Spaniard feels guilty when he drinks water,
it makes him feel less than a man.   But given the excuse
of medical need, combined with such horrible or ridiculous
suggestions as mixing the medicine with milk, beer or wine,
he can ease his conscience, laugh at his fate, and quench
his thirst simultaneously [James Booth, "The Romance of
Vichy Catalan," Atlantic, Jan. 1961, p. 138].   Therefore
Vichy water is a common drink in France and Spain among
the best people; and diplomats whose livers are too much
with them can drink it with their friends with sang froid
and full assurance that it is "proper."   As its bottle label
adds: "At the same time, it constitutes an excellent table
water, of agreeable flavour."   In other words, it is a
drink fit for kings and their ambassadors and they have not

failed to indulge in it while carrying out their policies and
diplomacy.

We are told that a village called Spa, in the Belgian
Ardennes, did the pioneering. The healing powers of its
springs and the celebrity of its drinkers (from Swedish royalty to Peter the Great) made the name generic by the end
of the 18th century. At a good "spa" one sipped from mineral springs to soothe the liver and placate the stomach;
one bathed in its radioactive waters to improve the body
tone and to relax the heart. It is curious to recall that because of its healthful as well as social attractions, there
was an interesting clause in many German marriage con-
tracts during the 19th century. The clause spelled out the
wife's right to one spa visit a year.

Any great resort, of course, had to have its crowned
sipper. Brighton--threatening Bath's supremacy--had the
Prince Regent, complete with Beau Brummel, dandies, and
members of the demi-monde. Napoleon III made Vichy the
imperial summer capital. In Austria, Bad Gastein flowered
under the visits of Franz Josef. Bohemia's Karlsbad
glowed with the presence of Balkan monarchs. Each summer for forty years the Empress Augusta rinsed her ex-
alted vitals in the springs of Baden-Baden.

Consider for example the renowned Bad Hamburg in
Germany, thirty minutes by car from Frankfurt. During
the last century, life there during the season was more
regal than practically anywhere in the world. Besides the
Kaiser and the Prince of Wales there came the kings of
Sweden, Spain, Siam and Bulgaria, the royal family of
Greece, including the child who became the present king,
the Czar of Russia, a whole mob of maharajahs, great
statesmen and generals of the Reich like Bismarck and Hin-
denburg, and an international constellation of tycoons like
Krupp, Opel, Jay Gould, the Harriman clan, and the brewing Buschs of St. Louis. Baron von Kosten-Gantzkow lost
a fortune there, and gambled away his horses, his carriage,
his estates, his patrimony, his silk jackets and trousers.
Prince Lucien Bonaparte, nephew of the Emperor, on the
other hand, broke the bank there in 1852. In 1863 Fyodor
Dostoievski went to Hamburg and kept returning to the casino for years--losing his royalties, his watch, even his
clothes to the croupiers; as usual, he turned his trials into
world literature. The "Siamese Temple," a flaming oriental vision in crimson and gold, was erected by Siamese

King Chulalongkorn in commemoration of his cured insides,
and was renovated in 1960 by his son, the present sovereign
of Thailand and also a Hamburg devotee. The Russian chapel
which rises minareted and onion-towered from the spa park
was inaugurated in 1899 by Czar Nicholas, and every week,
even today, some descendants of the court are said to still
worship in it.

Along with the services of the medicinal waters were
the attractions of roulette. "The casino in the Kurhaus was
not only luxuriously appointed, but alluringly snobbish in its
admission policy. Soon everything that was rich, outré,
sleek and adventurous landau'd to Hamburg in the summer.
From austere English statesmen like Gladstone to political
firebrands like Garibaldi; from coloratura princesses like
Adelina Patti (she would get five thousand gulden for a
single night's performance at the Kurhaus and lose it the
same dawn in the casino), to the Mephistophelean Paganini,
no one dared miss the season at Hamburg" [Frederic Morton, Holiday, Jan. 1962, p. 105].

Where there were kings and courts, there would also
be the ambassadors, impelled by bad livers as well as by
the lure of aristocratic society and the opportunity of gossip, scandal, intrigue, and diplomatic business. Their alibi
was of course the drinking of the restorative waters.

In the very early years of this century, the rich and
fashionable and diplomatic of London went for several weeks
to Carlsbad or Marienbad, both in Bohemia, in what is now
Czechoslovakia. The two spas are near each other on
small hills of pine forest; there all manner of social amenities were available, including vigorous rigid regimens of
eating and bathing.

> The center of attention was, of course, King Edward,
> who under the name of the Duke of Lancaster, used
> to spend a month every year at the Hotel Weismar,
> Marienbad. Punctually at eight o'clock every morn-
> ing His Majesty would be seen drinking his water at
> the Kreuzbrunsen; and afterwards strolling and chat-
> tering informally with his friends on the Promenade.
> ... Other famous men flocked thither when the King
> began to make his month's stay there part of his
> fixed annual programme. Celebrated politicians, like
> Haldane, Lloyd George, [Clemenceau,] and Rufus
> Isaac began to go there regularly ... during those

pleasant days before the war, mixing amusement with 'cure,' and also now and again with a little politics as well.   For there was a tradition, going back to Bismarck and Cavour, in favour of staging diplomatic conversations of a delicate character at one of the famous European spas [W. Watkins Davies, Lloyd George (1939), p. 421-2].

An ironic diarist in 1957, imitating Samuel Pepys, noted: "In goodly company yesterday when my hostess kindly asked me which I preferred with my whiskey: soda-water or plain water.   So I told her that generally speaking I took plain water, but in these days of shortage of rain I took soda-water and so conserved a more valuable fluid.   Mayhap when our wise Solons have provided everyone with a big catch and ample tankage, I may revert to plain water" [Ottawa Journal, June 7, 1957].

The attempt to disguise a beverage by substitution is not without its occasional embarrassments.   Mr. Eric Cleugh, British Ambassador in Panama, noted that diplomatic calls and return calls were numerous and usually made in the morning.   "As refreshments had to be offered he was faced with the dangers of drinking gin and tonic or whiskey and soda at inappropriate hours.   In my house I often substituted ginger-ale, since it looks like whiskey and soda, but once I was caught out by unthinkingly giving way to natural thirst and drinking all mine at one gulp.   This brought a look of astonished admiration to my caller's face and I had to confess in order to avoid acquiring an unwanted reputation for alcoholism" [Without Let or Hindrance, p. 197].

The American, Charles W. Thayer, speaks of the tendency of civilian nationals, or even fellow diplomats, to gain benefits from their diplomatic friends enjoying special diplomatic privileges of importations and customs exemption.   He recalls in his book Diplomat (p. 210) that once in the 1930's as he prepared to leave Moscow for a vacation in Turkey, several foreign diplomatic colleagues asked that he arrange for shipments of a Turkish mineral water called "Abali," from a springs northeast of Teheran.   His colleagues insisted it was the best water for mixing with Scotch in the world.   The quantity and the details were considerable and it took Thayer quite some trouble in Turkey to arrange for it.   Upon the time for his return to Moscow, several friends in the diplomatic corps in Teheran asked Thayer to arrange shipment of a natural sparkling water

known as "Narzan," from Soviet Georgia.   'It's the only de-
cent water to mix with Scotch!" they assured him.

According to the Marquess Curzon, these lines of
Byron's (from Don Juan, ii, stanza 180)--

> Not the first sparkle of the desert spring
> Nor Burgundy in all its sunset glow,
> After long travel, ennui, love, or slaughter,
> Vie with the draught of hock and soda-water.

are the first mention of soda water in English verse.

Lord Landsdowne, while Viceroy of India in 1892,
wrote to his mother about a tiger chase near Bombay.

> We had, as a matter of fact, one and a half hours'
> stiff climbing over very rough ground, and reached
> the ridge which we were to command in the last
> stages of exhaustion, the fat general collapsed alto-
> gether half way up and was only revived by having
> iced soda water poured into him and over him.   The
> feature of the place is soda water; wherever one
> goes, there goes also a small regiment of coolies
> staggering under a load of green bottles and lumps
> of ice carefully rolled in blankets.   The fat general
> and colonel drink a dozen and a half a day.   I am
> content with about half that amount, and feel like a
> 'ballon captif' [in: Lord Newton, Lord Landsdowne,
> p. 97]. *

I remember in my early diplomatic days in Japan a
similar situation in regard to our Canadian first secretary
and sometimes chargé d'affaires.   Dr. Hugh L. Keenley-
side, later ambassador and deputy minister, and his wife
were strictly teetotal, and in those early years never

---

*How ice could be carried for hours in the baggage train of an Indian tiger
hunt is a matter of surprised speculation, especially as in 1892 artificial
ice-making machines were doubtless rare in the Bombay Presidency.   Yet
as early as 1852 a shrewd Cape Cod marine trader was the first to conceive of making money by carrying ice to the tropical South Seas or Caribbean.   His first load, together with a knocked-down icehouse in which to
store it, he sold in Iquique.   Thereafter others followed suit, and made a
1000 per cent profit in the business.   Perhaps other shrewd navigators
could have transported ice by ship down the coast to Bombay; or perhaps by
the end of the century Bombay merchants were manufacturing it themselves.
Commercial refrigeration came into effect in the world between 1861 and
1880.

served wine at their dinners, but only sparkling imported
Canadian ginger ale, served often in champagne glasses.
This idiosyncracy brought him the local nickname of "Canada Dry." In fact, however, the majority of his private
dinner guests in the first year or two were local Canadian
missionaries and social workers, who scarcely minded.
Later, I think, the Keenleysides adopted a more liberal attitude toward provision of wines at the table, even though
they did not themselves drink of the grape.

Everyone knows how shipwrecked sailors, drifting for
days in lifeboats, suffer such craze of thirst that they cannot resist drinking the sea water around them, which tends
to drive them mad. It is extraordinary that in a modern
scientific age which produces moon rockets and interconti-
nental missiles, a simple and convenient converter of sea
water to fresh drinking water has not been generally adopt-
ed--although many experimental models have been invented
and many modern liners are now equipped with apparatus
for producing distilled water, as well as ice. Everyone
knows, too, how parched and almost dying desert travellers
have found water holes to be so brackish and chemically impure as to be undrinkable or to cause intense illness.
Many of the great rivers of the world are undrinkable. The
dirty "blue" Danube, the "life-giving" Nile, the polluted
Tigris passing through Bagdad, offer water in which one
may not swim and which one dare not drink without first
boiling. Even the crystal waters of Lake Ontario are very
polluted on the waterfront of Toronto and the clear fast-
running waters of Ottawa River are also so polluted by
sewage-dumping that the Canadian Federal Capital's water,
unless filtered or chemically decontaminated, is unsafe to
drink. But by these corrective measures, Canadians are
at least able to enjoy fresh tap water without the necessity
of boiling it first, as in so many backward and tropical
countries. Where indeed, in civilization can one enjoy the
Castalian fount of pure drinking water uncontaminated by
sewage, and unchemicalized?

No wonder that in so many cases, one must send
away for flagons of "pure spring" water, in bottles and
jars, to safeguard one's health. In some disadvantaged
spots, even teeth-brushing must be done with imported Vichy
water. This is one of the most unpleasant inconveniences
of diplomatic life in foreign countries.

One diplomat recounts how when he was giving a

party to his colleagues, his supply of soda water ran out.
One of his loyal and faithful servants offered to come to the
rescue and rushed out late at night to find some supplies.
He finally returned and the drinks were resumed. But afterwards everyone was incapacitated.   What he had produced was a supply of Eno's Fruit Salts!

Another narrative tells that when some travel-worn
American tourists visiting Moscow were invited to dine with
the American Ambassador, they found that the plumbing in
their hotel failed them in affording the requirements of a
bath; and they solved the urgent problem by buying one or
two dozen bottles of soda water, and making do with that
makeshift form of "bubble-bath."

Dr. Johnson was by principle a water drinker. For
a time, he confessed to Boswell, he was addicted to drinking wine in private, "in the first place, because I had need
of it to raise my spirits; in the second place because I
would have nobody to witness its effects upon me"; but then
he abandoned this indulgence, and said that "a man should
cultivate his mind so as to have that confidence and readiness without wine, which wine gives."   Boswell himself ad-
mits, in 1778 that he had become a water drinker "upon trial, by Johnson's recommendation."

But those who were so abstemious were not always
popular among the wine-drinkers. In the ancient Mycenaean
and Hellenic period of Mediterranean civilization, there were
no conscientious teetotalers and wine was the only alternative to water (and the water was often untrustworthy).   But
always among the Hellenic Greeks, wine was drunk mixed
with water.   Only barbarians, like the savage and "insolent
and oppressive" Scythians, drank their wine neat. At an Aegean feast or symposium, a krater, or mixing bowl, full of watered wine was brought in.   Shakespeare was not unaware of
the classic custom, apparently observed even in Roman days,
for in Coriolanus (II, i, 53) he makes Menenius Agrippa, ac-
cused of being the "humorous patrician," say "I am one that
loves a cup of hot wine with not a drop of allaying Tiber in it."*

*The condition of the polluted Tiber waters in the 15th century--the age of
Leonardo da Vinci, Cellini, and the Medicis--is well described in Irving
Stone's biography of Michelangelo, The Agony and the Ecstacy.   Shake-
speare's lines here parallel those of Richard Lovelace (1618-1658): "When
flowing cups pass swiftly round/With no allaying Thames" ["To Althea from
Prison," ii].

This reference to Tiber water, written by Shakespeare in 1606, reminds one of the remarks on the Tiber
written by the English traveller William Lithgow in 1632.

> This River of Tiber especially made muster of his
> extravagant disgorgements at that time when Pope
> Clement 8 was crowned Duke of Ferrara, anno 1589,
> and that same night he returned to Rome, Tiber
> waxed so proud of his arrival, that impetuously in-
> undating his bankes to make him welcome, he over-
> whelmed the better halfe of the Towne: And if it
> had not bene for the infinite charges of the Pope,
> and desperate toile of the people, the violent force
> of his rage swelling courtesie, had absolutely sub-
> verted and carried away the rest of the city. The
> like inundation was never seene of Tiber, as after
> this Coronation, portending, that as the first Ge-
> morah was destroyed by fire, so this second Sodome
> should be summersed by water [Rare Adventures...,
> chapter i].

If, as we have noted, there are groups of temperance or teetotal advocates, condemning the use of wine, it
would seem that there have also been some who condemned
the use of water as a beverage or a dilutant. When Ben
Jonson, poet laureate, founded the Apollo Club in the Devil
and St. Dunstan tavern in Fleet Street, where good wine,
good food and good conversation were prescribed in Latin
rules, a warning plaque written by Jonson was mounted under a bust of Apollo, on the due results of drinking nothing
but water:

> He the half of life abuses
> That sits watering with the Muses.
> Those dull girls no good can mean us;
> Wine, it is the milk of Venus.*

Another poet declared:

> Pure water is the best of gifts that man to man
>   can bring;
> But who am I that I should have the best of every-
>   thing?
> Let princes revel at the pump and peers with
>   ponds make free:
> Whiskey or wine--or even beer--are good enough for
>   me*

---

*Attributed both to the Hon. G. W. E. Russell and to Lord Neaves.

And then there is the old toast or invocation by Oliver Herford:

> Here's to Adam's crystal ale,
>   Clear, sparkling, and divine,
> Fair H$_2$O, long may you flow!
>   We drink your health--in wine.

Thackeray records: "I once heard the Head Physician of a Hydropathic establishment on the sunny banks of the Rhine, give the health of His Majesty the King of Prussia, and calling upon the company to receive that august toast with a 'donnerndes Lebehoch,' toss off a bumper of sparkling water. It did not seem to me a genuine enthusiasm. No, no, let us have toast and wine, not toast and water. It was not in vain that grapes grew on the hills of father Rhine" [Sketches and Travels in London].

Some readers will probably not need to be reminded of Stephen Leacock's spoofing tale of "A Butler of the Old School" [in Wet Wit and Dry Humour] in which the author was conducted through the cellars of the 1860 house he was visiting. Here he found vintage Rain Water from the year of the Johnstown flood, and rare Ditchwater with just the right body--a cheap commercial Ditchwater has "either got too much mud in it or it's so thin it has no strength." He found "French Tap Water bottled in Paris, Pump Water from the town pump of the early nineteenth century, Trough Water from an abandoned New England farm, English Pond Water in stone bottles, and Dutch Canal Water in tempting square bottles with yellow and green seals." The essay ended with an orgy as they swilled West Indian Bilge Water, a hundred years old.

If Leacock could satirize water-drinking, so could Thomas Meehan, who wrote a short satire for Esquire (February 1960): "Too Many Drops to Drink." It is a parody on the confessions of fallen women alcoholics, and concerns the fall and recovery of a movie-star named Glenda de Grand. In one brief passage of her diary she wrote about her love-at-first-sight meeting of Lance, a playboy-type who played water-polo professionally. "We were introduced at a party at Malibu and were married in Tijuana an hour and a quarter later," she said. After a time she discovered that he drank, after first being suspicious when she realized

he brushed his teeth an inordinate number of times

each day--four or five brushing an hour--and always
afterwards the glass of water.   Then I began to find
bottles of water hidden about the house, and on several occasions I came upon him sneaking the stuff
straight from the garden hose.   His speech was
slurred, he became giddy--and he had hang-overs.
... It was then I realized that Lance was a secret
water-drinker, a hydrolic!   When I caught him one
afternoon, at the edge of the swimming pool with a
ladle in his hand ...[h]e became angry and threatened
to leave me.   ... [T]o humor him, I too, took to
drinking.   At first, it was simply harmless social
drinking. ... Later, though, it was straight water
from big gin-glasses at the rate of fifteen or twenty
a day ...[but] despite everything ... after twenty-
three days of marriage, we were divorced.   Then I
really began to drink....

And Glenda de Grande goes on to describe her mad
and reckless career on the perilous water-wagon until she
was the worst case of chronic hydrolic.   Suddenly she found
her strength and kicked it.   Said Glenda de Grande to her
diary, "I brush my teeth with ginger-ale, stay out of swimming pools and rainstorms, and never go near ice-cubes.
I've learned my lesson, these days I drink nothing but
straight gin--a quart and a half usually sees me through to
sundown" [Esquire, Feb. 1960, p. 110].

My former minister in Buenos Aires, Justice W. F.
A. Turgeon, used to tell the story of a temperance lecturer,
who after an address on the poisonous effects of alcohol on
the internal system, put on a demonstration.   On his lecture table he placed a glass containing clear tap water, and
in front a projector was set up, with a screen at the back.
"Ladies and Gentlemen," he announced, "here is an ordinary glass of water.   The magnifying projector will show
what it looks like on the screen.   You see those little
specks drifting about on the screen; those are the little bac-
terial items, invisible to the naked eye, which exist in all
ordinary water.   They are, in fact, tiny organic organisms
of no deleterious consequence.   But now I shall place a
drop of alcohol in this glass on the table.   Please watch on
the screen the result."   On dropping his alcohol in the
glass, the magnification on the screen showed that most of
the specks dropped dead and descended to the bottom of the
glass.   "That shows, ladies and gentlemen, that alcohol is
a poison that kills all organic matter, including the cells

that make up the tissues of your stomach lining. It is a
lethal and destructive poison." Whereupon one man in the
audience raised his hand and asked permission to speak,
which was granted. 'Mr. Speaker," he said, "I have been
very impressed by your lecture, and particularly by your
demonstration of the floating animalcula in a glass of ordinary tap water. In future, I shall always make sure to puri-
fy my drink by putting some alcohol into it."

Apparently the customs regulations and protective
tariffs are often made under pressure of vested interests
and their legislative lobbyists. In the United States for instance, surely it must have been for the "protection" of
domestic soft drink producers, that imported mineral waters
were restricted by tariffs. But there can be found loopholes
in many customs regulations. A man who was shipping mineral water across the U.S. border from Eastern Ontario had
to pay duty until he got smart enough to freeze it first. Ice
was duty-free. (See Maclean's, Feb. 11, 1961, p. 1.)

In the days of American Prohibition it was difficult
to get even water through diplomatic channels, in Washington, D.C., which had no scarcity but merely bureaucracy
to overcome. Mr. J. Pouliot, then a member of the Canadian House of Commons and now Senator, related a story
in Parliament in 1933.

> One of the officials of the Kiwanis Club of the dis-
> trict of Washington wrote to the Secretary of State
> of the United States to ask if it would be possible to
> obtain a bottle of water from the House of Commons
> in Ottawa. There was a celebration to be held in
> Washington and the club wanted this water in order
> to drink a toast to Canada. The Secretary of State
> of the United States very gravely wrote to the Can-
> adian Minister in Washington to ask him if he could
> supply this sparkling fluid. The Canadian Minister
> wrote to the Department of External Affairs, and I
> was just wondering if the department communicated
> with the office of the Prime Minister.... If they
> did not communicate direct with the office of the
> Prime Minister, the subsequent actions were taken
> under the supervision of the Prime Minister. He
> gave instructions that his department should communi-
> cate with the Sergeant-at-Arms. The Sergeant-at-
> Arms gave instructions to the chief messenger to fill
> a clean bottle with water taken from a tap in the

House of Commons.   The chief messenger filled a
bottle with water and returned it to the Sergeant-at-
Arms.   It was then turned over to the Department of
External Affairs which sent it by special mail or ex-
press--or by diplomatic courier.   The bottle was
sent to the Secretary of State of the United States who
forwarded it to the Canadian Minister, who in turn
had it conveyed to the president of the club.

Mr. Malcolm: It did not turn out to be anything else, did it?

Mr. Pouliot: This was during Prohibition, and
probably the president of the Kiwanis Club thought
that there was something pleasant to the taste in the
water drunk by the members of the House of Commons.   The Prime Minister may be very busy with
matters of state, but if his time is taken up with
such things as sending a bottle of water from Ottawa
to Washington, he might better stay here and listen
to the speeches delivered by hon-members [House of
Commons Debates, April 28, 1933, p. 4400].

It is not usual, or even proper, to drink toasts with
water, although it is done in teetotal circles where alcoholic
beverages like champagne or beer are not served, or by
those individuals at a party who are abstainers.   Since a
toast is usually for someone's health, what better hygeia
could be drunk than water?   Somewhat akin to water, and
even soda-water, is milk, which President Kennedy was reported (Time, Feb. 3, 1962) to provide as an optional beverage at his private White House meals.   This called forth
a letter to Time (Feb. 9), as follows: "On behalf of the
bourbon drinkers of America, I protest.   Is this spiritless,
chalky liquid more worthy of the presidential accolade than
my beloved bourbon--or wine, or beer, or even sake?   Do
men toast their sweethearts with this bland fluid?   Does
the Government christen its boats with a magnum of milk?
Has any true American male, homeward bound, ever tarried
in his favorite bar to down a beaker of milk on the rocks?
Have you ever tried to warm the frigid inner man with a
cool goblet of milk--homogenized or otherwise?   Mr. Kennedy, you have done a disservice to bourbonites; and to sub-
bourbonites."   It is of interest to note that modern custom
in both America and England has been to create so-called
"milk bars" for those who value this beverage of nature.
The President's inclusion of milk at his table was typically
American (they are the greatest milk drinkers in the world),
and was also a gesture to show the public that the scare of

milk poisoned by "fall-out" was largely imaginary and need not be taken with too fearful anxiety.

The Canadian press noted that when Queen Elizabeth visited Canada in 1958, former Prime Minister John Diefenbaker proposed the royal toast by drinking milk. It pointed out that while toasts seem traditionally to call for alcoholic beverages, this deviation should cause no surprise, since Mr. Diefenbaker was a churchman and the particular denomination he belonged to took a strong stand against alcoholic beverages.

Speaking of Mr. Diefenbaker's abstemiousness, Jack Fishman, in the biography of Churchill's wife, My Darling Clementine, relates that Sir Winston Churchill found it hard to understand people who did not share his fondness for a mellow drink. "Canada's former Prime Minister John Diefenbaker went with some trepidation to dinner with the Churchills. He is a total abstainer. When he refused wine and asked for a soft drink, Winston began muttering and grumbling about prohibitionists in North America. Diefenbaker protested that he was not a prohibitionist, but merely a teetotaler. 'Ah,' said Sir Winston, 'that's not so bad, you believe only in doing harm to yourself' " [Ottawa Journal, Aug. 3, 1963]. W. Watson Davies records that in the home of David Lloyd George, a Baptist and an abstainer like Mr. Diefenbaker, while Chancellor of the Exchequer, never for many years was wine or other intoxicants allowed to appear on the table.

During the administration of President Rutherford B. Hayes, the White House was "dry." Mrs. Hayes was well known, but not always affectionately, as 'Lemonade Lucy"; she hid the key to the Executive wine cellars and sent to the attic all stemware and "paraphernalia for the taking of wines and spirits." During her arid reign she allowed only two drinks to be served--one each to the Grand Dukes Alexis and Constantine of Russia. When arrangements were being made for a dinner for the diplomatic corps, Secretary of State William Evarts called on Mrs. Hayes to explain that many, if not most, of the guests were accustomed to wine with their meals, and to ask her to make an exception in this case and to serve champagne. All in vain. The next day a friend of Evarts, who knew of his embarrassment, met him on the street and asked him how the dinner had gone. "Oh, fine," said Evarts sourly; "Water flowed like champagne" [Claude G. Bowers, Chile Through Embassy Windows, p. 106].

Ambassador Hugh Wilson recalls that after being
chargé d'affaires for two years, his new minister to Guatemala, Dr. Leavell arrived. "He was a Presbyterian clergy-
man of magnificent appearance, a face a sculptor would have
delighted to model and abundant snow-white hair.   Mrs.
Leavell was lovable, she cooked southern dishes like a master, and she had a sense of humor.   They were rigid prohibitionists and served no liquor at the table.   Their dinners
were either very solemn, or else the diplomats, warned of
their views, had taken more than adequate precautions in advance.   In the latter event, the dinner went with a rush as
far as the salad, and after that, collapsed" [The Education
of a Diplomat, p. 86].

In a world of liberal tastes, it must be supremely
difficult for national leaders to oppose convention by abstemiousness.   Even Muslim and African leaders, when thrown
into international society, find it more expedient to conform
to custom.   Mrs. Hayes was not beloved for her strict, puritan beliefs.   The second Prime Minister of Canada, Sir Alexander Mackenzie, was a total abstainer, but possibly this
was pardonable after the notorious example of his distinguished predecessor, Sir John A. MacDonald, a veritable
Sir Toby Belch.   The Rt. Hon. R. B. Bennett was a teetotaler.   I remember crossing the Atlantic once in mid-
winter with him after he had been defeated as Prime Minister in the elections of 1935 and was retiring from Canadian
public life to reside in England where he later received a
viscountcy.   His faithful and long-serving private secretary
Miss Miller was accompanying him.   When I invited her to
join me in an after-dinner drink in the saloon-lounge, she
asked me to wait until Mr. Bennett had retired to his cabin.   To a large extent former Prime Minister W. L. Mackenzie King was abstemious; his former secretary and later
biographer the Hon. J. W. Pickersgill, writes that "Mr.
Mackenzie King was not a teetotaler, but he was at all
times very moderate in his drinking.   During the War he
gave up drinking entirely, with only one or two exceptions.
At Mr. King's receptions, however, as I personally recall,
he allowed the usual alcoholic spirits and cocktails to be
served."   Ex-Prime Minister John Diefenbaker was a strict
teetotaler and sometimes surprised his guests at his receptions and garden parties by not serving any alcoholic drinks,
but only lemonade, fruit punch or ginger ale, along with
tea and coffee.   The former Minister of External Affairs,
the Hon. Howard Green, and the former Minister of Finance,
the Hon. Donald Fleming, and the Minister of National Reve-

nue, the Hon. Hugh John Fleming, were other members of
the Canadian Conservative Cabinet who practised an almost
Mohammedan abstention.   There may be others.   This only
reflects a private taste or a private principle; it does not
reflect national public policy or official practice.   Nor does
it prove any particular point, regarding health or longevity.
Sir John A. Macdonald, though heavily bibulous, survived,
like Winston Churchill, to a very ripe old age.   Sir William Mulock, a former postmaster-general, was a heavy
drinker (a bottle of Scotch a day), but lived to the age of
101 years!   Lord Strathcona, not an abstainer, remained
Canadian High Commissioner in London until he died en
poste in his eighties or nineties.   The American cocktail-
addict Senator Theodore Green survived 99 years.   One may
live to be a nonagenarian or a centenarian in spite of (or
perhaps because of) inhibiting strong drinks; or, equally, by
virtue of being abstemious or a teetotaler.

But in modern public life, the complete abstainer is
not only an anachronism, but is a martyr.   The Hon. Howard Green, as Minister of External Affairs, and thus constantly confronted with current diplomatic practices, has admitted that he has had to endure so much orange juice or
lemonade, in lieu of customary wines and spirits, that his
stomach was revolted.   A British borderman once declared
his nationality by saying that he was English by extraction
and Scotch by absorption; and he added that water was only
for external use; it has a tendency to rust pipes.

It must not be overlooked that at every diplomatic
conference table, whether in the United Nations Committee
rooms, or at international discussions elsewhere, there is
always the pitcher of iced water and a tray of tumblers.
Cocktails and liquor are only the optional social aftermath.

VI

THE COCKTAIL CIRCUIT

In our sociological and diplomatic commentary on drinks and the diplomats, we have left for a special chapter the most conspicuous of them all: the "cocktail." This is because it is not only a distinctive form of alcoholic beverage, differing from those we have already mentioned, but also because it has contributed to a way of life no less important to the profession and business of diplomacy than is the business of dining and dinners. In the social life of modern diplomacy, there are two essentials; the dinners and the cocktail parties.

Puritans, originating from the Reformation and the Cromwellien Republic of England and continuing into our own day, and entering America with the Plymouth Brethren, look askance at all this; and the sect of Teetotalers, which has so many worthy political adherents, will deprecate this emphasis on a historical and present-day factor of diplomatic life. But, like other natural circumstances and foibles of human kind this tranche de vie cannot be excluded from a realistic sociological study of the diplomatic profession, or from contemporary social life generally, whether or not it warrants deprecation and condemnation. The water drinkers to which we have just referred are in the minority. Diplomats have, in the majority, succumbed to the current vogue of the cocktail party. And this is what we find in our Looking Glass.

MIXED DRINKS

The history of "mixed drinks" and "cocktails" runs in parallel lines. A cocktail is essentially a mixed drink with a spirit base--whiskey, vodka or most commonly gin, colored or flavored with another liquid, often a heavy wine, usually vermouth. Other mixed drinks are frequently known as punches--most often having a rum base with various fruit juices and other liqueurs added. But, outside the cocktails and punches, the pharmacopoeia of mixed drinks is infinite.

235

The medical prescription "the mixture as before" was transferred to the bar and suggestions to amateur bartenders or
hosts were proffered--"How to Mix Good Drinks." In fact
a cocktail server might be given the name of a modern ap-
pliance and be nicknamed the "Mix-master." One reads in
the newspaper advertisements of special schools for training bartenders; everyone today must be a professionally
trained specialist.

Among the earliest alcoholic mixed drinks was that
made from fermented honey. The Greeks and Romans had
such drinks under the names of hydromel; mulsum was a
form of mead with the addition of wine. Mead itself was
commonly drunk during the Middle Ages throughout Europe;
it was mainly a mixture of fermented honey and water.
Sometimes, under the name of Metheglin, it was a medi-
cated or spiced form of the drink, taking its name from the
Welsh meddyglyn, from meddyg (Latin, medicus, healing)
and llyn (liquor). Mead was probably drunk as a standard
beverage even in the courts and diplomatic circles, and
probably for toasts and wassails, as well as among the common people.

Hippocrates, we are told, in 400 B.C. created his
own lusty infusion of wine with almonds and resin, or some
say, with cinnamon, cloves, sugar, mace, nutmeg and other
rare aromatics. Roman wines were made not only from the
grape but from turnips, radishes, asparagus, parsley, thyme,
mint, hyssop and almost anything else that spring up around
the villa. Cicero pointed with pride to his own private concoction of wine mixed with dittany leaves. One bitter ingredient used since the 17th century is quinine; its familiar
zest is present today not only in most apertif wines but also in all tonic waters.

In similar manner, a simple product of distillation,
such as vodka, becomes, by its flavoring of juniper, gin;
by its flavoring of anise, aquavit; by its flavoring of fruit
juices, slivovitz. Punches are spirits "braced" with spices
and condiments. And there are various indescribable concoctions which go beyond any name or classification and can
only be termed "witches' brews." Remember the nonsense
song sung to Alice in the Looking-Glass House:

> Then fill up the glasses with treacle and ink,
> Or anything else that is pleasant to drink;
> Mix sand with the cider, and wool with the wine.
> And welcome Queen Alice with ninety-times nine.

In early Canadian days, the habit of weird mixed drinks was as crazy as in Alice's. In the early 1800's, a main staple was whiskey or "whoop-up bug juice" as the Blackfoot tribe preferred to call it. They would trade robes, pelts, weapons, horses and squaws for it until they had nothing left. "Bug-juice" was not a good whiskey. One recipe from those days was to mix together a quart of whiskey, a pound of chewing tobacco, a handful of red pepper, a bottle of Jamaica ginger, and a quart of molasses, dilute the whole with water, heat it to make a true fire-water, and sell it by the mug. Another formula combined "Perry's Famous Painkiller" with Hostetter's Bitters, tobacco, molasses, and a dash of red ink for color. (See W. G. Hardy, From Sea unto Sea.)

We may rightly shudder at such incredible concoctions, but I recall how in Tokyo, after every legation dinner, large or small, the Japanese servants cleared away all the glasses, many of them containing half-finished whiskeys or martinis, champagne, wines and liqueurs, and in the back kitchen, poured all these together into one large bowl, making an amazing "punch" which they surreptitiously imbibed as their after-share of the diplomatic dinner. When I first heard of such undiscriminating procedure, I was shocked to imagine the sort of witches' brew they concocted. But having read the records of other such infamies, I ceased to be shocked. At least the servants' "cocktail" had ingredients of the very best quality!

PUNCH

Punch, by definition, is the name of a drink composed of spirits--usually rum--water, sliced lemons or limes, or lemon juice, together with sugar and spice, and served hot. The word is the English representative of the Hindustani panch ("five"), from the number of ingredients, and was introduced from the East. Bernard Mandeville (1670-1733), a Dutch-born English physician and satirist, refers to a bowl of punch in these words:

I don't doubt but a Westphalian, Laplander, or any other dull stranger that is unacquainted with the wholesome composition, if he was to taste the several ingredients apart, would think it impossible they should make any tolerable liquor. The lemons would be too sour, the sugar too luscious, the brandy, he will say, is too strong ever to be drunk in any quan-

tity, and the water he will call a tasteless liquor,
only fit for cows and horses; yet experience teaches
us that the ingredients I named, judiciously mixed,
will make an excellent liquor, liked of and admired
by men of exquisite palates.

Lord Frederic Hamilton, a young diplomat at the
Court of Berlin in the 1870's, recounts that

A feature of the Berlin State balls was the stirrup-
cup of hot punch given to departing guests.   Knowing
people hurried to the grand staircase at the conclusion of the entertainment; here servants proffered
trays of this delectable compound.   It was concocted,
I believe, of equal parts of arrack and rum, with
various other unknown ingredients.   In the same way,
at Buckingham Palace in Queen Victoria's time, wise
persons always asked for hock cup.   This was compounded of very old hock and curious liquors, from
a hundred-year-old recipe.   A truly admirable beverage.   Now, alas! since Queen Victoria's day, only
a memory [The Vanished Pomp of Yesterday, p. 42].

"Wassail," meaning "to your health," was the toast
proposed originally in England at Christmas to offer greet-
ings and good wishes.   The Wassail bowl of Merrie England
contained hot punch; apples, oranges, and chestnuts roasted
in front of an open fire, the fruit usually with a few cloves
tucked in them.   When they were added into the bowl, the
heat of the fruit made the hot punch steam.   It was a cheering sight on a cold and frosty evening.

The Wassail Bowl, as Washington Irving noted in his
Sketch Book, was sometimes composed of ale instead of wine,
with nutmeg, sugar, toast, ginger, and roasted crabs; in this
way the nut-brown beverage is still prepared in some old families, and around the hearths of substantial farmers at Christmas.   It is also called Lamb's Wool, * and is celebrated by
Herrick in his "Twelfth Night."

---

*The old compound of roasted apples, ale, and sugar, which our ancestors
knew as "Lam's Wool," is thought to have derived its name as follows:
the words La Mas Ubal are good Irish, signifying the Feast, or day of the
Apple, and pronounced "lama sool," the sound of which soon degenerated
into "lamb's wool."   The mixture was drunk on the evening of the Feast
day, which was supposed to be presided over by the guardian angel of fruits
and seeds.

> Next crowne the bowle full
> With gentle Lamb's Wool;
> And sugar, nutmeg, and ginger.
> With store of ale too;
> And thus ye must doe
> To make the Wassaile a swinger.

In earlier times the Wassail Bowl was passed around, wherefrom every guest drank. But the custom of drinking out of the same cup gave place to each having his cup.

A custom of New Year's wassail is still maintained in various places. Among some Americans it nowadays takes the form of a morning eggnog party instead of the hot punch. I recall that in my Tokyo days, American Embassy secretaries gave such New Year's morning eggnog parties, to which their junior diplomatic colleagues and friends were invited for an extended session of celebration and good cheer. Even the ambassador, at that time the Hon. Joseph C. Grew, used to turn up, in top-hat and morning coat, on his way back from attending church, to spend a pleasant quarter of an hour with the convivial juniors and to make wassail to their health and happiness. It was a pleasant annual custom, which no doubt is duplicated in many other diplomatic posts in foreign lands or at home.

On one occasion a modern wassail in Ottawa was accompanied by a certain small misfortune. Governor-General Georges P. Vanier was holding his New Year levée in the Senate Chamber on January 2, 1961. Afterwards, the guests repaired to the Railway Committee Room, where a lavish buffet was laid out. In accordance with custom, there was served a hot richly spiked punch, consisting of a mixture of rum, cognac, ginger ale, hot water, sugar and cinnamon. At the right moment, this was brought in and poured into the great punch bowls on the side tables. But one of the huge crystal or glass bowls was unfit for such a hot brew; it cracked, and shattered, and before anything could be done, the hot savory concoction had flooded like a river the polished floor of the hall, around the feet of the growing crowd of guests. The pungent aroma of warm alcohol perfumed the chamber with a tavern-like cheer.

COCKTAILS

From "witches' brews" to punches, and thence to

"cocktails" was but a step. The hot drink, mainly reserved
for toasts and Christmas or New Year anniversary celebration, gave way to the iced drink, indulged in at any occasion.

It may be mentioned that the use of ice in drinks
long preceded the Cocktail Age. Dr. Doran, in 1859, has
reported: "To talk of the fierceness of a Russian summer
seems paradoxical, but it is simple truth; and probably the
court of Naples itself, throughout its long season of heat,
does not consume as much ice as their imperial Muscovite
majesties [and citizenry] do in the course of their slow-to-
come, quick-to-go, and sharp-while-it-lasts summer. ...
They eat it and drink it, surround their larders with it, and
mix it with the water, beer, quass [kvass]--in short, with
whatever they drink [Table Traits, p. 435].

In the Sultan's vast Seraglio at Stamboul in the 18th
century, among other mysterious rooms and corridors of
the Palace, we are told of "great ice-pits, where snow,
wrapped in flannel, was brought on mule-back some seventy
miles from Mount Olympus, and was stored for the making
of sherbet and other cooling delicacies" [Lesley Blanch,
The Wilder Shores of Love]. In fact, long before Turkish
and Russian civilizations, it is said that Nero saw to it that
ice houses were built, the contents of which enabled thousands to quaff the cool beverage which is so commendably
spoken of by Aristotle. In our own day, with ice cubes
automatically created in every refrigerator, no cool drink
is acceptable without ice, either as an outside cooling agent,
as in the cocktail-shaker, or in the drink itself. The pleasant sound of tinkling ice-cubes against the glass is an aesthetic and gustatory satisfaction, but as the melting ice
cubes tend to dilute the beverage, the absurd subterfuge has
been invented of plastic or glass cubes, which will tinkle
but not melt.

It has been suggested that a form of mixed drink related to the cocktail name might be traced back to the
Greeks and Romans, for whom the cock was the bird of
sacrifice and for whom sacrifices were associated with drinking. In one of the Odes of Horace there are these lines:

> Be joyous, Delius, I pray;
> The bird of morn, with feathers gay,
> Gives us his rearward plume;
> For mingled draughts drive care away
> And scatter every gloom.

In England, in the 18th century the name of cocktail was applied to beer which was too fresh, with the foam on it.   In stock breeding terms, it was applied to a horse which had a touch of impure blood, and was therefore a mixture.   These animals, usually hunters, or coach horses, had their tails docked, as thoroughbreds did not, and were thus called cock-tailed horses.   "I can't afford a thoroughbred," says a character in Thackeray, "and hate a cocktail."   "Nearly full-bred" was another phrase applied to a horse, "the least bit of cocktail in the world."   The word was even extended into the human field to cover a man who was not quite a gentleman.   In The Newcomes we find "such a selfish, indolent coxcomb as that, such a cocktail"; while the true country gentleman considered that "to breed tame fowls and then blow them away from the end of the gun is snobbish and cocktail."

Oscar Wilde visited the United States on a lecture tour in 1882.   In recounting his experiences at a repast given to him in the depths of a silver mine by a party of miners, he said: "At the bottom of the mine we sat down to a banquet, the first course being whiskey, the second whiskey, and the third whiskey.   The amazement of the miners when they saw that art and appetite could go hand in hand knew no bounds.   And when I quaffed a cocktail without flinching, they unanimously pronounced me 'a bully boy with no glass eye' " [Hesketh Pearson, The Life of Oscar Wilde].

It is also recorded that "cock-ale" was already known as a mixture of spirits fed to fighting cocks in training, and the spectators at cockfights used after the contest to toast the cock with the most feathers left in its tail, the number of ingredients in the drink corresponding with the number of feathers.

It became a recognized name in America for mixed drinks during the following century.   In 1806 it was referred to in an American periodical The Balana, where the statement appeared that "Cocktail is a stimulating liquor, composed of spirits of any kind, sugar, water and bitters-- it is vulgarly called bittered sling and is supposed to be an excellent electioneering potion."   It seems to have reached England by the 1850's, when Tom Hughes mentions it in Tom Brown's School Days: 'Bill ... the half-hour hasn't struck.   Here, Bill, drink some cocktail."   Thackeray mentions it in The Newcomes--"Did ye iver try a brandy

cocktail, cornel?"--while in America Hawthorne describes
a character who was "famous for nothing but gin cocktails."

But the father of the modern cocktail is said to be
a bartender from New York and San Francisco named Jerry
Thomas, who in the 1860's published his Bon Vivant's Companion; or, How to Mix Drinks. He it was (quotes Lord
Kinross) who, a few years before the Civil War, "gave the
aid and encouragement of his genius to the cocktail, then a
meek and lowly beverage pining for recognition and appreciation, and by self-sacrificing work in the laboratory raised
it to its rightful place among the drinks. A perfect flood of
new mixtures soon showered upon a delightful world." At
that time the cocktail was, as a rule, a bottled drink, popular rather in the morning than in the evenings. "The
cocktail," Thomas wrote, "is a modern invention and is generally used on fishing and other sporting parties, although
some patients insist that it is good in the morning as a tonic." "In the morning," he wrote again, "the merchant, the
lawyer or the Methodist deacon takes his cocktail. Suppose
it is not properly compounded. The whole day's proceedings go crooked because the man himself feels wrong from
the effects of an unskillfully mixed drink."

That popular nabob of San Francisco and Nevada,
Lucius Beebe, whose heart is still in the aristocratic 19th
century, wrote nostalgically that

> In the past, businessmen recognized the pleasant
> privilege to which their estate entitled them. They
> enjoyed three or four cocktails and wine with their
> lunch, and, in anywhere from an hour to three hours,
> made their way through three courses of good food in
> a club or topnotch restaurant. The cocktail, indeed,
> rose to esteem in America as the mid-morning drink
> of bankers and brokers in downtown New York, who
> went across the street for a couple of Manhattans
> along about ten-thirty or at what is now the time for
> the coffee-break. In San Francisco, early in this
> century, all ranking executives of the Bank of Cali-
> fornia, the Southern Pacific Railroad and Wells Fargo
> & Co., would meet at noon by mutual agreement at
> the Bank Exchange for two of Duncan Nicol's ineffable
> Pisco Punches, and then go on to an elaborate lunch
> ["Party of One," Holiday, Sept. 1960, p. 12].

The origin of the modern "cocktail" is a matter of

dispute.   The coquetel, a mixed drink, is said to have been known in Bordeaux for centuries; but its direct relation to our present drink is dubious.   It is also suggested by some that the cocktail came to us from pre-Columbian Mexico. Supposedly a Toltecan noble invented a concoction, apparently from a potent cactus juice, and sent a sample via his daughter Xochitla, to the king, who gratefully dubbed it a xoctl.   But by general concurrence, the modern cocktail as we know it had its origins in North America, although even there various claims exist.

The word "cocktail," according to H. L. Mencken, originated in New Orleans at the turn of the 19th century. A Frenchman, one Antoine Amedée Peychaud, arrived in New Orleans by way of San Domingo in 1801.   He opened an apothecary shop near the waterfront and quickly became friends with several riverboat captains.   When these lusty characters returned from their trips up and down the Mississippi, it was their custom to drop in on Peychaud, who served them a special blast he had concocted.   The drink consisted of French brandy, sugar, water, and bitters.   The secret of the drink lay in the bitters, which Peychaud had brought with him from San Domingo.   The pharmacist had no toddy glasses, so he used double-ended eggcups, called cocquetiers (pronounced "kok-tyay").   The rugged boatmen called them "cock-tays" and later, "cocktails."   Gradually, cocktail came to mean any drink containing hard liquor, a dilutant and an aromatic flavoring.

Another, even more widely accepted story of the origin of "cocktail" leads us to a "Betty Flanagan" of Yonkers, New York--in reality a Mrs. Hustler of Lewiston, Niagara Falls.   Mr. & Mrs. Thomas Hustler kept a tavern on the Niagara River at Lewiston before and after the War of 1812. James Fenimore Cooper, then (1809) a young U.S. Naval officer on Lake Ontario, was put up at the Hustler place and Cooper was in a way fascinated by the belligerent Mrs. Hustler who it is said eventually became the Betty Flanagan of his revolutionary tale, The Spy.   (Apparently Cooper drew the character of Mrs. Hustler so accurately as Betty Flanagan that her daughter is said to have thrown The Spy into the fireplace upon reading it.)   Her husband, a veteran of General Wayne's campaign, became Sergeant Hollister of the same story.   Unconfirmed rumor had it that Mrs. Hustler was a sutler to the American troops near Yonkers, New York, during the Revolution and that she was present at a tavern there in 1779 when an American raiding party

brought in wine, brandy and chickens after a successful venture against the headquarters of nearby British officers.
Mrs. Hustler is supposed to have given a chicken feast, and for a "bracer," to have mixed several liquors with wine and to have placed a tail feather of a rooster in each glass before she served the mixture to the American and French officers who were present.   Upon tasting the concoction, a young French officer was said to have stood and toasted her sutlership with "Vive la cocktail!" or perhaps "Vive la coquetal!" (See Raymond F. Yates, A Picture Story of Niagara.) Rumor also has it that years later, the tavern which she ran at Lewiston was the only building left standing when the British burned Lewiston during the War of 1812.   British officers stationed across the river could not bear the thought of destroying a resort to which they had journeyed to enjoy Mrs. Hustler's (alias Betty Flanagan's) cocktails.

Someone once wrote that there should be a monument erected in honor of one who had so influenced the tribal customs of America and the world, by inventing the ubiquitous cocktail and the social custom of cocktail parties.   Such a monument should equal that of Bacchus, Pan, or Cupid. But apparently all that exists are the weather-worn and all but forgotten gravestones of Catherine and Thomas Hustler, the hero and heroine (called Betty Flanagan) of Cooper's The Spy, in a quiet corner of an old Lewiston burial ground.

PROHIBITION

But, whatever the origins, the modern vogue of the cocktail and of cocktail parties as forms of Western social life clearly recommenced in the United States during and immediately after World War I.   It was a paradoxical by-product of the era of Prohibition.   By another paradox, the mixed character of the cocktail was in fact nothing more than a means of disguising the raw taste of "bootleg gin" by means of more tasty additions.   Cocktails were the unintentioned by-products of "side-effects" of the noble experiment of Prohibition.

While the 18th Amendment and the Volstead Act are generally regarded as the Prohibition epoch, they were in fact only the crowning act in a long series of preparatory steps.   When the United States Congress voted in December 1917 that prohibition should be extended to the whole territory, it had already been rigidly applied in 27 states.   Nine pioneer states had even adopted it prior to 1914.   By 1920, when the 18th Amendment came into force, 33 states had already gone dry on their own initiative.   All these measures were directed at preventing drunkenness and eliminating the evil saloons.   During the war, they were also aimed at improving the health and efficiency of the vast industrial and manufacturing population and in theory, at safeguarding those in the Armed Forces.

The 18th Amendment, carried by Congress on December 1917, was not ratified until January 16, 1919, and provided for implementation one year after that date.   Even at that time, prohibition was to a great extent an accomplished fact, for when the United States went into the War in 1917, very severe restrictive measures had been taken by the government.   Later, on July 1, 1919 a law entitled the "War-Time Prohibition Act," which had been prepared while America was at war, had decreed the immediate closing of all distilleries, breweries and saloons.   The Volstead Act was passed on October 28, 1919; enforcement began as of New Year's Day, 1920.

Three effects resulted from all this legislation. First, it drove drinking underground into secret bars and "speakeasies" for those who could afford this illegal and more expensive indulgence.   Secondly, it produced illegal manufacture in the home or in illicit stills, and a vast network of illegal "bootleg" smuggling of wines and liquors from outside the country, notably Canada.   Thirdly, because the bootleg liquor was usually of bad quality, it fostered the development, at least in the "smart sets" of society, of mixtures and concoctions generally known as "cocktails."

"At first glance," one writer ironically wrote,

there is some evidence to support the impression that prohibition was a noble experiment.   The Volstead Act, there can be no doubt, did much to further convivial affection in the bosom of the family, bringing together golden head and grey over the bathtub as droplets of glycerin and aromatic essence of juniper were decanted carefully into drugstore alcohol.   But such a gain pales into insignificance when one reflects that the act was actually framed, not to encourage such instructive and praiseworthy home industry, but, unbelievable as it may seem, to keep people from drinking.   In every community there were a few arid individuals who because they them-

selves did not relish the flavor of spiritual beverages
or perhaps were ignorant of their medicinal value,
strove to keep others from enjoying them. It was
civil war, brother against brother [G. S. Albee, "The
Snowbound Jury," Sat. Eve. Post, Feb. 6, 1960].

And so by passing the law, the legislators thought they could
stop drinking. They were shortsighted, for they only succeeded in increasing it in certain quarters and forcing it out
of the taverns and pubs into the thousands of "blind pigs"--
anonymous unobtrusive blank buildings, entered through basement doors with peepholes, or behind shops--that sprang up
all over every large city. Kenneth Allsop wrote:

In New York, where there had been 15,000 legal saloons, 32,000 speakeasies spangled like dandelions in
spring.... Shops opened specializing in hops, yeast,
malt, corn meal, grains, copper tubing, charred
kegs, bottle tops, crocks and kettles--the entire do-
it-yourself kit for the home moonshiner.... The fo-
cal point of any party became the bathroom, where
the gin was being prepared to wither tongues and
scarify the stomach linings of guests at that night's
whoopee party.... Americans drank oceans of bootleg alcohol, but they did not hold it in high regard,
as the vast glossary of slang terms in the use at the
time implies. With a kind of affectionate revulsion
it was called coffin varnish, craw rot, rotgut, bust-
head, squirrel-juice, horse liniment, razors, taran-
tula juice, junk, strike-me-dead, belch, sheep-dip,
and a hundred other horror comic names. The tribu-
taries of the eerily varied thirst-quenching liquids
that were poured down their throats were as diverse
["The Bootleggers," Ottawa Journal, Oct. 26, 1961].

A glimpse of how these mixed drinks were concocted
in private houses during Prohibition days has been given by
the world renowned Canadian photographer-artist Yousuf
Karsh in his recent memoirs. After emigrating to Canada
at the age of 16, he was apprenticed for a time to his fellow Armenian, the great photographer Garo, of Boston.
Garo used to give studio parties to a brilliant collection of
artistic and musical friends.

Garo secured his supply of chemical from the bar I
operated from a bootlegger. He was a very honest
bootlegger, however, who did not charge too exorbi-

tant a price. The chemical was brought to the door,
and handed to Garo in turpentine tins. Then I would
go to the drugstore to buy the flavoring. This might
be gin flavor, or rye flavor, or rum flavor, or bourbon flavor, even Scotch flavor for the epicures. The
flavors came in tubes, and we would use one tube to
so much alcohol, and add so much water. If we ran
a little short of alcohol, there was always more
water [In Search of Greatness, p. 30].

A gin drink was nicknamed a "nitric acid" and the humorous
code word for bourbon was "hypo."

One of our secretaries on the Washington legation
staff in 1928-1929, who subsequently became an ambassador,
was a very popular bachelor socialite from Ontario, who had
been a fraternity boy at Toronto University, had taken ad-
vanced studies at the Ecole des Sciences Politiques in Paris
and acquired fluent French, and who was also a brilliant
pianist and entertainer. Everybody liked him. He "invented"
a new concoction which he called the British Empire Cocktail. His recipe, if not remaining a secret, was at least
unknown to me, his old classmate and close colleague in
Washington. In principle I believe that it contained such
Empire ingredients as either Scotch or Rye, sweetened with
Canadian maple syrup, and some Jamaica Rum. Whether
or not it also included some South African or Australian
sherry, or some other ingredients of colonial origin, I do
not know. At any rate it was a sweet and potent cocktail,
and was much enjoyed. Its inventor was invited to a great
many Washington parties, diplomatic and otherwise, and was
so popular as a cocktail-mixer that he was always asked to
"do the honors," as lady guests are asked to "pour tea" at
tea parties. He would stalk around the room talking to other guests, while shaking up the drinks in the host's silver
cocktail shaker. He used to wink at me and say sotto voce:
"I'm doing my daily dozen!"; this exercise evidently kept
him in great physical trim.

Mr. Patrick Gavin Duffy, the author of a small booklet, The Standard Bartender Guide, which somehow came into my possession a few years ago, makes the remark:
"Where and how most of these cocktails originated, like our
jokes and jazz pieces, history may never reveal." He
points out however that of 'a considerable number which
were created here during the period of Prohibition, some
are obviously of irresponsible origin. During these years,

the huge traffic in liquor was conducted by the inexperi-
enced and lawless element of the nation and the great hotel
restaurant and legitimate saloon men who were the backbone
of the business had absolutely no part in it.   For this spirit
of resignation and law-abiding behavior, the public did not
accord due credit. "

Oddly enough, Canada, which during United States
Prohibition days had been largely responsible for exporting
illegal or smuggled liquor into the neighboring country, with
many diplomatic problems accruing, was later to reverse
the American Repeal and to introduce in many Provinces, a
similar form of regulation or prohibition, which the Americans had abandoned.

THE MARTINI

As gin became purer--no longer homemade and bootlegged, requiring additives for disguise--the variety of mixed
cocktails became reduced and simplified.   The most popular
of all cocktails became the "dry martini, " a combination of
trustworthy gin and honest vermouth.   At first it was half-
and-half; but gradually the vermouth portion decreased while
the gin component increased, until sometimes it is almost
straight gin, merely touched with a drop or two of vermouth
and decorated by an olive or a slice of lemon.

The American poet William Rose Benét, in "The
Martini, " exclaimed:

> Chilled Martini like Ithuriel's spear
> Transferring all dubiety within
> Oiled by an olive and shred of lemon-peel!

And another modern American poet, Ogden Nash, in "A
Drink with Something in It, " wrote:

> There is something about a Martini,
> A tingle remarkably pleasant;
> A yellow, a mellow Martini:
> I wish that I had one at present.
> There is something about a Martini,
> Ere the dining and dancing begin,
> And to tell you the truth,
> It is not the vermouth,
> I think that perhaps it's the Gin.

The American diplomat Charles Thayer relates an episode in which, when he was appointed to protect British interests in Germany in World War II, he was instructed to help a British vice-consul in Hamburg who had been thrown into jail while awaiting repatriation, in retaliation for the arrest of a German consul in Glasgow. When Thayer arrived at the German jail, the director had the British vice-consul called from his cell, and Thayer gave him pajamas, shirts, socks, a toilet kit and other comforts. He then brought out a bottle of sherry, instructing the director to serve it to the prisoner before lunch. The director took the bottle without complaint. Next, Thayer produced champagne, explaining that it should be served, properly chilled, with the vice-consul's supper. The director of the jail looked pained but accepted it. Then came a bottle of gin and one of vermouth and a shaker, with the explanation that this was for the prisoner's evening martini. As Thayer began to recite--"four parts gin, and one part--," the director exploded in anger: "Verdammt! "I am willing to serve sherry and champagne and even gin to this prisoner, but he can damn well mix his own Martinis!" [Diplomat, p. 91].

President Franklin D. Roosevelt always preferred to mix drinks or cocktails himself for his guests. It is related that on one occasion he invited a group of political leaders on a cruise. Included among the guests was the then Senator from Kentucky, Alben Barkley. Before dinner, F.D.R. served drinks, which he mixed himself. They proved to be powerful concoctions and generous. One of the guests took a sip and gasped. Turning to Barkley, he whispered hoarsely: "His drinks are as radical as his politics." "I think," the Senator corrected, "they are more liberal than radical!" Robert E. Sherwood tells of Roosevelt's standard cocktail ceremony in the Oval Study of the White House at 7.15.

> The President sat behind his desk, the tray before
> him. He mixed the ingredients with the deliberation
> of an alchemist but with what appeared to be a cer-
> tain lack of precision since he carried on a steady
> conversation while doing it. His bourbon old-fash-
> ioneds were excellent, but I did not care for his Mar-
> tinis, in which he used two kinds of vermouth (when
> he had them) and sometimes a dash of absinthe.
> Hopkins sometimes talked him into making Scotch
> whiskey-sours, although he didn't really like them.
> The usual canapés of cream cheese or fish paste on

small circles of toast were served, also popcorn.
Roosevelt was an extremely mild drinker--he did not
have wine with meals except at large, formal dinners,
and I don't recall ever having seen him drink brandy
or other liquors or a highball; but he certainly loved
the cocktail period and the stream of small talk which
went with it [Roosevelt and Hopkins (1948)].

That cocktails have had the sanction of certain kings
and presidents is shown by the tastes of sovereigns like King
George VI and Edward VIII and, among others, President
Roosevelt.   During the visit in 1939 of George VI and Queen
Elizabeth, they were to spend a day at the Hyde Park home
of President Roosevelt.   As Eleanor Roosevelt reports in her
reminiscences

> We sat in the library waiting for them.   Franklin had
> a tray of cocktails ready in front of him, and his
> mother sat on the other side of the fireplace looking
> disapprovingly at the cocktails and telling her son that
> the King would prefer tea.   My husband, who could be
> as obstinate as his mother, kept his tray in readi-
> ness, however.   Finally the King and Queen arrived.
> In a short time they were down in the library.   As
> the King approached, my husband said: 'My mother
> does not approve of cocktails, and thinks you should
> have a cup of tea.'   The King answered: 'Neither
> does my mother,' and took a cocktail [This I Remem-
> ber].

The kindest and most authoritative words that have
been spoken for drink in many years came out of a symposium on drinking which a group of physicians, psychiatrists,
sociologists and biochemists held in 1961 at the University of
California School of Medicine.   The cocktail party, in particular, was singled out for praise by an Italian doctor who
said that every man must have periods when he can be inefficient and relax and recharge his batteries."

Mr. Dean Acheson tells of a Berlin reception given
by General Maxwell Taylor, then commander of the U.S.
sector in Berlin.   He invited the other commandants, but,
he said, General Chuikov would probably not come; he had
not attended any Western social function for months.   The
reception had been going on for an hour, when there was a
great clatter at the door and in came not only General Chuikov but all his staff.   Up came a waiter with a tray of cock-

tails on a large tray. Chuikov took a solemn appraising look
and began to drink them, before his mistaken assumption of
a challenge was realized. "You don't have to drink all those,
General," Acheson assured him. He looked immensely relieved. "Good Lord," Acheson went on. "You must have a
tin stomach!" It was translated. He shook his head. "No,"
he said: "steel" [Sat. Eve. Post, March 25, 1951, p. 69].

COCKTAIL PARTIES

Thus commenced what is nowadays euphemistically
called "social drinking" in the new form of cocktail parties
instead of Bierabends and other convivial "routs," as some
of the pre-war diplomats called them. And this new social
device supplemented the growing number of illicit speakeasies
of the Prohibition period by introducing "social drinking" into private homes, in place of the Victorian tea parties. Before the 1920's such drinking in the pleasant company of
friends was done in public bars and thus was very largely a
man's occupation. But after the advent of Prohibition, the
living room became a social drinking center and of course
women were welcome participants. There was in the Prohibition era much more gaiety and excitement automatically
generated by a coctail party--there was something bold (and
illegal) and jaunty about it. Recipes--mainly of far-fetched
concoctions designed to disguise the ugly taste of the homemade stuff--were constantly sampled and passed around.
Hostmanship included a sort of rivalry for the most daring
the most different, the cleverest drinks. Wines, steak
sauces, egg yolks, soft drinks, honey, bitters, milk, sugar,
fruits--all these and many more ingredients were tried and
discussed.

Once established, cocktail parties continued unabated
even after Repeal took the fun out of the illegality of it. It
was a national habit, perhaps even a nostalgic one, long after their necessity ended. Another reason quickly arose,
however: during the Depression many could not entertain a
large number of guests; throwing a cocktail party for them
was the way to do it.

There was more truth perhaps than he intended when
Norman Douglas, in South Wind, remarked, almost propheti-
cally, "many a man who thinks to found a home discovers
that he has merely opened a tavern for his friends." One
contributor to The Compleat Imbiber, referred to it as "that
inhospitable way of working off people who do not rate a
meal."

The national capital, Washington, seat of the legislation nationally forbidding the manufacture, sale, transpor-
tation or consumption of alcoholic beverages, was one of
the most flagrant violators of that legislation.   During my
diplomatic sojourn there in 1928-29, there were said to be
365 speakeasies in Washington, one for each day of the
year.   And of course in every diplomatic house, privileged
under the laws, there was bootleg drinking; in many American homes there was bootleg drinking; and the surreptitious
carrying of hip-flasks and imbibing therefrom at dances and
parties, as an act of defiance and mischief, was notorious.

One reason for the vogue of private cocktail parties
is that as houses grow smaller, and the great mansions of
our grandfathers' day have been taxed out of occupation, it
is not so easy to give large dinner parties; and it is relatively easy to crowd any number of friends and acquaintances
into smaller rooms for stand-up refreshments.   Another
economic reason is that in these modern days household
servants, chefs, scullery maids, butlers and other servi-
teurs are scarce and formal dinners therefore are difficult.
But a host and hostess can themselves serve cocktails, or
hire a bar-boy and maid for a couple of hours to lend assistance and if necessary, sandwiches and canapés can easily be supplied by caterers.   Another feature is the informality; there is no need to dress up for a cocktail party,
as there is for a dinner.   While there is less intimacy or
serious conversation, there is more movement.   If one is
bored by another, he or she can move on to join another
group without notice or offense.

Cocktail parties are a facile way for newly-arrived
diplomats to become widely acquainted, especially with the
leaders of local society.   But it is sometimes disturbing
to find that one's permanent butler or maid in the official
residence is so well acquainted with the local guests that
he or she will take advantage, and do a little private diplomacy or "visiting" with the guests behind the back of the
host or hostess.   I recall one post where I was a newcom-
er, yet head of mission, anyhow, where I gave cocktail
party receptions at which my permanent housekeeper used
to hobnob with the well-known guests while she was carrying the tray or passing around the drinks.   She had recently acquired a "budgie" of which she was inordinarily proud.
On more than one occasion I noticed her amid the throng,
talking to the prime minister's wife or some other famous
lady, and surreptitiously exhibiting her budgie-bird which

she had smuggled under her apron. It was a good excuse
or pretext to make "friends" with society people and to gossip. To my surprise some of these ladies shared her enjoyment of malicious gossip! One never quite knows what
may happen at a cocktail party, especially when the domestic servants assume charge.

Although in modern times the cocktail had its major
vogue in America during the 14 years of Prohibition, it
had earlier quickly spread to Britain, and thence, by wealthy
travellers and Anglo-Saxon diplomats, into other foreign
countries where western types of social practices were
adopted among the élite. In Britain it became fashionable,
in perhaps a more respectable form than among the quick-
drinking and indiscriminating Americans. Gin had been
scarce during World War I but after, despite new and higher
duties, it returned in triumph to give to the 1920's the name
of the Cocktail Age. The cocktail bar became the resort of
the élite. The cocktail party came into being--introduced
into London, probably, in the late Twenties by an American-
born hostess named Madame Alfredo de Peña, to fill in for
her friends the blank period between tea-time and dinner-
time. It reached Oxford at about the same time, introduced
by a small group of American undergraduates. In due
course, this new social convention, by then well established
in the fashionable English set, found its way into stage plays,
even as ales, sack, wines and other potables of the Elizabethan Age were referred to in Shakespeare's plays. Frederick Lonsdale is said to have served the first cocktail on
the stage, in a play Spring Cleaning (1925). Noel Coward
repeated this, in This Year of Grace, in The Vortex, in
Fallen Angels, and in Words and Music. But the cocktail
party reached its apotheosis in T. S. Eliot's The Cocktail
Party.

Poet Laureate John Masefield, however, struck a
slight warning note in The Everlasting Mercy:

> Meanwhile, my friend, would be no sin
> To mix more water in your gin.
> We are neither saints nor Philip Sidneys,
> But mortal men with mortal kidneys.

Canada was apparently a contributor to the development of the cocktail in the United States. "The best English spirits," remarks Lord Kinross, "it is true, were
smuggled into the [United States] on a large scale; Booth's
'House of Lords' gin found its way there from Vancouver in

Canada, and from the French island St. Pierre-Miquelon off
the coast of Newfoundland, the cases being dumped into the
sea and floated ashore in sacks. But before being sold as
'right off the boat,' the gin was almost invariably diluted
with raw alcohol, becoming a species of fire-water!'' As a
point of departure for the Prohibition period smuggling trade,
Canada was an important base of operations; and if a complete history were to be written of this neighborly traffic,
the story would be as dramatic and colorful and astonishing
as any tales of the earlier Gold Rush days in the wild and
woolly West. Although the orators boast of the century-old,
exemplary "undefended border" between Canada and the United
States, there was a period of anti-smuggling "defence"--
coupled with an infinite amount of diplomatic business--
which produced Coast Guard cutters, even gunboats, and Internal Revenue policing guards, in the boundary waters between the two countries. The vogue of the cocktail party in
the United States had a lesser-known background of international smuggling and skulduggery.

The Russians in upper-class circles (there never was
a "classless society" in Russia) adopted the Western cocktail party in foreign and diplomatic circles. Sir Bruce
Lockhart claims that the cocktail was first introduced into
Moscow social life by the British Consul-General, Charles
Clive Bayley, at the time of the Bolshevik Revolution of
1917-18. In the 1930's, the popular Russian Ambassador
in Tokyo, Mr. Troyanovsky, whose embassy I visited on a
number of official occasions, was renowned for his receptions, with grand buffet, champagne, vodka, and various
cocktails.

When Ivan Mikailoff was promoting wrestling matches
in Winnipeg, it is related that he "invented a pre-war Molo-
tov-Cocktail which was believed to be composed of two parts
of Scotch whiskey and one part of Benedictine. After one
accident, cigarette-smoking was forbidden in Ivan's apartment when the master was concocting and consuming this
potion. A wrestler, who was smoking when he lifted the
glass to his lips, suffered severe flash burns which left his
face resembling the relief map of Alberta" [Jim Coleman,
Ottawa Citizen, Sept. 17, 1962, p. 13].

When the Hon. Lester B. Pearson was entertained
by Mr. Molotov at a party in Moscow, he is reported to
have jokingly saluted his host, glass in hand: "Here's to
your co-existence cocktail: half-gin, half-vodka!'' (A less

dangerous type of "Molotov Coctail.") His host replied:
"Well, how does it feel?" Mr. Pearson, hand on stomach,
answered: "I can't say that I feel very peaceful yet." To
which Molotov, the inscrutable, replied enigmatically: "Ah,
but it takes time; it takes time."

Bruce Hutchison notes that although Mr. Khrushchev
may regard the American Revolution as a poor bourgeois
affair, he too uses the American cocktail party as the chief
apparatus of diplomacy, providing a setting sometimes for
most shattering pronunciamentos. "In vino veritas."*

In our era of Babel and multiplicity of languages and
ideologies, cocktail parties seem to provide one unifying influence, the salutation which, though phrased in various
tongues, has but a single and unifying import. In this cate-
gory belong such amicable terms as "cheerio," "Here's how,"
"bottoms up," "prosit," "skol," "na zdrovie," "gambei,"
"here's mud in your eye," and "down the hatch." They
form an Esperanto; spirited and spirituous and perhaps even
a spiritual "brotherhood" of good will. One touch of nature
(not denatured) makes the whole world kin. But, alas, it
leaves all the Islamic countries out. Not even the substitute
of Coca Cola or lemonade can contribute, as cocktails do,
to international fraternity, amity, and cordiality.

COCKTAIL NOISE

Anyone who has given or attended cocktail receptions,
as all diplomats have to do, is familiar with two quirks of
human character that such parties promote. One is the
gregarious instinct. It is customary to invite more guests
than are expected to come, based on an observation of average practice and a calculation of probability. But even on
such a calculation, based on room space, and other factors,
the crowd that turns up usually exceeds the expected. There
are extra gate-crashers, or unannounced "companions" of
the guest, or that marginal group which statistical averages
and experience had led one not to expect, but who do turn
up. One does one's best to accommodate the throng. If
one has two large reception rooms, the guests make their

---

*There was once reported a bitter quarrel between the British and Czech
governments because Prime Minister Harold Macmillan, delicately balancing
a martini in one hand, a canapé in the other, remarked to the ambassador
from Prague that he hoped the Communist government of Czechoslovakia
wouldn't last very long!

way gregariously into one of those rooms, like a flock of
sheep, where they will all stand crushed together, fighting
for air, elbows bumping and spilling drinks over one another, while the other room with perhaps an exquisite buffet,
remains empty.   Then one tries to suggest that some colleagues or secretary or aide lead a few of the guests into
the adjoining room.   In a few minutes, everyone in that
room, all rushed together, fighting for air, elbows bumping, and spilling drinks over one another.

When I was ambassador to Egypt, I had a de luxe
apartment of great spaciousness, and above it a very hand-
some roof-garden terrace, illuminated either by a silvery-
white Nile moon or by festoons of multicolored electric
lights among the potted shrubbery.   At a large cocktail reception, my guests would be received and would congregate
in the downstairs apartment of several connecting salons,
where there were a huge buffet and a bar and several
waiters.   But when the crowd became too pressing, I would
suggest that some of them investigate the roof-garden above,
where I had another large buffet, a bar, and several additional waiters.   The transition at first was slow, since
guests seemed reluctant to be led away from the main
crowd; but their curiosity to see the Nile moon above the
roof-garden shrubbery overcame their hesitation and they
made the upstairs trek.   In ten minutes or so, everyone
had followed this Pilgrims Road, and before long, my whole
crowd was upstairs on the roof-terrace, while the spacious
apartment below was almost deserted.   This is what I call
the migratory instinct of gregarious society.

The other characteristic, noticeable everywhere, is
the mathematical relationship of numbers and noise.   A few
persons in a salon might maintain a quiet conversational
hum of sound; but as more and more people gather, the
hum grows higher and more strident; when the room becomes well filled, the conversational pitch goes up rapidly,
until it sounds almost like a bedlam of shouting--everyone
of a hundred guests talking at the top of his voice until
almost shrieking to be heard.   To a newly arriving guest,
it sounds like pandemonium in the monkey-house or an avi-
ary of raucous parakeets.   I once conceived the definition
of such parties as an occasion of "belles and decibels."
To a detached and somewhat scientific observer, it is difficult to explain this gradual but inevitable rise in pitch and
fortissimo in proportion to the increase in numbers.   Even
a large orchestra can still play pianissimo; but crowd-be-

havior, if uncontrolled by some disciplinarian conductor or host banging loudly for "silence, please: a speech is to be made!," inevitably produces an ever-rising volume. It is a characteristic of crowds confined in limited spaces, which means that it is a characteristic of cocktail receptions.

Leigh Hunt, in Table Talk, foreshadowed the modern cocktail party garrulousness when he described the after-dinner retreat of the gentlemen to the smoking-room.

> During the wine after dinner, if the door of the room be opened, there sometimes come bursting up the drawing-room stairs a noise like that of a tap-room. Everybody is shouting in order to make himself audible; argument is tempted to confound itself with loudness; and there is not one conversation going forward, but six, or a score. This is better than formality and want of spirits; but it is no more the right thing, than a scramble is a dance, or the tap-room chorus a quartet of Rossini. The perfection of conversational intercourse is when the breeding of high life is animated by the fervour of genius."

But, according to modern experience, the perfection and effectiveness of conversational intercourse at cocktail parties is measured by the fervor of the shrill and noisy chatter.

My old acquaintance in Chile, the U.S. Ambassador Mr. Claude G. Bowers, tells of a reception in Santiago to which he was invited by the President of Chile to meet the visiting dictator of Argentine, Juan Domingo Perón and then the reception that followed at the Argentine Embassy.

> I was delayed in reaching the embassy, and when I arrived the room was packed with my colleagues, who were scarcely recognizable in the thick cloud of tobacco smoke; the chattering was deafening. I could not locate the two presidents to greet them, and the clamor was so great I could not make myself heard when I tried to make inquiries. At length, with the aid of my elbows, I reached Perón and Ibáñez, shook hands, and withdrew into the crowd. Even so, that evening a radio station, not unfriendly to the dictator, solemnly announced that 'when the American Ambassador entered the Argentine Embassy a dead silence fell upon the room.' The noise had been so great I had not heard the silence [Chile Through Embassy Windows, p. 359].

A team of Canadian noise researchers of the Canadian National Research Council recently made a study of this peculiarity, and published a report for the Acoustical Society of America. First, they found that there was little difference in degree of "noise" at coffee-parties and at cocktail parties: "The nature of the beverage served seems of minor importance ... at least in the range from coffee to cocktails." ("The coffee party," they reported, "was staged to maintaining quiet.... [yet] despite this handicap, they managed to hold their own with the true cocktail party-goers.") Secondly they reported that, by and large, all-male parties are somewhat less noisy than mixed gatherings. Thirdly, they found little or no evidence to back up a previous researchers' theory that at a critical point at every cocktail party, the party changes abruptly from a quiet to a noisy one, "corresponding to the difference between conversational and declamatory speech." All their findings pointed to cocktail parties being fairly noisy right from the start, with rapid rises in the noise levels, and "with no evidence of a 'quiet plateau'." (See Frank Carey, Ottawa Citizen or Ottawa Journal, Feb. 15, 1960.)

Everyone who has read Parkinson's Law is familiar with the erudite author's chapter on "The Cocktail Formula," in which he tries to prove that guests who wish to be noticed will arrive at approximately 7:10 at a 6 to 8 o'clock party, for at that critical moment they will not be too early and unobserved, and after that time some of the observant guests will have left. Professor Parkinson also develops his statistical and mathematical theory of the clockwise rotational movement of most cocktail guests in an enclosed or four-sided room.

If we combine the two known facts, the lefthand drift and the tendency to avoid the center, we have the biological explanation of the phenomenon we have all observed in practice: that is, the clockwise flow of the human movement. There may be local eddies and swirls--women will swerve to avoid people they detest, or rush crying "Darling!" towards people they detest even more--but the general set of the tide runs inexorably round the room. People who matter, people who are literally "in the swim," keep to the channel where the tide runs strongly. Those who appear to be glued to the walls, usually in deep conversation with people they meet every week, are nobodies. Those who jam themselves in

the corners of the room are the timid and feeble.
Those who drift into the center are the eccentric or
merely silly.

The New York Times, we are told, recently examined this question and adopting Parkinson's Law, proposed a
set of rules to codify, regulate and legitimize the cocktail
party by a set of international rules.   The first rule, said
the New York Times, is to enter the customary brawl and
circulate clockwise, to keep talking and never finish a sentence, above all to hear nothing but the din.   To this the
Canadian Bruce Hutchison takes strong exception.   "That
sounds easy but it requires a long education, hard atheltic
training, a wide tolerance to alcohol and people, plus a sure
sense of equilibrium.   To tell the truth I have yet to master this many-sided craft.   I can't tell which direction is
clockwise and which anti-clockwise, and besides, as any
hostess will tell you, nobody pays any attention to the clock.
The party scheduled for six o'clock to eight hardly ever
ends before midnight when host, food and bottles are exhausted."   Bruce Hutchison adds:

> One rule is to talk about something non-controversi-
> al.   The weather, for example.   I tried that, too.
> When a strange lady of massive proportions fixed me
> with a glittering eye I said the weather was fine,
> hoping to encourage a pleasant stream of small talk.
> That lady said to heck with the weather (not her
> words), and what in the heck did I mean by criticiz-
> ing Mr. Diefenbaker and Mr. Pearson in print?   I
> didn't get her point clearly because, in the middle of
> a sentence, she began to circulate very clockwise
> and not too vertically either [Ottawa Citizen, Dec.
> 22, 1958].

The American columnist Sydney J. Harris has written about the problem of manipulating a cocktail in one hand
and other refreshments in the other while at a stand-up reception or coctail party.

> One of the great benefactors of mankind ... may
> easily turn out to be an Iowan named Wayne Norland
> [who] has devised a shelf that hangs from one's
> shoulders, rests against the stomach and is adjust-
> able to size, shape and sex.   This shelf, which may
> come to rank with the wheel and the abacus as pri-
> mary inventions, is designed for the aid of all party

guests who nowadays stand around juggling a drink,
a plate of hors d'oeuvres, a cigarette and assorted
silverware during those lunatic crushes known as
cocktail parties.

The cocktail party is a menace to civilization at best;
but under current physical conditions it also repre-
sents a peril to clothing, limbs and dignity.   The
Norland Shelf ... will also prove an inestimable boon
to people like me, who were born without a lap. ...
I usually end up eating off the fireplace mantle, or
sitting cross-legged on the floor, bending down to my
plate like some carnivorous animal, snarling with
greed.   With the Norland Shelf nonchalantly hanging
from my shoulders, I can become the debonair guest
I have always wanted to be-- ... I will feel like a
doge instead of a dog.

CRITICISM

The cocktail party, in respect to official and diplomatic life, has now become a fixed feature on the social
landscape.   No sociologist or historian of contemporary
mores can ignore it.   It reflects itself in our diplomatic
Looking Glass world.   Nevertheless, there are many critics
of the contemporary custom, and many who are repelled by
such a form of social intercourse.   So ineffectual have cocktail parties seemed to many persons of high social standing
that they have been denounced in highly eloquent diatribes.
This protest was expressed even by Shakespeare in Othello
(II, iii, 35).   "I have very poor and unhappy brains for
drinking; I could well wish courtesy would invent some other custom of entertaining. "

Sir Joseph Pope, founder of the Department of External Affairs of Canada and its first Undersecretary of
State (1909-1926), used to say that "life would be tolerable
if it wasn't for its amusements. "   No wonder the American
Ambassador Mr. Charles Dawes once complained that diplomacy is not too hard on the head, "but is devilishly hard
on the feet"--although one of his caustic friends, Ambassador Fletcher, remarked, "It all depends on upon which end
you make most use of. "

Sir Lawrence Evelyn Jones, in the fourth volume (I
Forgot to Tell You) of his autobiography and reminiscences,
expresses his "repulsion" for coctail parties.

> It is not that, being six foot four in height, I can
> only see the tops of women's hats, and hear with
> difficulty the sweet nothings that are uttered from
> below them, nor because of the fatigue, akin to that
> felt in a geological museum, which overpowers me.
> It is that I can never think of anything to say, and
> my neighbours never say anything to make me think.
> The truth is that we are all unhappy together.   No-
> body really enjoys noise and chatter and heat. ...
> At each party, I add to the number of people whom
> I shall offend, by forgetting their faces, at the next,
> and cut, unaware, those met at the one before.
> Cocktail parties debase social intercourse, spoil our
> dinners, and diminish good will towards men.   They
> ought to be abolished by common consent.

Not long ago I desired some information concerning
one of the posts to which I had formerly been accredited.
I contemplated writing a personal letter to the country's
representative in Ottawa, but decided to await an opportunity
of meeting him at a forthcoming diplomatic reception.   I
met him, and forthwith made my inquiry; but before I could
listen to his sympathetic reply, we were both interrupted by
the intrusion of other "cher collègues" and I failed to get
my information on the spot.

One of the most renowned hostesses in Washington,
Miss Elsa Maxwell, apparently revolted against the institution.   She has been quoted as saying:

> I cannot bear them.   There are a number of people
> in this world whom I don't care to meet, and when-
> ever I go to a cocktail party, there they are!   Cock-
> tail parties are full of noisy chatter, wretched
> people, horrible hors d'oeuvres made with rancid
> mayonnaise and tired tomatoes, poisonous little-
> finger sandwiches, warm drinks made with inferior
> liquor.   Cocktail parties are boring dull and ineffi-
> cient--the most miserable form of entertaining there
> is, and also the cheapest.   I avoid them like the
> plague.

In an interview with the Canadian artist-photographer Rudolph
Beny, Miss Maxwell was quoted as saying: "There aren't
any great parties any more.   Cocktail parties are deadly,
and certainly sitting about in night clubs as the young
people do today isn't any fun" [Chatelaine, April 1962, p.
148].

Nevertheless, the diplomats cannot escape them, or avoid giving them. Another great Washington social hostess, Mrs. Pearl Mesta ("Call me Madam"), when Minister to Luxembourg, could hardly "avoid like the plague" this ubiquitous and endemic diplomatic custom; nor, I suppose, could Ambassador Clare Booth Luce in Rome. They had to conform to the masculine diplomatic tradition, although even the males would also no doubt like to see the custom decline into desuetude. Former Foreign Secretary and Prime Minister Anthony Eden, once declared this as his personal opinion; but then he was suffering from an internal ailment. For the ladies, there is at least the special appeal of fashion; the rivalry in cocktail dresses, the desire to display their own, or to examine the others; but at the same time come headaches as to "what to wear."

According to British diplomat Eric Cleugh, there is a story of a young reporter who wanted to investigate first hand the phenomenon of the wandering eye, the inattentiveness except to the comings and goings of those with senior rank, that characterizes diplomatic cocktail reception.

> [The reporter] went to a diplomatic reception at which he made the same remark to a number of different people. 'I was sorry,' he would say casually, 'to hear that your mother died last night.' The reply, accompanying the wandering look to which I have referred, would be. 'Yes, too bad isn't it; are you going to the Russians (French, Indonesians, Swedes, etc.) tomorrow night? They have such wonderful caviar (champagne, curry, smörgasbord, etc.)!' It takes a little getting used to, realizing that nobody listens to what you say at cocktail parties, but you learn to and it is probably just as well anyway [Without Let or Hindrance, p. 178].

These parties were enjoyed by the oldsters as well as by the gilded youth of Scott Fitzgerald's generation. But the venerable, and perhaps slightly dessicated Oxford Professor of English Literature Sir Walter Raleigh (1861-1922), somewhat enviously, was once moved to write some wistful "Wishes of an Elderly Man," at a garden party in June 1914:

> I wish I loved the Human Race;
> I wish I loved its silly face;
> I wish I liked the way it walks;

I wish I liked the way it talks;
And when I'm introduced to one
I wish I thought 'What Jolly Fun!'

Once George Bernard Shaw, bored at a party, retired
to a corner, away from the other guests. Observing him,
his hostess approached and asked: "Are you enjoying yourself, Mr. Shaw?" "That's all I am enjoying," replied the
playwright.

My former colleague in Warsaw, American Ambassador Mr. Stanton Griffis, who was a Wall Street tycoon and
millionaire, was something of a maverick during his diplomatic service in Poland, Egypt, Argentina and Spain. In
his memoirs, Living in State, he criticized the inefficiency
of the State Department, and some of the futilities of the
ambassadorial role. Although rich, he pooh-poohed the assumption that American Ambassadors had to be men of
wealth, and commented on the wasteful cost of entertaining
and cocktail parties. Probably with tongue in cheek he un-
dervalued the usefulness of diplomatic dinner parties (although much of his business success, as he recounts, resulted from his dinner parties), and also discounted "cocktail parties" which, though he gave them regularly, he regarded as futile. He thought it was "no treat" for already
hard-worked ambassadors and others to have to attend parties and dinners at the American Embassy, which, he states,
seldom result in any positive outcome. 'But the tradition
remains and the entertainment can be made as lavish or as
primitive as the ambassador desires. Unfortunately, the
whole theory of 'we must have a cocktail party' spreads
through the corps down to the lowliest secretary, and in the
last analysis that is what sometimes makes the diplomatic
life so expensive. Yet no one who really loves the game
of diplomacy, no one who would deeply desire to spend his
life with the State Department, should ever refuse it on account of its cost" [p. 158].

The greatest cocktail addict in the United States was
perhaps the venerable Senator Theodore Green of Rhode Island, recently retired in his 90's. He is said to receive
invitations to about six parties in Washington almost every
day of the week, and tries to attend most of them. At one
of them, a friend noticed him in a corner, back to the
crowd, stealthily perusing a little pocket notebook. The
friend came up, patted him on the back, and said: "Well,
Senator, what are you doing? Looking to see where your

next cocktail party is?"   'No," shyly replied the embarrassed statesman, "I'm looking to see where I am now."

Truly it may be said that the institution of the cocktail sometimes is enough to drive a man to drink!

Diplomatic receptions and cocktail parties in Ottawa
apparently follow closely the pattern in diplomatic circles in
other world capitals. Because residences are smaller than
they used to be, and servants are scarcer, such parties
are growing less formal. It is reported that Ottawa parties
run about two hours. There's seldom any entertainment; it
cuts down the talk. It is said that in comparison with other
world cities, Canada's capital rates about average socially
--although 'way behind Moscow and Washington. Diplomats
compare it with Oslo or The Hague. The biggest party of
the year is always the French Embassy's "Prise de la Bas-
tille" celebration in July, with more than a thousand guests.
The United States Embassy and the Embassy of the U.S.S.R.
with their own large staffs, also throw large national day receptions. Other missions, such as one-man Cuba or Ice-
land, of course hold much smaller gatherings and give fewer cocktail parties.

It is said that junior diplomats in Ottawa go to about
70 parties a year. Seniors may get to more than 150. At
the height of the winter season, few have an evening off.
There are several score diplomatic missions in Ottawa,
each giving at least a national day reception, besides special parties for distinguished nationals or other visitors, or
for some other anniversary or occasion.

Perhaps, on the other hand, cocktail parties are not
always an ineffectual waste of time. The United States Ambassador to Thailand from 1945 to 1953, Mr. Edwin F.
Stanton, has recorded his impression in this respect.

When I returned to the house at night there were always guests in the garden. Iced tea helped to re-
vive flagging energies and made it possible to climb
upstairs and, in the stifling heat of our sun-baked
bedroom, dress for the round of evening cocktail
parties and dinners. These were useful; sometimes
I could transact more official business at a party
than in the office. After a while one became adroit
at maneuvering one's way through the crowds at a
reception and cornering the person with whom one

wanted to talk about official matters. Within an
hour the views or replies extracted might be on the
air to Washington, or later dispatched by one of the
Embassy's faithful code clerks. These parties were
not 'pink teas' but really hard work [Brief Authority,
p. 205].

Vice President Nixon's tour of South America in
1958 led to criticism of the diplomats, and to the criticism
that cocktail diplomacy isolates too many foreign representatives within a select circle, and from the people. To this
the Boston Herald [May 21, 1958] commented:

Protocol exists for a number of sound and excellent
reasons. The business that transpires among Ambassadors is not only formal, occurring over the ex-
panse of an office desk, but informal, occurring in
the artificial atmosphere of the banquet and the ballroom. To expect a representative to go out and
mingle with the people is a misunderstanding of the
aims of diplomacy.... If the United States is under
a handicap because of so-called "cocktail diplomacy"
it is a handicap shared with the other nations of the
globe.... It is difficult to imagine beer diplomacy
as a substantial improvement over the cocktail variety.

Notwithstanding the general misgivings or even private repugnance toward the modern social system of cocktail parties, as emphasized in the foregoing pages, it is
possible that they sometimes do have a diplomatic value,
as luncheons and dinners do. The distinguished British diplomat Sir George Rendel, for example, relates how in 1947
he, as United Kingdom representative, attended his last
conference of the Preparatory Commission of the International Refugee Organization. The newly designated head was
an American. According to Rendel, the organizational
sense of the Americans and the British were quite different.
Englishmen seemed to prefer a vertical structure with clear
lines of authority and responsibility. The Americans liked
better a horizontal structure with overlapping responsibili-
ties--as he termed it, "a sort of bungaloid system." The
two differing points of view produced some clashes. But
then Rendel relates:

Towards the end of the proceedings the Canadian
delegate decided to give a cocktail party, but, to

make it a little out of the common, he chartered a
lake steamer and we cruised in circles around the
lake of Geneva for a couple of hours while the party
proceeded. The main drink provided was a really
remarkable cocktail made, I understood, on a basis
of Canadian whiskey and maple syrup. It was good
and plentiful and spirits rose as the trip proceeded.
As it happened, we had had quite a serious difference of opinion with the Americans during the previous few days. The subject was raised again, and
suddenly we discovered a mutually satisfactory solution. We made a note of it then and there, and I
am glad to say that we all confirmed it in writing
the next morning. I have often regretted that I did
not obtain the recipe for this admirable concoction
from my Canadian colleague at the time. Its effects were obviously not only beneficial but lasting
[The Sword and the Olive, p. 256].

There is one theory that at a cocktail reception,
business executives or diplomats may meet one another informally, go off into a secluded corner, and negotiate private business. I have often seen this appear to happen.
Sometimes, negotiators almost immediately and automatically move over to a corner and go into a private "huddle"
of business, ignoring the rest of the party. But all too
often I have also seen such efforts of private and confiden-
tial conversation, afforded by a cocktail party with the cup
that cheers and the glass in hand that eases restraint, interrupted most inconveniently by other intrusive guests who
wish to join in the conversation and think that they have
every uninhibited right to do so. A cocktail party is an occasion of jolly informal chatter; guests can hardly conceive
of it as an opportunity for serious conversations or delicate
private negotiations. Footloose men will intrude to share
chit-chat of golf or fishing, while some serious diplomatic
or business conversation is going on. Footloose and charming ladies will crash in to seek some masculine attention
and to put an end to grave serious talk. This so invariably happens that I have long been disillusioned as to the
serious "utility" of cocktail receptions. Their primary value
is in being "introduced" to other guests, some of whom
may be important persons. The serious talks must be
sought at later and more private rendezvous. In this respect only are such informal breezy and noisy receptions
of much practical value. They are a means of making
"contacts." Much as I dislike the overcrowded, noisy dip-

lomatic receptions and cocktail parties, in place of a small
intimate group of friends invited informally and privately
for "drinks," I must admit that, even in a large crowd, I
have often re-met old acquaintances and friends and have
been introduced to new people of either social or political
importance.

The adventure of the private and illicit cocktail party
came to an end with the Repeal of Prohibition.   It became
no longer exciting but merely a legitimate custom.   For
one reason, no alternative attraction in beverages has been
introduced.   Even the modern ubiquitous Coca Cola, so
largely a favorite of teenagers and small fry, can scarcely
displace the more enlivening spirituous beverages.

Only recently (December 1960) was it announced in
Ottawa that because the public were now more inclined to
resort to the "cocktail lounges" than the predominantly male
and gloomy taverns and beverage rooms, leading hotels in
Ottawa would shut down their separate tavern facilities.
The general trade preferred to mingle with the "carriage
trade" in the more attractive cocktail lounges.

Nevertheless "cocktails," as such, seem to be losing
their appeal, though cocktail parties have not.   There is
some indication that the fad for mixed drinks, of fancy
names and exotic ingredients, or for disguised or flavored
gin (originating because the home brew or bootlegged gin
tasted so bad), is gradually diminishing in favor of single
martinis or straight gin or whiskey drinks.

In September 1960 the chairman of the British Bartenders' Guild said that he believed that the cocktail is on
its way out.   "Sensible drinkers ask for spirits unmixed,"
Charles Tuck of London told reporters, "Only pretentious
people ask for cocktails nowadays."   The popularity of
"straight" drinks, sometimes neat, sometimes diluted with
water or just "on the rocks," is apparently increasing.
When a foreigner was lately studying English, he was asked
by his teacher to spell "straight" and having done so correctly, was asked to explain the meaning of the word.   He
promptly replied: "Straight--without water or ice."

But who can say how long this 20th-century social
custom will endure?   In diplomatic circles at least, it has
become a convention and a formality, rather than a spon-
taneous family picnic improvised at short notice out of joie

de vivre.   We have not yet reached the stage when the cocktail party will decline and grow outmoded like the coffee
houses, the gin palaces and the tea drinking "At Homes."
Those forms of social conviviality faded because their po-
tions were displaced by some other popular beverage, and
because of changes in mode of living and the passing from
the scene of servants.

It is true that the vogue of "mixed" drinks or true
cocktails may be replaced by simpler wines and spirits and
that cocktail parties may become so formalized or fatuous
as to lose their popularity.   But there will always remain
the attraction of some form of convivial alcoholic cheer.
This has been so through the millenia.   The gregarious human urge must be served.   Here's looking at you through
the looking glass.

INDEX

Abdul Hamid, Sultan 81-2, 128
abolitionists 153
Acharnians (Aristophanes) 125
Acheson, Dean G. 144, 250-1
Adams, Henry 52
Adams, Samuel 129
Addington, Henry see Sidmouth
  Henry Addington, Viscount
Addison, Joseph 63
Adventures of a naval captain
  (Theonge) 146
Agamemnon 10
Age of faith, The (Durant) 41-2
Age of reason begins, The
  (Durant) 48-9
akvavit 179-81, 183
Albec, G. S. 245-6
Alexander I, Czar of Russia 72,
  169
Alexander III, The Great, King
  of Macedon 9, 21
Alexandra, Queen of England
  109-10
Alexis of Russia, Grand Duke
  232
Alfonso XII, King of Spain 220
Alfred, King of England 72
Alice in wonderland and Through
  the looking glass (Lewis)
  42, 79, 111-2, 123, 133,
  147, 197, 236
Allsop, Kenneth 246
Alphand, Hervé 115-6
Amadeus, King of Cyprus 131
Ambassador extraordinary (Hatch)
  121
American diplomat in China, An
  (Reinsch) 102-3, 117, 149
Amicitia, De (Cicero) 86
Andrews sisters 201
Antony see Marcus Antonius
Arabian nights 137
Archestratus 39

Argentina
  cattle raising in 13
  control of meat trade by
    Britain in 13-4
  "gran seca" 13
Argentine diary (Joseph) 14
Argosy 175, 186
Argyllon, Robert 78
Aristophanes 125
Aristotle 240
Armour, Jean 199
Armstrong-Jones, Anthony, Lord
  Snowdon 217
Art culinaire, L' (Cussy) 62-3
art of cooking
  China 42-3, 45
  diplomats 73-4, 76
  England 49-52, 62, 80
  France 80, 83-4
  Japan 43-4
  royalty 72-3
  U. S. 52-5 see also chief cooks
Arthur, King of England 36, 46
Arundel, Henry, 3rd Baron of
  Wardour 140
Asahi Brewery, Japan 215
Athenaeus 10, 38
Athens, lack of food 11
Atkinson, Amy 54-5
Atlantic 118-9, 220
Atlantic advocate 129
Attic room, An (Coffin) 53
Attila 9
Aze 99, 101

Bad Gastein, Austria 221
Bad Hamburg, Germany 221
Baden-Baden, Germany 221
Balana, The 241
Ballantine Distillery, Dumbarton
  190
Barkley, Alben 249